The New England Orchard Cookbook

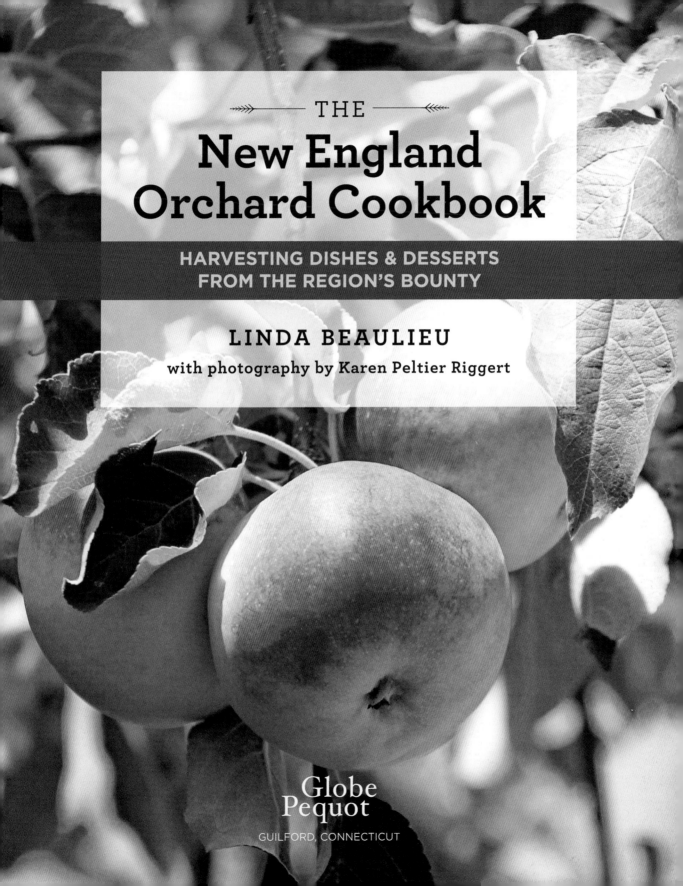

THE
New England Orchard Cookbook

HARVESTING DISHES & DESSERTS
FROM THE REGION'S BOUNTY

LINDA BEAULIEU

with photography by Karen Peltier Riggert

Globe
Pequot

GUILFORD, CONNECTICUT

This beautiful book is dedicated to Mike and Karen.

Globe
Pequot

An imprint of Rowman & Littlefield

Distributed by NATIONAL BOOK NETWORK

Copyright © 2016 Linda Beaulieu
Photos taken at the orchards in New England by Karen Peltier Riggert
All others images © Thinkstock

British Library Cataloguing in Publication Information Available

Library of Congress Cataloging-in-Publication Data available

ISBN 978-1-4930-2540-4
ISBN (e-book) 978-1-4930-2541-1

∞™ The paper used in this publication meets the minimum requirements of American National Standard for Information Sciences—Permanence of Paper for Printed Library Materials, ANSI/NISO Z39.48-1992.

Contents

Introduction

I keep trying to retire, but then I get wonderful writing opportunities—like this one, *The New England Orchard Cookbook*. Once again I jumped (as well as I can at my age) at the chance to write about something I love.

"Orchard" is defined as an area of land devoted to the cultivation of fruit trees or a place where people grow fruit trees. Many farms have orchards on their land, and this book is devoted to the fruits of those orchards, not farm crops in general. So we are talking apples, cherries, nectarines, peaches, pears, plums, and quince. Here and there we've included a blueberry recipe or a zucchini dish that could not be ignored. We also included an amazing pumpkin recipe from Rhode Island, but for the most part this book is a celebration of tree fruit.

For six months I immersed myself in the research needed to write this book. With my husband Brian as navigator and our dog, Beau, along for the ride, we hit the highway that led us to country byways, on to the sometimes hidden, always beautiful land of orchards. We watched the summer sun set in Connecticut and watched the fall foliage turn to red and gold in Massachusetts. We felt the chill of winter in the northern states of Vermont, New Hampshire, and Maine. I realized during these travel experiences that I love each one of these states for all kinds of different reasons.

APPLES

Whenever I embark on a new book project, I always learn so much and meet the nicest people. For instance, I had no idea that there were so many New England apples—more than 120 varieties according to the New England Apple Association, a nonprofit organization dedicated to educating consumers (some experts claim it's more like 200). Of that total, about forty varieties are grown commercially with McIntosh making up about two-thirds of the New England crop. Heirloom or antique apples as well as new varieties are increasingly available at mom-and-pop orchards.

Apples come in four colors: red, green, yellow, and russet, with variations. And the names! From Akane to Zestar! (that exclamation point is part of the name). There are so many more than the Cortland and Empire apples we see year-round in our favorite supermarket.

Apples ripen at different times during the harvest season, from August through November. Aficionados will visit a spectrum of orchards seeking out the more obscure varieties, and they will return monthly to see what is now ripe. Many of us make only an annual trip to a nearby orchard on a perfect fall day. I now realize they are deserving of much more of my time.

The New England apple has a rich history. There were no apples, as we know them today, only wild crab apples in the New World when the first settlers arrived. The Pilgrims landed at Plymouth Rock in Massachusetts in 1620. Three years later the first cultivated apples appeared, thanks to the seeds brought over by the French, Dutch, German, and English.

(For a wonderful read, check out the online version of "Wild Apples" by Henry David Thoreau (1817-1862), one of America's foremost writers. His essay laments the destruction of the wild apple species.)

Today the six-state region of New England produces between 3.5 million and 4 million (forty-two-pound) boxes of fresh apples every year. By acreage, here are the state-by-state statistics:

Massachusetts	3,100 acres
Maine	2,700 acres
Connecticut	1,800 acres
Vermont	1,700 acres
New Hampshire	1,300 acres
Rhode Island	230 acres

As for statistics on New England orchards, I was unable to find answers to my questions. There are plenty of statistics on the farms of New England, and many but not all of those farms do have orchards. Based on my experiences during the past year, I feel confident in saying there are at least one thousand orchards, large and small, in this northeast corner of America. And there's more than apples in those many orchards.

Apples tend to be the main crop at New England orchards, with cherries, peaches, nectarines, pears, quince, and plums as the supporting crops.

CHERRIES

The cherry trees in a mixed orchard are the first to bear fruit. Cherry blossoms cheer us in the spring with their color and beauty. The cherry has a very short growing season, and the peak season is brief as well, only about three weeks from late June to mid-July. Sweet cherry cultivars include Black Gold and Lapins that you can eat right off the tree. Sour or tart cherry cultivars, which are meant more for cooking, include Dwarf Northstar, which is considered the best, and Montmorency, great for baking pies.

Parlee Farms in Tyngsboro, Massachusetts, has nine varieties in a two-acre cherry grove with 1,400 trees. This is a precious fruit, and New England's winter weather can ruin the following summer's crop. After having below-zero temperatures in February 2015, most of the cherry crop was lost, and there was no cherry picking at Parlee Farms that summer. So, as they say at Parlee Farms, enjoy this wonderful fruit when you can.

PEACHES AND NECTARINES

Kissing cousins—that's how orchard owners describe peaches and nectarines. The only difference between these two juicy fruits is fuzz. A peach has fuzz. A nectarine is a peach without the fuzz. They are so closely related that a peach tree will occasionally bear nectarines, and vice versa. Some experts also claim a slight difference in flavor with peaches being musky and nectarines lighter and almost lemony. Look for fruits that have an orange-gold background color, for they are the sweetest. There are hundreds of peach and nectarine cultivars, classified as either freestones or clingstones. The flesh of freestones separates easily from the pit. The flesh of clingstones clings tightly to the pit.

Like cherries, peach trees have a brief but juicy season. Red Haven and Canadian Harmony peach trees are popular in Massachusetts. Other New England peaches include Ernie's Choice, Madison, Cresthaven, and Garnet Beauty. Reliance peaches can be found in many orchards beginning in July. The Fantasia nectarine is another favorite. Parlee Farms has 15 varieties of freestone peaches and three varieties of nectarines.

PEARS AND QUINCE

Pears and quince belong to the same family. We're all familiar with pears, while quince is a new fruit to many of us. As for pears in New England, orchards grow Bartlett, Bosc, D'Anjou, and Kieffer. The small but very sweet Seckel pear is very popular. Asian pears are new to New England and tend to be grown in Boston-area orchards with Shinko considered the

best for flavor. Other names you may see at farm stands are Luscious, Parker, Patten, and Summercrisp.

Bright golden yellow when ripe, a quince looks like a pear. It's usually cooked, although in warmer climates quince can ripen more and be eaten raw. Quince trees are rarely grown in large amounts with usually only one or two trees in a mixed orchard.

PLUMS

There are more than 100 species of plums with about thirty of them indigenous to North America. Commonly found in New England, especially the southern half, are the wild red plum, *Prunus americana*, and the beach plum, which is good for preserves. Small and usually purple, European plums such as Green Gage and Damson are the top choice for the colder regions of New England. Green Gage has green skin and flesh even when ripe. With purple or black skin and green flesh, Damson plums are rather tart and used mostly for preserves or cooking. The other European plums are good for canning and sweet enough to be dried for prunes. Many are excellent for simply eating fresh out of hand.

Parlee Farms has eight varieties of plums that are harvested from early August into mid-September. Some of the varieties grown in New England include Santa Rosa, Empress, Polly, President, Seneca, Stanley, Blue Damson, and the Italian Plum. Only one inch in diameter, the American plum—red, yellow, and orange—is grown in all six New England states.

The Orchard Cycle

For years I have visited local orchards and stopped at rustic farm stands only on beautiful summer and fall days. It's one of the ways I enjoy life, and it makes me feel good. But having learned so much of what it takes to be an orchard owner, I now realize the orchards have a yearlong cycle.

As I write this introduction in February 2016, fruit trees throughout New England are resting amidst a blanket of pure white snow. The trees are dormant, and it's time for pruning. Every fruit tree is pruned every year. This not only removes dead branches, it also encourages more fruitful growth.

The folks at North Chester Orchards in Maine informed me that blossom time is around the third week of May for their apple trees. This is when the honeybees kept at the orchard and wild bees do their job of pollination. The pollen from the flowers of one variety of apple must be moved to another for the apples to grow. Every apple begins as a beautiful blossom.

When summer comes around, orchard owners use fertilizers and sprays to ensure a good, healthy crop. Many orchards now use Integrated Pest Management (IPM), which permits the use of less spray. Insect traps are set, and pest monitoring lets farmers know when certain insects and pests are present.

The cherries are the first to ripen, followed by the peaches, nectarines, apples, pears, and quince, from early summer into the autumn months. That's the busiest time in the orchard cycle. Orchard owners and their staff must pick what's ripe, and they must deal with the public. If it's a pick-your-own orchard, customers must be taught how to pick fruit correctly. An apple, for instance, is picked by holding the apple in the palm of your hand and lifting up with a twist. You should never pull down on an apple. Doing so breaks off the twigs that should bear next year's fruit. It's very important that the children in an apple-picking group learn how to do this.

Many orchards are open only for the picking season, but just as many stay open until Thanksgiving or even Christmas. Fruit that isn't sold can be kept in cold storage, and some winterized farm stores remain open all winter long—when it's time for the orchard cycle to start again with that all-important *pruning*.

Orchard Etiquette

There are the dos and don'ts of how to behave when visiting an orchard, especially pick-your-own places. Some orchards post their specific rules on their websites, while others go a step further and have signage (often humorous) on the property. Here is a compilation of the Ten Commandments at various orchards:

1. Remember you are a guest, and respect the orchard the same way you would want visitors to respect your property.

2. Supervise children at all times for two reasons—they must be kept safe, and they must not do any harm to the orchard any farm animals on the property.

3. If there is a petting zoo, you can pet and feed them, but never chase a farm animal.

4. No vehicles are allowed in the orchard without special permission.

5. Do not climb on the trees or shake branches. This causes damage.

6. Sampling the fruit while picking your own is expected, within reason.

7. Do not throw the fruit around. Do not waste fruit.

8. Thou shalt not steal fruit by hiding it. Remember this is someone's livelihood.

9. Watch out for moving cars and farm equipment.

10. Do not litter. Use the trash receptacles on the property.

Dogs are another matter. Many orchards do not allow dogs on the property, while some are happy to have dogs visit as long as they are on a leash. If dogs are allowed, it's asked that you keep them away from the petting zoo. You must clean up after your dog. And do not let your dog do his business on the pumpkins or bales of hay. Be considerate of other people in the orchard. Not everyone loves dogs as much as you do. Of course, guide dogs and service dogs are always welcome.

With all that said, I hope you like the recipes in this book as much as I do, and I hope you are inspired to go exploring. Visit orchards near and far. I promise it will make you feel good.

Linda Beaulieu
Lincoln, Rhode Island
February 14, 2016

Massachusetts

Massachusetts has many claims to fame, among them folk hero Johnny Appleseed who was born in the Bay State. John Chapman (1774-1845) became known as Johnny Appleseed as he established orchards throughout America. Born in Leominster, the eccentric frontier nurseryman traveled extensively, planting trees that produced small, tart apples that were good for making hard cider.

With a Bible tucked under his arm and a sack full of seeds, Johnny Appleseed was quite the character, usually barefoot and wearing raggedy clothes and a hat made of tin. He was a staunch believer in animal rights and a practicing vegetarian in his later years. After his death, the pioneer folk hero became a legend. Johnny Appleseed statues dot northeastern and midwestern states, and festivals are held in his name. The story of Johnny Appleseed has been told for decades in countless children's books. He is the official folk hero of Massachusetts, and the Honeycrisp apple is the official state fruit.

We can thank John Chapman for the hundreds of apple orchards in this state alone, from the Berkshire region in western Massachusetts to the Greater Boston area, on to Cape Cod and the islands of Martha's Vineyard and Nantucket.

According to the Orange Pippin website, there are well over one hundred orchards in Massachusetts. The first was planted in 1625 in Boston by William Blaxton, an English preacher.

Orange Pippin is the definitive source of information when it comes to orchards and their fruits. Their curious name, Orange Pippin, comes from an apple variety regarded as an excellent dessert apple. Pippin is an old English word for seedling.

Massachusetts played a major role in American history. The Pilgrims fled England on the *Mayflower* to find their "New England," landing in Plymouth, Massachusetts, in 1620. A year later the first Thanksgiving was held in that area with the Pilgrims and Native Americans breaking bread and giving thanks for having survived their first year in the new world. Today visitors can visit Plimoth Plantation for a real-life glimpse of what life was like back then. Agriculture was the main economy until the Industrial Revolution brought about manufacturing.

In the past centuries, Massachusetts has become well known for its educational institutions such as Harvard University, its medical facilities, and technology. The famous Kennedy family has always called Massachusetts home, whether they served in political office or vacationed at the family compound in Hyannis Port on Cape Cod. Today Massachusetts is the fastest growing state in New England, largely due to a high quality of life and a well-respected higher education system.

Like much of New England, Massachusetts has a transitional climate with warm to hot summers and wet winters. Average temperatures range from about 35°F in the winter to 81°F in the summer. This ever-changing range has brought about an often-heard comment: "If you don't like the weather, just wait five minutes."

WHICH APPLE DO YOU LOVE?

The Cox Orange Pippin is widely considered the most delicious dessert apple, combining complex hints of pear, melon, orange, and mango.

The Big Apple

(And we don't mean New York City)

On the first day of fall in 2015, we drove down country roads that led to The Big Apple farm stand in Wrentham, Massachusetts. On this quintessential autumnal weekday, the farm stand was busy but manageable. On weekends, The Big Apple is mobbed with families, young couples on dates, and individuals in search of that perfect apple.

Located in a huge white barn attached to the family residence, The Big Apple offers twenty-six varieties of apples (and so much more), handpicked in the surrounding orchards on 200 acres of land. It started out as a farm prior to the American Civil War. This property was named Pine Hedge Orchards in 1930, but people started calling it The Big Apple because of the huge carved wooden apple that still hangs above the entrance to the barn. Since 1950, the Morse family has owned and operated The Big Apple. Today the spacious

barn is a modern fruit processing facility with a viewing platform where you can watch the apple grader sort the apples. Children especially like to watch the old-fashioned doughnuts being made in the on-site bakery.

In addition to the basic Baldwin and the exotic Fuji apple, the historic barn holds plenty of pumpkins, freshly picked vegetables, seasonal fruits, baked goods (I recommend the blueberry pie), jams, jellies, preserves, maple syrup, honey, fudge, and even penny candy. The back wall is devoted to freshly pasteurized pure apple cider, available by the cup, half-gallon, and gallon. The richer and sweeter Russett Apple Cider is a fall favorite and available only at Thanksgiving. Peaches, cherries, pears, plums, nectarines, and apricots round out the orchard offerings. The apricots are a choice find, not available at many local farm stands.

The opportunity to pick your own apples is available on weekends only, starting after Labor Day. We like to drive directly into the orchard, but you also can park near the farm store and enjoy a hayride to and from that part of the orchard that's been selected for pick-ing on that day. The variety to be picked depends on recent weather. All the picking fruit is within easy reach for adults and children.

Every piece of fruit in The Big Apple farm store is picked by hand. At the height of the season, you'll see professional pickers with large open sacks slung across their shoul-ders, which allow them to pick with both hands, even when they climb to the top of their wooden ladders. The sacks of apples are gently deposited into large wooden crates that

are lined up beside the trees, waiting for a tractor to haul the fruit into the barn for grading.

The apple grader washes, dries, polishes, and sorts the fruit by weight onto bagging tables. It's really something to see. Workers then carefully place the shiny apples into sturdy white and red paper bags that end up lining the shelves inside the farm stand, waiting to go to a good home. Some apples are destined for the candy apple cauldron, where they are quickly dipped and turned to coat all sides. After drying on wax paper, the candy apples are wrapped and put on display. Another contraption called "the Pease apple peeler and corer machine" peels, cores, and slices 32 apples per minute. These sliced apples are used to make The Big Apple's famous apple pie and apple crisp.

Don't forget to help yourself to a free apple from their apple barrel.

JUST WHAT ARE DROPS?

They are the apples that drop from the trees and are lying on the ground. Some orchards allow customers to collect the drops, usually at a lower price. But many orchards no longer sell their drops, nor do they use them to make cider. A few years ago, a New York orchard made cider from their drops. Those drops were lying on the same ground where their cows roamed. The orchard did not do a good enough job washing the apples, and customers who drank that cider got sick. Drops can be used to make cider, but the cider makers must follow stringent rules and regulations. Buyers beware.

Apple Pie

Piecrust dough, rolled out, top and bottom

½–⅔ cup sugar

⅛ teaspoon salt

1–1½ tablespoons cornstarch

¼ teaspoon cinnamon

⅛ teaspoon nutmeg

5–6 cups peeled and thinly sliced apples

Preheat oven to 450°F. Line the bottom of a 9-inch pie pan with a rolled out piecrust dough.

In a large bowl, combine the sugar, salt, cornstarch, cinnamon, and nutmeg. Gently mix the apple slices in until they are well coated. Place the apples in the pie pan. Cover the apples with the rolled out dough for the upper crust. Be sure to prick holes in the top crust for venting.

Bake in the 450°F oven for 10 minutes. Reduce the heat to 350°F and bake for 35–50 minutes, or until golden brown and done. Oven temperatures vary so watch carefully.

Makes 6 servings.

Note: You can also use this recipe for Peach Pie by substituting sliced peaches for apples. I like to use brown sugar instead of white granulated sugar when I make an apple pie. I'm too busy to make pie dough from scratch so I use ready-to-bake piecrusts with great success. They are available in the refrigerated section of most supermarkets. One package contains two 9-inch piecrusts for the top and bottom of a basic pie. Make sure you let the dough come to room temperature before use. That way it will unroll easily without creasing or folding.

Pie for Breakfast

Did you know that many New Englanders eat pie for breakfast? It's a centuries-old tradition brought over from England by early American settlers. We also like a wedge of sharp Vermont cheddar cheese with our apple pies. When you think about that combination of apple pie and cheese, it's the perfect breakfast made up of carbs, fruit, and dairy. With this in mind, we've selected this quintessential apple pie recipe from The Big Apple in Wrentham, Massachusetts, as the first recipe in this book celebrating the beautiful orchards of New England.

From the Cherry Orchard

I've been making these muffins for years, and I love the tang of the cherries mixed in with the wholesomeness of the oats. I always spray my muffin tin with a light coating of non-stick veg-

etable spray instead of greasing the muffin cups with butter. That way I don't feel so guilty when I grab another muffin to go with my morning coffee. New England cherries have a very short sea-son—only about three weeks from late June to mid-July. If you are lucky enough to live near a cherry orchard, such as Parlee Farm in Tyngsboro, Massachusetts, near the New Hampshire border, you can make this recipe with fresh, local cherries. It's amazing how some-thing so delicious is so fast and easy to make. As for the ingredients, I once substituted allspice for the nutmeg, and vanilla extract for the almond extract, and these muffins came out even better.

Cherry Oatmeal Muffins

1 cup old-fashioned or quick-cooking oats, uncooked

1 cup all-purpose flour

½ cup firmly packed brown sugar

1½ teaspoons baking powder

¼ teaspoon ground nutmeg

¾ cup buttermilk

1 egg, beaten

¼ cup vegetable oil

1 teaspoon almond extract

1 cup tart cherries, coarsely chopped

Preheat oven to 400°F. In a large bowl, combine the oats, flour, brown sugar, baking powder, and nutmeg.

In a small bowl, combine the buttermilk, egg, oil, and almond extract. Pour the buttermilk mixture into the oats mixture. Stir just to moisten the ingredients. Quickly stir in the chopped cherries.

Spray a muffin pan with non-stick spray. Fill the muffin cups two-thirds full. Bake in the 400°F oven for 15–20 minutes.

Makes 12 muffins.

CHERRY FACTS

Cherries are very perishable and do not ripen after pick-ing. So pick fully ripe cherries and refrigerate soon after purchase. These can remain fresh in your refrigerator for at least two days.

Studies have shown cherries to have many health bene-fits. They are high in antioxidants, low in cholesterol, fat, and sodium. They are also a good source of vitamin C and fiber.

Autumn Hills Orchard

Autumn Hills Orchard is perfectly named. Located on three rolling hills, the 84-acre orchard offers spectacular views of hills and mountains in Massachusetts and southern New Hampshire. On a clear day, as the song goes, the scenery is quintessential New England, especially during fall foliage season. A working orchard for more than sixty years, Autumn Hills is in historic Groton, Massachusetts, northwest of Boston. Family operated, the orchard grows more than twenty-five varieties of apples, as well as peaches, pears, plums, and grapes. They consider themselves to be a small operation, with more than 4,000 semi-dwarf trees. Autumn Hills relies on Integrated Pest Management techniques, and their goal is to grow the best fruit possible in a sustainable manner with the least amount of impact on the land and the critters that live in the area.

PAYMENT AT AUTUMN HILLS

Autumn Hills has a small "honor system" farm stand where you can purchase apples or other fruit in season. The stand is located in the barn where there is a cooler stocked with apples. Customers must bring exact change or a check to drop in the honor box.

Owner Ann Harris loves to talk about apples, pointing out there's so much more cooks can do with apples beyond the traditional apple pie. She says apples can be prepared in a variety of ways and don't always need to be the primary ingredient in a dish. From her personal recipe collection comes a recipe for Oven Cakes with Apples and Bacon. Oven cakes are light pancakes, much like popovers. They can be baked in a large pan or in smaller skillets and ovenproof ramekins. Ann likes to use small cast-iron pans, six inches in diameter, for individual servings. A second favorite recipe from Ann is for crepes that are lighter and sweeter than most because they are made with wheat flour and cornstarch.

Oven Cakes with Apples and Bacon

FOR THE BATTER:

3 large eggs

2 tablespoons granulated sugar

¼ teaspoon freshly grated nutmeg

¼ teaspoon salt

½ cup unbleached all-purpose flour

½ cup milk

2 tablespoons unsalted butter

FOR THE APPLE MIXTURE:

2 medium-size apples

1 tablespoon butter

1 tablespoon sugar

¼ teaspoon cinnamon

FOR SERVING:

4 slices cooked bacon

Maple syrup, as needed

Adjust oven rack to middle position. Preheat oven to 425°F.

In a large bowl, whisk the eggs with the sugar, nutmeg, and salt until well blended. Add the flour, whisking until smooth. Add the milk, continuing to whisk until smooth.

Heat 2 small ovenproof skillets for smaller oven cakes or use one larger skillet to make a single oven cake. Melt 1 tablespoon of butter in each pan, and then pour in the batter, half in one pan and half in the other. If you are making a single oven cake, melt all the butter and pour all the batter into the one large skillet.

Bake in the 425°F oven until the pancake is puffed and golden, about 20 minutes. Refrain from opening the oven door to check during the baking, as the pancake may not puff up as much.

While the oven cake is baking, peel and core the apples, slicing them into ¼-inch slices. In a large skillet, melt the butter and sauté the apples, sugar, and cinnamon for about 10 minutes, or until the juices start to caramelize and the apples soften. Remove from heat.

Using tongs and a spatula, gently remove the oven cake from the pan, and serve on a plate. Spoon the cooked apple slices into the center of the oven cake. Top with bacon strips and drizzle with maple syrup.

Makes 2 servings.

Crepes with Boiled Cider Sauce

FOR THE CREPE BATTER:

½ cup cornstarch

¼ cup wheat flour

3 large eggs

3 tablespoons unsalted butter, melted

2 tablespoons sugar

1 tablespoon Calvados or other apple brandy

1 teaspoon vanilla extract

¼ teaspoon coarse kosher salt

2 tablespoons of butter, clarified for pan

FOR THE BOILED CIDER SAUCE:

1½ cups apple cider

TO MAKE THE CREPES:

It's best to let your crepe batter sit for at least an hour before making crepes. Prepare in advance by whisking all the batter ingredients in a large bowl until smooth. Cover and refrigerate if sitting for more than 1 hour.

Heat a medium-size non-stick skillet or seasoned crepe pan. Pour 1 teaspoon of clarified butter into the pan and brush to coat the entire surface.

Add 2 tablespoons of batter to the pan, spreading the batter evenly over the pan by tilting it or by using a crepe stick to distribute the batter.

Cook until the center of the crepe is cooked through and the edges are lightly browned, usually 1 minute or less.

Run a spatula around the crepe to loosen it, and flip the crepe over. Cook the second side for about 15–30 seconds, just to brown it a bit. As each crepe comes off the pan, you can place them on a plate, separating each crepe with parchment paper or a paper towel.

Serve with boiled cider sauce drizzled over the crepes. If serving this as a dessert, add vanilla ice cream for a special treat. Alternatively, you can serve the crepes one at a time by folding them in quarters and dipping the crepe into the boiled cider sauce, coating part of the crepe with the sauce.

TO MAKE BOILED CIDER SAUCE:

Place 1½ cups of fresh apple cider in a small saucepan, and boil on high heat until the cider becomes thick and has the consistency of maple syrup.

The cider will lose up to 80 percent of its volume, which may take 20–30 minutes depending on the heat setting. Test by pouring off a spoon of the cider. When the cider starts to drip off the spoon in a wider stream or more slowly, like maple syrup, you can turn the heat down to a lower temperature, just to keep it warm while you make the crepes. Makes about ¼ cup of boiled cider sauce.

Shortcut: Boiled cider jelly is available in some gourmet stores and markets in New England that feature regional foods. In a small saucepan, combine ½ cup or so of the prepared boiled cider jelly and 1–2 tablespoons of water. Heat until the jelly becomes a thick, warm syrup.

Makes about 18 crepes of medium size.

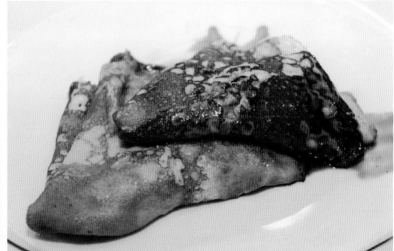

Westward Orchards

When you pull up to Westward Orchards in Harvard, Massachusetts, you can smell the freshly made apple cider doughnuts from the parking lot. That's just the start of your sensory experience here. The big red farm store is a turn-of-the-century dairy barn now stocked with fresh fruits and vegetables, gourmet foods, baked goods. It is a quaint place to grab a bite to eat. Breakfast (think Belgian waffles with seasonal fruit, maple syrup, and whipped cream) and lunch (sandwiches, salads, and soups) are offered daily, and you can dine on the large covered porch. That porch is the scene for live bluegrass music jam sessions every Sunday afternoon from June through mid-October.

Now run by Karen Green, Westward Orchards is a fourth-generation, family-owned farm on 275 acres in Nashoba Valley, one of the state's best apple-producing areas. They grow blueberries, peaches, pears, plums, and of course apples—primarily Cortland, Delicious, Macoun, McIntosh, and Spartan. Folks can pick their own, and they can take a wagon ride down to the pumpkin patch. The Holiday Open House in early December is always a big draw.

Clarkdale Fruit Farms

Clarkdale Fruit Farms in Deerfield, Massachusetts, is one of those quaint destinations that has New England written all over it. The barn red-and-gray farm stand beckons, especially in the fall with its open windows and a riot of color surrounding its portals—bright orange pumpkins, green winter squashes, and warm yellow mums. Rustic wooden bins and barrels hold fresh produce. The store is open daily from 8 a.m. to 5 p.m., August through March.

From April through July, the Clark family at this fourth generation fruit farm is busy tending to its one hundred-plus varieties of apples, peaches, pears, plums, nectarines, quince, cherries, and grapes. Much of the summer fruit is available only in August and September, while the pears are offered through December, while supplies last. The yellow- and white-fleshed peaches include antique varieties and "super sweet" low-acid peaches. The Clarks proudly sell only tree-ripened fruit that just hours before hung on the trees.

Consider the apples grown there, more than forty varieties, from Duchess to Spigold, names you won't see in your supermarket. New varieties are planted every year. The farm still has heirloom apple varieties from trees planted by the first generation of Clarks. They offer pick-your-own McIntosh apples every fall. For more than half a century, the Clarks have produced apple cider from their own apples. Their fruit and cider can be found on the menus of local restaurants and at local farmers' markets. The Clark family strongly believes in sustainable agriculture.

I am always surprised at how wonderful apples and onions go together. A perfect example of that combination can be found in Clarkdale Fruit Farm's Apple Onion Cheese Gratin. And, for dessert, how about old-fashioned apple dumplings? Or a modern twist on the classic apple crisp?

Apple Onion Cheese Gratin

1 tablespoon butter

1 tablespoon unbleached white flour

1 cup milk, scalded

½ teaspoon salt

½ teaspoon ground nutmeg

Pinch of ground cloves

4 cups peeled and sliced apples

1 cup chopped onions

2 tablespoons brown sugar, optional

2 cups grated cheddar cheese

1 cup chopped walnuts

1 cup bread crumbs

Preheat oven to 350°F. Lightly grease an 11 x 7-inch baking dish.

In a pot, melt the butter and whisk in the flour to make a roux. Slowly add the scalded milk, whisking continuously until the sauce starts to thicken. Add the salt, nutmeg, and cloves, and stir for 1 minute or until thick. Remove from the heat and set aside.

Spread the apples and onions evenly in the prepared baking dish. For a sweeter gratin, mix in the brown sugar.

Sprinkle the grated cheese over the apples and onions, and pour the sauce on top. Scatter the walnuts and bread crumbs over everything.

Bake uncovered in the 350°F oven for 45 minutes, or until top is golden and crisp.

Makes 6 servings.

Apple Dumplings

3 cups flour

1 cup shortening

½ cup cold water

½ teaspoon salt

5 apples, peeled, cored, and sliced

⅔ cup sugar

1 teaspoon cinnamon

½ teaspoon nutmeg

3 cups brown sugar

3 cups boiling water

2 tablespoons butter

Whipped cream or vanilla ice cream

Preheat oven to 350°F.

In a bowl, mix together the flour, shortening, cold water, and salt. Roll thin like a piecrust in a rectangular shape.

Sprinkle the apples with the sugar, cinnamon, and nutmeg. Mix well and spread on the dough. Roll up the dough like a jellyroll, and slice into 12 pieces. Place the pieces in a 9 x 13-inch baking pan.

In a separate bowl, mix the brown sugar, boiling water, and butter. Pour over the apple rolls.

Bake in the 350°F oven for 30–40 minutes. Serve with whipped cream or vanilla ice cream.

Makes 12 servings.

Apple Ginger Crisp

4 cups peeled and sliced apples
(tart apples are recommended)

½ cup brown sugar

¼ cup butter, softened

1 teaspoon cinnamon

1½ cups crushed ginger snap
cookies

Vanilla ice cream (optional)

Preheat oven to 375°F.

Layer the apples in a 9-inch square pan. In a bowl, combine
the remaining ingredients, and spread over the apples. Bake
in the 375°F oven for 30 minutes.

Serve warm with a scoop of vanilla ice cream if desired.

Makes 6 servings.

Keown Orchards

A true New England treasure, that's how regular customers view Keown Orchards and its owner, Foppema's Farm. These two entities are now one large farming organization in central Massachusetts. Yet their fans still see this seasonal operation as a family farm.

The 175-acre spread was originally owned by Arthur and Alice Keown back in 1924. Two generations of Keowns currently work on the property.

Away from the pristine farmland, the farm stand is located in scenic Sutton, about fifty miles outside of Boston. It is open Thursday through Saturday from mid-September through October for apple picking and hay wagon rides through the orchard.

More than fifty varieties of apple are grown at Keown Orchards, including many antiques and some so new they have yet to be named. The cultivars from before 1900 include Dutch Sweet Apple and Golden Russett. Their farm stand also offers twenty varieties of peaches and nectarines as well as plums, cherries, and pears. The aroma of freshly baked fruit pies fills the air along with the scent from apple wood burning in the stove. Fresh pressed cider is always available. In cool weather, there's also mulled cider to chase away the chill.

Here are four of their best recipes, sweet and savory, with one dessert calling for very ripe pears, and the other for perfectly ripe summer peaches.

Sherry Peach Salad

¼ cup fresh lemon juice

3–4 tablespoons sugar

¼ cup dry sherry (substitute cranberry juice if desired)

3 medium peaches, peeled and sliced, about 2 cups

2 bananas, sliced ¼-inch thick

1 cup seedless grapes

In a medium bowl, combine the lemon juice, sugar, and sherry. Stir until the sugar is dissolved. Add the peaches, bananas, and grapes to the dressing. Toss gently until well coated. Cover and refrigerate until it's time to serve.

Makes 4 servings.

Apple and Beet Salad

8–10 beets

Oil, as needed

Salt and pepper, to taste

¼ cup walnuts

2 tablespoons butter

2 cups balsamic vinegar

1 cup maple syrup

2 McIntosh apples

2 Cortland apples

Mesclun lettuce mix, as needed

Blue cheese, as needed

Preheat oven to 350°F. Peel and trim the beets, lightly oil, and season with salt and pepper. Place the beets in a roasting pan. Roast the beets in the 350°F oven until tender, about 25 minutes.

In the meantime, heat the walnuts in the butter in a skillet over medium heat. Pour in the balsamic vinegar and maple syrup. Simmer until reduced and thickened.

When the beets are cooked and the salad is about to be served, cut the apples thinly and in the shape of a half moon (approximately 1 cup after coring). Cut the beets into slices.

On a large platter, lay the beets and apple slices over the top of the mesclun mix that has been tossed with the balsamic vinegar dressing. Crumble the blue cheese over the top of the salad and serve.

Makes 4-6 servings.

Pear and Gingerbread Pudding

4 large, very ripe, yellow Bartlett pears

2 cups honey

1 cup brandy

4 tablespoons freshly grated ginger

1 teaspoon ground cardamom

1 teaspoon ground nutmeg

1 loaf day-old white bread

1 cup golden raisins or dried cranberries (optional)

1 cup sliced almonds (optional)

1 quart light cream or half and half

2 cups heavy cream

8 large eggs

Preheat oven to 350°F. Remove the cores from the pears, and dice the fruit into 1-inch cubes. Mix the pears with the honey, brandy, ginger, and spices, and allow them to sit for several hours in a sealed container.

Remove the crust from the bread, and cut the loaf into 1-inch cubes. Place the cubes into a 7 x 12-inch baking dish. If desired, evenly distribute the raisins and almonds in the dish as well.

In a bowl, whisk together the cream and eggs, and pour the mixture over the bread. Allow the bread to soak in the cream mixture for several minutes, until soft.

Add the marinated pears over the bread and cream mixture, making sure to mix in all of the juices. Add some almonds to the top of the bread pudding, and drizzle with honey.

Bake the bread pudding in a 350°F oven for 30–45 minutes until just set, or until a knife inserted in the center of the pudding comes out clean. Serve with whipped cream, or simply drizzle with a little more honey.

Makes 12 servings.

Peach Cake

½ cup butter or margarine

1¾ cups sugar

2 eggs

2½ cups flour

½ teaspoon baking soda

Pinch salt

1 cup plain yogurt

Zest of 1 lemon

2 cups sliced peaches, sprinkled with sugar to taste

Whipped cream, as needed

Preheat oven to 350°F. Grease and flour a 9 x 13 x 2-inch baking pan.

In a bowl, cream the butter and sugar until smooth. Add the eggs. Blend completely.

In another bowl, combine the dry ingredients and add the butter mixture alternately with the yogurt. Add 1½ table-spoons of lemon zest to the cake batter. Mix well. Pour the batter into the prepared pan.

Bake in the 350°F oven for 40 minutes, or until the cake tests done. Cool the cake on a rack. Serve with sliced peaches and whipped cream.

Makes 12 servings.

Wilson Farm

Wilson Farm is spread across 500-plus acres in two towns in two states—Lexington, Massachusetts, and Litchfield, New Hampshire. They produce more than one hundred varieties of fruits, vegetables, and herbs. Almost everything they grow is sold within hours of being harvested. Their impeccable fruit includes berries of almost every color, stone fruit, juicy pears, and a large variety of apples including heirlooms.

The farm stand at Wilson Farm is nothing less than amazing with its award-winning bakery, a cheese shop with more than 200 kinds of cheese from around the world, and premium selections of fine foods, meats, and seafood. This is a whole lot more than your typical "farm" stand. They even have an executive chef, Raymond Ost, who conducts cooking classes. Open year-round, the farm stand usually has a Wilson or two—Scott, Calvin, or Jimmy—on the premises to answer any questions a visitor may have.

It all began in 1884, when fresh from Ireland, James Wilson and his brother-in-law George Reynolds farmed sixteen acres in Lexington. Four generations later, a huge timber barn sits on thirty-three acres of land along with a massive greenhouse. That is the heart of the Wilson Farm.

This is one of those rare places where you can purchase quince, which they grow in their orchards. Quince? Just what is a quince? Only a handful of orchards grow quince, which is related to apples and pears. Quince trees with their eye-pleasing pale pink blossoms are grown mostly in the Middle East and China. In America, quince trees were first grown in the eighteenth-century New England colonies, where there was always a quince tree in the lower corner of every garden. The mature quince looks much like a pear with a bright golden-yellow color. Most varieties are too hard and sour to eat raw, so quince is usually cooked. They are high in pectin, which is needed to make jam and jelly. They can be roasted, baked, and stewed.

In this first recipe from Lynne Wilson at Wilson Farm, the quince is simmered until tender along with exotic flavors from far-off worlds. The second recipe from Wilson Farm is for a creative pizza right out of the orchard, made with pears, walnuts, and figs.

Quince and Goat Cheese Tarts

2 quince, peeled, cored and cut into eighths

1 quart pomegranate juice

Zest from 1 navel orange

1 cinnamon stick

½ teaspoon allspice

½ cup brown sugar

½ cup goat cheese

½ cup crème fraiche

¼ cup ricotta

1 tablespoon honey

2 eggs, beaten

Pinch of black pepper

Pre-baked mini tart shells, as needed

Apple cider, as needed to taste

Preheat oven to 325°F. Place first six ingredients in a pot. Simmer until the quinces are just tender. Remove from the heat and let cool completely. Remove the quinces and cut into small pieces. Set aside both the quince and the liquid in which it cooked.

Add the goat cheese, crème fraiche, ricotta, honey, eggs, and black pepper to a food processor. Pulse until blended.

Put 3–4 pieces of quince in each tart shell. Add a spoonful of the goat cheese mixture on top. Bake in the 325°F oven until golden brown, 15–20 minutes. Serve with the leftover pomegranate juice mixed with apple cider and reheated.

Makes 4 servings.

Pizza with Pears, Walnuts and Figs

1 pound fresh pizza dough

3 tablespoons butter

5 Bosc pears, peeled, cored, and thinly sliced

1 jar fig spread (available in gourmet stores)

1 cup walnuts, chopped

Gorgonzola cheese, as needed

Preheat oven to 450°F. Divide the pizza dough into 4 equal pieces. Spread out each piece to make individual pizzas.

In a large sauté pan over medium high heat, heat the butter to melting. Add the sliced pears and brown lightly. Remove the pan from the heat.

Spread a thin layer of the fig spread on the pizza dough going almost to the edge. Add the pears. Sprinkle with walnuts, and dot with Gorgonzola cheese.

Bake in the 450°F oven until golden brown, 5–6 minutes.

Makes 4 servings.

Boston Baked Beans

My mother-in-law, who was from Maine, always cooked her Saturday night baked beans in a traditional bean pot in the oven. Dot Beaulieu made classic Boston baked beans with navy beans, molasses, and salt pork, just as her mother taught her.

This classic dish originated with Native American Indians, who taught "bean hole cookery" to early American colonists. This method of baking was done in a dirt hole that was filled with very hot stones on which an earthenware pot of beans was placed. More hot stones were put around the pot, then dirt to fill the hole. The beans would bake for hours.

In and around the city of Boston, Massachusetts, the very religious Puritan women would bake their beans on Saturday and serve them that night for dinner. Enough baked beans would be made also to serve at Sunday breakfast and again at lunch, usually with brown bread and codfish cakes. Cooking was not allowed on the Sabbath, which ended on Sunday evening. So a huge pot of baked beans was put to good use every weekend. That tradition continues to this day in some Yankee households.

Once in a while I will make franks and beans on a Saturday night. For years I relied on canned beans, especially the B&M Brick Oven Baked Beans brand out of Portland, Maine. And, then, one day I made my own.

The first time I tried cooking baked beans, I did so in a crockpot. Since then I've tried other methods, but "low and slow" is the only way I like to make them now. The hot crockpot helps to warm the kitchen, and the aroma of the baking beans warms my soul. This is New England comfort food, especially in the fall and winter. Slow cooked in a flavorful sauce, baked beans are low in fat and high in fiber. It's almost magical how one cup of dried beans turns into more than two cups cooked.

Centuries ago someone figured out how to preserve autumn's apple cider by reducing it into a luscious dark syrup. It became a pantry staple in many households, from Appalachia to Maine.

Baked beans are now prepared a bit differently from state to state. I add apple cider to my mixture (I doubt if Dot would approve of that). Old-fashioned Vermont baked beans are made with yellow eye beans and a generous amount of maple syrup. In New Hampshire, salt pork is essential to good baked beans. Those of French-Canadian descent always put a whole onion into the pot. It's traditional in every New England state to serve baked beans with brown bread. In Massachusetts the baked navy bean is the official state bean.

If the beans you are baking today are to be eaten tomorrow, it's best to leave the beans juicy for they will absorb the liquid overnight. When you try this slow cooker method, check your crockpot from time to time. If it looks too thick and dry, add some boiling water or, as I like to do, add more hot apple cider.

Crockpot Apple Cider Baked Beans

2 cups dried white navy beans, picked over, washed, and soaked

1 small onion, diced

4 tablespoons molasses

4 teaspoons Dijon mustard

2 tablespoons ketchup

½ teaspoon salt

2 teaspoons black pepper

2 teaspoons dried thyme

1 small bay leaf

1 teaspoon cider vinegar

4 teaspoons soy sauce

1⅓ cups apple cider, boiling

Boiling water, as needed

Pour the beans onto a flat surface, such as your countertop, in a single layer. Pick out rocks, dirt, off-colored and broken beans, and discard. Wash the beans in two changes of cold water. Place the beans in a large pot, and cover with 3 inches of cold water. Allow the beans to soak for 8–10 hours or overnight.

If you prefer the quick-soak method, cover the picked-over beans with 3 inches of cold water, and bring to a boil. Boil for 1 minute, turn the heat off, and let stand for 1 hour or more.

Drain the beans, reserving their liquid. Bring that liquid to a boil.

Pour the beans into a crockpot. Add all the ingredients, stir, and add enough reserved boiling liquid to cover beans. Cook on high for 6–8 hours. Check periodically to make sure the beans are cooking in enough liquid. If it seems to be drying out, add 1–2 cups of boiling water.

Makes 8 servings.

Notes: You may substitute the dried beans with canned beans by using 3 (15-ounce) cans of navy beans or great northern beans. Drain and rinse. Proceed with step 4) of the recipe. Alternatively, you can always doctor up canned baked beans. That is, in a large slow cooker, combine 3 (28-ounce) cans of baked beans with 1 cup of chopped onions, 1 cup of barbecue sauce, 1 cup of brown sugar, and 4 tablespoons of prepared mustard. Cover the slow cooker and cook on high for 2–3 hours. Feel free to doctor up this recipe to suit your own tastes—add more or less of the barbecue sauce, brown sugar, mustard, and any other ingredients (like bacon, as shown here) that you like to flavor your beans.

Carlson Orchards

Walter and Eleanor started farming on a remote hilltop in Harvard, Massachusetts, in 1936. Their property turned out to be an excellent place for growing apples. As soon as they had apples to pick, the family started making cider. In the late 1960s, the farm specialized in fruits with apples as the main crop.

The second generation now runs Carlson Orchards, a 140-acre working farm. Bruce, Frank, and Robert Carlson, the three sons of Walter and Eleanor, are dedicated to continuing the family tradition.

Almost half of the Carlson property consists of fruit trees with the balance occupied by berry patches, a pumpkin field, and a frog pond noted for its abundance of dragonflies. The fruit trees produce four varieties of nectarines, six varieties of peaches, and twenty varieties of apples, from the ever-popular McIntosh to the lesser-known Cameo and Crispin. The annual Peach Festival in mid-August is always a popular event with hayrides into the orchards, live music, and a cookout.

The Carlson clan has come a long way since 1936. On a busy fall day they now bottle as much as 8,000 gallons of freshly pressed and pasteurized apple cider in a solar-powered state-of-the-art facility. Annually more than 500,000 gallons of cider are produced.

The retail store, with its dark green front doors, is open seven days a week. If you stop in during the slow season, don't be surprised if there's no one there, with customers expected to pay through the honor system.

Tougas Family Farm

The Tougas Family Farm in Northboro, Massachusetts, has been in operation for more than three decades, with Maurice and Phyllis Tougas purchasing the "home farm" in 1981 and adding acreage through the years. They now own about 120 acres, well stocked with apple, peach, and cherry trees, various berries, and pumpkins. The apples are the heart and soul of this farm. Maurice has devoted a great deal of energy bringing new varieties and modern growing techniques to this corner of New England. Currently there are more than 30 apple varieties available from mid-August to mid-October. USA Today listed the Tougas Family Farm as one of 10 great places to pick your own apples.

Over the years, the farm has grown, enabling the family to experiment with dwarf cherry trees and new apple varieties such as the explosively juicy Honeycrisp and the tart Crimson Topaz. The farm is located on an excellent site for fruit-growing site. Maurice with son Andre has been working diligently to learn how to grow sweet and tart cherries for reliable harvest in order to further diversify their fruit offerings.

Three Tougas children were born and raised on the farm. Andre, who went to Cornell University to study Pomology and Farm Finance, is now back on the farm full time. The family is dedicated to producing fruit in the safest and most environmentally friendly manner. In 1986 the farm was preserved under the Agricultural Preservation Restriction Program run by the state of Massachusetts.

People of all ages can enjoy this farm with its barnyard of baby animals and a professional kitchen turning out apple cobbler in September and apple cider doughnuts in October.

For many people, breakfast wouldn't be breakfast without some homemade jam smeared on toast or an English muffin. You can buy delicious jams at the Tougas Farm store, or you can make them yourself at home. (A basic knowledge of canning is required.) The Tougas family offers canning instructions and a bevy of recipes for you to try on their website (www.tougasfarm.com) including these three yummy jams, made with and without pectin. From the beverage section of the Tougas family recipe collection, we also offer three drink recipes, one for adults only and the other two for all to enjoy.

Peach Jam

8 cups peeled and crushed peaches

⅓ cup water

6 cups sugar

Combine the peaches and water in a heavy saucepan. Cook gently for 10 minutes. Add the sugar, and slowly bring to a boil, stirring until the sugar dissolves. Cook rapidly until thick, about 15 minutes. Pour the hot mixture into hot jars; adjust lids. Process for 10 minutes in a boiling water bath.

Makes about 8 half-pint jars.

Note: This jam is made without added pectin.

Spiced Blueberry-Peach Jam

4 cups chopped or ground peaches (about 4 pounds peaches)

4 cups blueberries (about 1 quart fresh) or 2 (10-ounce) packages frozen unsweetened blueberries

2 tablespoons lemon juice

½ cup water

5½ cups sugar

½ teaspoon salt

1 stick cinnamon

½ teaspoon whole cloves

¼ teaspoon whole allspice

Place the fruit in a large heavy saucepan; add the lemon juice and water. Cover, bring to a boil, and simmer for 10 minutes, stirring occasionally.

Add the sugar and salt; stir well. Add the spices tied in cheesecloth. Boil rapidly, stirring constantly until mixture reaches a temperature of 9°F above the boiling point of water, or until it thickens.

Remove from the heat; take out bag of spices. Skim any foam from the top. Pour the hot mixture into hot jars; adjust lids. Process 10 minutes in a boiling water bath.

Makes 6 or 7 half-pint jars.

Note: This jam is made without added pectin.

Raspberry-Peach Jam

2 cups peaches, finely chopped

2½ cups raspberries, crushed
(strain to remove seeds)

2 tablespoons fresh lemon juice

1 package powdered pectin

6¼ cups sugar

Place the fruit, lemon juice, and pectin in a large heavy saucepan. Bring the mixture to a full boil. Stir in the sugar and return to a full boil. Boil for exactly 1 minute. Remove from the heat. Skim any foam from the top.

Ladle quickly into clean jars. Wipe the tops of the jars, and cover with hot lids. Screw on the bands. Process in a water bath canner for 5 minutes.

Makes about 8 half-pint jars.

Note: When using commercial pectin, read and follow the directions enclosed with it carefully. After the addition of sugar, the mixture must be brought to a full boil and cooked for 1 minute. Purchase pectin designed to be used with less sugar to reduce the sugar content. Do not attempt to reduce amounts of sugar in regular pectin recipes, as the product will not jell.

JAM VERSUS JELLY

Jams and jellies are fruit products preserved by sugar and jellied to some extent. Jam is made from fruit, which has been crushed; it holds its shape but is less firm than jelly. Jelly is made from fruit juice, is clear, and firm enough to hold its shape. Jams made without commercial pectin take longer to cook than those made with added pectin.

Peach Smoothie

1 cup sliced peaches

1 scoop ice cream or frozen yogurt

⅔ cup water

1 cup ice

Place all the ingredients in a blender. Process until smooth.

Makes 1 serving.

Strawberry Sunrise Smoothie

1 cup vanilla yogurt

½ cup frozen strawberries

¼ cup apple juice or cider

1 banana

Place all the ingredients in a blender. Process until smooth. Serve in tall glasses.

Makes 2 servings.

The Old and the New

Here's an old-time dessert for you to try in your modern-day kitchen—a fruit buckle from Tougas Family Farm in Northboro, Massachusetts. It's just as it was made by the early settlers of New England. At the opposite end of the dessert spectrum is a recipe for a crisp that's easy as pie because it's done in a microwave oven.

Fruit Buckle

1 cup flour

½ cup sugar

1 teaspoon baking soda

¼ cup butter or margarine

½ cup milk

½ teaspoon salt

1 teaspoon vanilla

1 egg

1 cup fresh fruit (apples, blueberries, blackberries, raspberries, etc.)

FOR THE CRUMB TOPPING:

½ cup oats

½ cup sugar

½ cup flour

¼ cup butter

1 teaspoon cinnamon

½ teaspoon nutmeg

Preheat oven to 350°F. Grease a 9 x 9-inch or a 9 x 12-inch pan.

In a bowl, combine the flour, sugar, baking soda, butter or margarine, milk, salt, vanilla, and egg. Mix well and spread into the greased pan. Layer the fresh fruit on top.

In a bowl, combine the crumb topping. Sprinkle on top of the fruit.

Bake in the 350°F oven for 40 minutes, or until a tester comes out clean.

Makes 6–8 servings.

WAY BACK WHEN

· A stone tablet found in Mesopotamia from 1500 B.C. documents the first recorded sale of an apple orchard at a cost of three sheep.

· Egyptian pharaoh Ramses ordered apples to be grown in the Nile Delta in 1300 B.C.

· In 55 B.C., Julius Caesar's armies carried apple seeds with them as they conquered parts of Europe, planting orchards after each victory.

Microwave Peach Crisp

4 medium peaches, sliced (about 3 cups), or 2 (16-ounce) cans sliced peaches, drained

¼ cup biscuit baking mix

½ cup quick cooking oats

½ cup brown sugar, packed

3 tablespoons butter, softened

½ teaspoon cinnamon

¼ teaspoon nutmeg

Arrange the peaches in a microwave-safe 8 x 8 x 2-inch dish.

In a bowl, combine the remaining ingredients. Mix until crumbly, and sprinkle over the peaches.

Microwave on high for 6 minutes, then rotate the dish a half turn. Microwave until the peaches are tender, another 4–6 minutes.

Serve with ice cream or whipped cream, if desired.

Makes 6 servings.

Conventional oven directions: Bake in a preheated 375°F oven until the peaches are tender, 30–35 minutes.

Summer Peaches

"Fresh fruit, fresh air, and family fun"—that's the slogan at Tougas Family Farm in Northboro, Massachusetts. Their vast compendium of favorite recipes includes these two gems, which make excellent use of fresh summer peaches.

Peachy Praline* Pie

¾ cup granulated sugar

3 tablespoons flour

4 cups sliced peaches

1½ teaspoons lemon juice

Unbaked 9-inch piecrust

PRALINE:

⅓ cup brown sugar, firmly packed

¼ cup flour

½ cup chopped pecans

3 tablespoons butter or margarine

Preheat oven to 400°F. In a large bowl, combine the granulated sugar and 3 tablespoons of flour. Add the sliced peaches and lemon juice.

In a small bowl, combine the brown sugar, ¼ cup of flour, and pecans in a small bowl. Cut in the butter until the mixture is crumbly.

Sprinkle ⅓ of the pecan mixture over the bottom of the pie shell. Pour in the peach mixture, and sprinkle the remaining pecan mixture over the top of the pie.

Bake in the 400°F oven for about 40 minutes, or until the peaches are tender.

Makes 6 servings.

Note: Praline is a confection, usually made up of almonds and caramelized sugar that has its roots in classic French cuisine. French settlers brought the recipe to Louisiana, where New Orleans chefs used pecans instead of almonds, giving birth to the classic American praline.

Peach or Apple Blackberry Pie

Blackberries add a depth to this pie that is equally good with peaches or apples. For the pie top, both a lattice crust or a crumble topping work well, although remember to level the mixture in the plate if you prefer a lattice top.

FOR THE PIE:

3 cups peeled and sliced peaches or apples

2 cups blackberries

½ cup sugar

2 tablespoons flour

½ teaspoon cinnamon

½ teaspoon nutmeg

1 single 8-inch unbaked piecrust

IF YOU PREFER A LATTICE TOP:

1 single 8- or 9-inch unbaked piecrust cut into strips

IF YOU PREFER A CRUMBLE TOPPING:

½ cup flour

¼ cup sugar

¼ cup butter or margarine

Preheat oven to 400°F. Combine the filling ingredients and place in the unbaked piecrust.

Top with a lattice crust OR to top with a crumble topping combine the flour and sugar in a bowl. Cut the butter into the flour and sugar mixture. Spread evenly over the filling.

Bake in the 400°F oven for about 40 minutes, or until the filling is bubbling.

New England's Best-Kept Secret?

It's been called New England's best-kept secret in the fall. Historic Russell Orchards in Ipswich, Massachusetts, is family owned and operated. The 120-acre fruit farm is idyllic, especially in autumn when the colorful leaves start to fall, and you can detect the aroma of newly made apple cider doughnuts coming from the old red farmhouse.

It started out as the Goodale Farm with its first trees planted in 1920, and a successful cider mill was established in the 1950s. An agricultural preservation restriction was imposed to ensure the property would always be a working farm. After a series of owners, the Russell family purchased the farm and changed its name to Russell Orchards with Max planting fruit trees and berries, and Meredith starting up a bakery known for its made-from-scratch doughnuts. You can watch the doughnuts being made from a viewing platform. What is the secret ingredient? The cider pressed on the premises.

Current owners Doug and Miranda Russell took over in 2008, the second generation to farm the land. A winery was added, and you can sample their fruit wines in the tasting room. For the youngsters, they can feed the barnyard animals. On fall weekends, the entire family can enjoy a hayride out to the picking area. Plenty of picking advice is on their web site (www.russellorchards.com) as well as a slew of recipes. Here are two of their breakfast dishes for you to try at home—a rather elegant crepe with caramelized apples and a classic German apple pancake.

Crepes with Caramelized Apples

FOR THE CREPE BATTER:

2 eggs

½ cup milk

½ cup water

1 tablespoon sugar

¼ teaspoon salt

1 cup all-purpose flour

2 tablespoons butter, melted

FOR THE CARAMELIZED APPLES:

4–5 tart apples

2 tablespoons butter

2 tablespoons maple syrup, honey, or brown sugar

½ cup sweet hard cider (or regular cider)

4 sprigs fresh mint, optional

....

Note: A blender makes short work of these crepes, and the batter will keep well in the refrigerator. If you have no blender, whisk the ingredients in a large bowl.

....

TO MAKE THE BATTER

Blend the eggs, milk, and water together with the sugar and salt. Add the flour and melted butter. Blend or whisk until smooth.

Ladle some of the batter onto a hot griddle or frying pan. Smooth the batter into a thin layer with the back of the ladle or swirl by tipping the pan. When the surface is set, turn the crepe over and cook the other side. Remove to a warm plate.

TO MAKE CARAMELIZED APPLES

Peel, core, and coarsely chop the apples. Melt the butter in a 12-inch skillet. Add the maple syrup. Be careful not to burn. Add the apples and cook over medium high heat until the apple bottoms start to brown and caramelize. Stir frequently with a wooden spoon to caramelize all sides. Add the cider, cover, and cook down until the apples are softened and the cider has evaporated. If apples don't seem soft enough, add a bit more cider and continue to cook. Cinnamon or vanilla extract can be added with the cider, if desired.

TO SERVE

Crepes may be stacked and filled later, or filled and served immediately. Fresh berries, jam, or chocolate are also good with the crepes. Garnish with fresh mint if desired.

Makes 4 servings.

CIDER IS GOOD FOR YOU

According to the folks at Russell Orchards, apple cider has been used as a health tonic since the days of Hippocrates. A sip or two a day aids in digestion and eases sore throats. Packed with enzymes and high in potassium, apple cider vinegar boosts the immune system. Studies show it helps with weight control and removes toxins from the body. Leftover cider vinegar can be used after shampooing to make hair shiny, or, when mixed with water, it's a natural skin toner for the face. You can also add some to bath water to ease sore muscles. New Englanders would agree this is an all-purpose item.

German Apple Pancakes

3 eggs

⅓ cup milk

⅓ cup flour

¼ teaspoon salt

2 tablespoons butter or
shortening

¼ cup thinly sliced apples

Sugar and cinnamon, as needed

Preheat oven to 400°F. In a bowl or blender, beat the eggs with the milk, then add the flour and salt, and beat until smooth.

Melt the butter (or shortening) in a heavy 10-inch skillet. Tilt the skillet from side to side so all surfaces will be coated with the melted fat.

Quickly pour the egg mixture into the hot skillet, and sprinkle the apple slices on top. Bake in the 400°F oven, uncovered, for 20 minutes.

Remove the skillet from the oven, and serve pancakes immediately with a sprinkling of sugar and cinnamon.

Makes 2 servings.

Thanks to the Earl of Sandwich

Linguistic experts believe that the word "lunch" can be traced back to the 1500s, when the Spanish used the word *"lonja,"* which means a slice. A slice of bread or a slice of meat may have been an entire meal for some back then. That brings us to the word "sandwich," defined as a dish of sliced bread with a variety of meats, cheeses, and condiments. The sandwich is named after the John Montagu, Earl of Sandwich, in eighteenth-century England. A notorious gambler, Montagu would request a slice of meat between two pieces of bread so his fingers would not soil the playing cards. He would be amazed to see a modern-day lunch menu with so many sandwiches from which to choose, from pita pockets to gyros, and even sandwiches made without any bread. A sandwich and a fresh apple, peach, or pear is the perfect lunch.

Fruity Sandwiches

I grew up on the all-American grilled cheese sandwich. I remember on summer nights when it was too hot to cook a full meal, my mother would make perfectly golden grilled cheese sandwiches with potato chips on the side. We would dine outdoors in a yard that was enclosed with lilac bushes and pink rambling roses along a stone wall that my father built. A beautiful childhood memory, but this is boring food by today's culinary standards. It's a bit more work, but as an adult I prefer these savory grilled cheese sandwiches. I hope my mother would approve.

I collect grilled cheese sandwich recipes that appeal to adult taste buds such as the following two. The first is from my personal recipe collection. I like combining butter with olive oil for cooking, and I love how sweet an onion can be if it's sautéed properly. But what really makes this first sandwich sing is the apple cider jelly. As they say in that television commercial for potato chips, you can't eat just one.

The second modern-day grilled cheese sandwich is in the form of a panini, the Italian word for sandwich. Ideally you should make it on a panini grill or in a sandwich press, but you can also use a regular frying pan with a weight (such as a brick wrapped in foil) on top of the sandwich. Done that way, you will need to turn over the sandwich to get it brown on both sides. Once you have this adult grilled cheese sandwich, courtesy of Russell Orchards in Ipswich, Massachusetts, you won't want to go back to the plain variety.

Not Your Mother's Grilled Cheese Sandwich

3 tablespoons butter, divided

1 tablespoon olive oil

1 large onion, very thinly sliced

Salt and pepper, to taste

8 thick slices crusty bread

Apple cider jelly or a chunky apple chutney, as needed

8 ounces your favorite cheese (Gruyere, cheddar, or Brie are recommended), sliced

In a large skillet, melt 1 tablespoon of the butter in the oil. Add the onion, cover, and cook over high heat, stirring occasionally, for about 5 minutes. Lower the heat and uncover the skillet. Continue cooking over medium heat, stirring occasionally, until the onions are caramelized, about 25 minutes. Season with salt and pepper.

Spread one side of the bread with the remaining butter. Arrange the bread buttered side down on an immaculate work surface (some cooks like to do this on aluminum foil).

Spread a layer of apple cider jelly on each slice of bread. Top half of the slices with equal amounts of the cooked onions and the cheese (about 1 ounce per slice). Close the sandwiches.

Preheat a skillet or panini press (which I prefer). Grill the sandwiches over low heat until the bread is toasted and the cheese has melted, about 10 minutes. If you are using a skillet, press down on the sandwiches with a large spatula and flip them over halfway through the cooking process. When done, remove the sandwiches and cut them in half. Serve immediately.

Makes 4 servings.

Caramelized Apple and Gorgonzola Panini

4 cooking apples (Jonagold, Braeburn, or Granny Smith)

2 tablespoons butter

4 tablespoons honey

8 slices sourdough bread, thickly sliced (or your preference)

Gorgonzola cheese, as needed

Chutney (peach, mango, cranberry, or your preference), as needed

Peel and core the apples, then cut them into slices. Place the slices in a bowl of cold lemon water to prevent discoloration. After 5 minutes, drain the apples and pat them dry with a paper towel.

In a large skillet, melt the butter and honey, blending well. Add the apple slices and cook over medium-high heat for approximately 5 minutes, or until the apples begin to brown. Turn the slices over several times to brown evenly. The apple will start to caramelize and should be tender.

Assemble the panini by putting a layer of the caramelized apples on a slice of bread, then a layer of the cheese topped with some chutney. Close the sandwich. Butter both sides of the panini. Place in a panini or sandwich press, and close. (Follow the manufacturer's recommendations for cooking times.) The panini is done when both sides are golden brown.

Makes 4 servings.

....

Variations: You can also make these sandwiches by adding chopped walnuts, dried cranberries, chicken, or turkey.

....

Apple Sangria

An Orchard with a Winery

Doug and Miranda Russell, owners of Russell Orchards in Ipswich, Massachusetts, were married in the orchard and now have two children who love the farm as much as they do.

Their crops include apples, apricots, cherries, nectarines, peaches, pears, and plums as well as berries. What sets Russell Orchards apart from its peers is its winery. A cozy tasting room is located in the barn. In cold weather the huge fieldstone fireplace is a perfect spot to sip on the various (more than thirty) wines available. The apple-blueberry, cherry, peach, and pear wines have won awards. I'm a fan of their ciders, no less than seven types, including the very smooth Dry Cider Reserve, barrel aged in oak for sixteen years.

Here are three of their recipes that make excellent use of their extraordinary fruit wines, and a salsa recipe to go with your delicious sangria.

Apple Sangria

2 firm apples such as Pink Lady, Honeycrisp, or Baldwin

1 bottle Baldwin apple wine

½ cup triple sec

¼ cup honey

2 oranges, quartered

1 lemon, quartered

1 lime, quartered

2 cinnamon sticks

3 whole cloves

Club soda or ginger ale, as needed

Mint leaves, for garnish

Peel, core, and chop one of the apples. Set aside.

In a bowl, combine the wine, triple sec, and honey. Add the chopped apples, one quartered orange, all the lemon and lime, cinnamon sticks, and cloves. Refrigerate for at least 4 hours.

Strain the mixture into a pitcher. Peel, core, and finely chop the remaining apple. Peel, section, and chop the remaining orange. Mix the apple and orange in a bowl.

Fill glasses with ice. Pour in the sangria until three quarters full. Top with a splash of club soda or ginger ale. Garnish with a spoonful of the chopped apples, oranges, and a sprig of mint.

Makes 1 pitcher.

Ginger Summer Sangria

2 oranges, sliced

2 lemons, sliced

2 limes, sliced

1 bottle summer fruit wine such as raspberry, cherry, blackberry, strawberry, or peach

12½ ounces white grape juice

6¼ ounces ginger brandy or liqueur

12½ ounces ginger beer

Seasonal fruit, for garnish

Fill a pitcher to halfway with ice and the citrus slices. Add the wine, white grape juice, and ginger brandy. Stir to combine. Top with the ginger beer, and garnish with fresh fruit appropriate for the wine you're using.

Makes 1 pitcher.

Peachy Keen Cocktail

6 ounces peach or raspberry peach fruit wine

2 ounces fresh orange juice

1 ounce Campari

Orange and/or peach slices, for garnish

Fill a tall glass with ice. Add all the ingredients and stir to combine. Garnish with fresh orange or peach slices.

Makes 1 serving.

Peach Salsa

1⅓ cups diced peaches

¼ cup diced red bell pepper

¼ cup chopped green onions

2 tablespoons fresh lime juice

2 tablespoons chopped fresh cilantro

1 tablespoon minced jalapeno, seeded

1 teaspoon minced fresh ginger, peeled

1 garlic clove, minced

In a serving bowl, combine all the ingredients. Mix well. Season to taste with salt and pepper.

Makes about 2 cups.

Brining

Brining has become a popular trend in recent years, first at innovative restaurants and then with home cooks. Brining is much like marinating, but the usual purpose is to moisten the meat rather than to add flavor. Here the talented cooks at Russell Orchards in Ipswich, Massachusetts, share their recipe for brining a turkey with cider, followed by their method to braise a pork shoulder in hard cider.

Cider Brined Turkey

2 quarts plus 1 cup apple cider

1 cup kosher salt

½ cup light brown sugar

1 cup soy sauce

16 whole black peppercorns

8 whole star anise pods

6 garlic gloves, smashed

6 scallions, white parts only, trimmed, split lengthwise

6 (¼-inch-thick) slices unpeeled fresh ginger

5 dried shiitake mushrooms

2 cinnamon sticks

2 sprigs of cilantro

1 (12- to 14-pound) turkey

Salt and freshly ground black pepper, to taste

2 sweet-tart apples (Crispin, Cortland, or Granny Smith) cut into 6 pieces each

Melted unsalted butter or vegetable oil, for basting

In a very large pot, bring the 2 quarts of cider and next 11 ingredients to a boil, stirring to dissolve the salt and sugar. Let cool to room temperature. Stir in 1½ gallons cold water.

Add the turkey to the brine and press down to submerge. Cover and refrigerate overnight.

Remove the turkey from the brine and pat dry with paper towels. Discard the brine. Season the turkey lightly inside and out with salt and pepper.

Place it, breast side up, on a rack set in a large heavy roasting pan. Tie the legs together with kitchen twine. Let stand at room temperature for 1 hour.

Preheat oven to 375°F.

Combine the remaining cup of cider and 3 cups of water in the roasting pan. Scatter the apples around. Brush the turkey with butter. Flip the turkey to breast side down. Roast the turkey, basting occasionally, for 1 hour in the 375°F oven.

Using paper towels to protect your hands, flip the turkey. Roast, basting occasionally, until a meat thermometer registers 165°F, another 1–1½ hours.

Transfer the turkey to a platter and let it rest for 20 minutes before carving.

Meanwhile, strain the juices from the roasting pan into a saucepan, reserving the apples. Simmer over medium heat until the juices have thickened, about 10 minutes. Serve the cider jus alongside the turkey and apples.

Makes 8 servings (with leftover turkey for sandwiches).

How to Brine a Fresh Turkey

1. Select a brining recipe. There are many such recipes online.

2. Buy a fresh turkey or completely thaw a frozen bird.

3. The night before you plan to roast your turkey, remove the giblets and turkey neck. Rinse the bird inside and out. Pat it dry with paper towels.

4. Prepare the brine, making sure that all of the salt is dissolved. The brine should be at room temperature.

5. Use a container made of food-grade plastic, stainless steel, or glass, large enough to hold your turkey and small enough to fit inside your refrigerator.

6. Place the turkey breast side down in the container. Add the brine. The entire turkey should be covered.

7. Place the container in the refrigerator for the recommended amount of time. Allow one hour for every pound. For example, a 12-pound turkey should brine for 12 hours.

8. After the recommended brining time, remove the turkey from the brine. Rinse and pat dry with paper towels. Roast the turkey as desired.

Pork Shoulder Braised in Hard Cider

3 thyme sprigs

3 fresh flat-leaf parsley sprigs

½ teaspoon whole black peppercorns

3 pounds pork shoulder

Salt and pepper, to taste

Olive oil, as needed

1 small leek, white and pale green parts, finely chopped

3 garlic cloves, peeled and minced

½ cup peeled and diced parsnip

½ cup peeled and diced celery root

4 cups sweet hard cider, divided

½ cup chicken stock

FOR GARNISH VEGETABLES:

3 medium leeks, white and pale green parts, halved lengthwise and washed

3 medium parsnips, peeled and halved lengthwise

1½ small celery roots, peeled and cut into 1-inch wedges

FOR THE SAUCE:

1 tablespoon unsalted butter, at room temperature

1 tablespoon all-purpose flour

¼ cup heavy cream (optional)

2 teaspoons grainy mustard, plus more for serving

Preheat oven to 400°F. Wrap the thyme, parsley, and peppercorns in a small piece of cheesecloth and tie with kitchen twine to form a sachet. Season the pork with salt and pepper.

Heat a large Dutch oven or other pot with a tight-fitting lid over high heat for 2 minutes, then add enough oil to barely coat the bottom of the pot and heat until shimmering. Cook the pork in the pot until well browned on all sides, turning with tongs once each side is seared. This will take a total of 12-15 minutes. Remove the pork from the pot.

Reduce the heat to medium, and add the leek, garlic, parsnip, and celery root. Season with salt and pepper. Stir frequently and cook until the leek is translucent, about 2 minutes.

Return the pork to the pot, and pour in 1 cup of hard cider. Bring to a boil and deglaze the pot, scraping up browned bits from the bottom. Add the remaining 3 cups of cider and the stock along with the herb sachet. The liquid should come about halfway up the sides of the pork. Add more stock if needed. Bring to a boil on top of the stove. Cover, and put in the oven. Reduce the oven temperature to 325°F. Cook until pork is very tender (it should offer little resistance when pierced with a knife), about 2-2½ hours, turning over with tongs about halfway through so the meat cooks evenly.

Finish the braising with garnish vegetables. Transfer the pork to a large plate and strain the braising liquid through a fine sieve, pressing on the solids to extract as much liquid as possible. Discard the solids. Return the liquid and the pork to the pot and add the garnish vegetables, nestling them into the liquid. The liquid should almost reach the top of the vegetables. Bring to a boil on the stove, then return the pot to the oven and cook until vegetables are tender, about 30 minutes.

Lift out the vegetables and arrange them on a serving platter. Transfer the pork to another plate. Cover both and keep warm.

Continued next page.

Make a sauce by rubbing together the softened butter with the flour in a small mixing bowl until completely incorporated. Pour off and measure the cooking liquid remaining in the pot. You should have about 2 cups. Return it to the pot and boil until reduced to 1 cup, about 6 minutes. Whisk in the butter mixture and continue whisking until the liquid comes to a boil, then lower heat and simmer for 1 minute (to remove the raw starchy taste). Turn off the heat and stir in the cream (if using) and mustard.

Use a fork to shred the meat into large chunks. Transfer the pork to the platter with vegetables. Serve with the sauce and more mustard on the side.

Makes 12 servings.

What's Old Is New Again

Farro is an ancient grain that is now undergoing renewed interest by chefs and home cooks. It was cultivated by the Romans and served as a basic part of their diet until wheat became more plentiful. Farro can be used to make soups and salads. Here it's served as a side dish at room temperature, flavored by the cider in which it cooks and Pecorino. Pecorino is a sharp hard Italian cheese made from ewe's milk. This recipe comes from Russell Orchards in Ipswich, Massachusetts.

Apple Cider Cooked Farro

2 cups apple cider

2 cups water

1 bay leaf

Kosher salt, to taste

1 cup semi-peeled farro

2 tablespoons cider vinegar

2 tablespoons olive oil

½ small celery root (celeriac), peeled and julienned

½ medium sweet-tart apple, cored, cut into matchsticks

¼ small red onion, thinly sliced

½ cup chopped fresh parsley leaves

¼ cup coarsely chopped black olives

1 ounce Pecorino, shaved

Salt and pepper, to taste

In a medium saucepan, combine the apple cider, water, and bay leaf. Season with salt. Bring to a boil, reduce the heat to medium high, and add the farro. Simmer until *al dente*, 25–30 minutes, and drain.

Spread the farro out on a baking sheet, and allow to cool.

In a large bowl, toss the farro, vinegar, and oil. Add the celery root, apple, onion, parsley, olives, and Pecorino, and toss to combine. Season with salt and pepper.

Makes 4 servings.

New Twists

We've all heard of strawberry rhubarb pie, but cherry rhubarb? That's a delicious variation of the classic summer dessert. This recipe comes from Russell Orchards in Ipswich, Massachusetts. Far more delicious than it sounds, this is for you if you're tired of apple and berry pies (heaven forbid).

Cherry Rhubarb Pie

4 cups rhubarb cut in ½-inch slices

1 pound tart red cherries, drained

1 cup sugar

½ teaspoon nutmeg

¼ cup minute tapioca

Pastry dough for a two-crust pie

Preheat oven to 400°F. Combine the rhubarb, cherries, sugar, nutmeg, and tapioca. Let stand for 15 minutes while preparing the pastry.

Line a 9-inch pie plate with thinly rolled pastry dough. Pour in the filling and cover with the second sheet of thinly rolled pastry (or make a lattice crust, if desired). Crimp the edges of the pie to seal tightly.

Bake the pie in the 400°F oven for 40–50 minutes, or until the rhubarb is tender and the top crust is browned.

Makes 6 servings.

Twice Baked

From old-fashioned pleasures to modern-day trends, apples are a key ingredient. In this biscotti recipe from Russell Orchards in Ipswich, Massachusetts, dried apples are essential. Biscotti are Italian cookies that are baked twice. A flattened cookie loaf is baked, removed from the oven, cut into slices, and then returned to the oven for the second baking. The results are crisp cookies, perfect for dunking.

Apple Maple Walnut Biscotti

2 eggs

⅔ cup sugar

⅓ cup butter, melted

⅔ cup maple syrup

2½ cups flour

½ tablespoon cinnamon

½ teaspoon nutmeg

2 teaspoons baking powder

½ teaspoon salt

2 cups chopped walnuts

1 cup dried apples (see recipe on page 58)

Preheat oven to 325°F. Coat a cookie sheet with non-stick spray.

In a mixing bowl, vigorously beat together the eggs, sugar, melted butter, and maple syrup. Sift in the flour, cinnamon, nutmeg, baking powder, and salt. Mix well. Fold in the walnuts and dried apples.

Form the dough into a uniform cylinder the width of the cookie sheet. Flatten to 1 inch in height. Bake in the 325°F oven for 25 minutes. Remove from the oven, and let cool for about 10 minutes.

Reduce the oven temperature to 300°F.

Using a serrated knife, slice into ½-inch pieces. Bake the biscotti in the 300°F oven for 6 minutes on one side, then turn the biscotti over, and bake for 6 minutes on the other side.

Makes about 24 biscotti.

Dried Apples

To make dried apples, all you need is a food hydrator or an oven. Follow these five steps:

1. Select firm, ripe apples, any quantity. Roma apples are recommended, usually yielding two cups of dried apples from five cups fresh. Wash the apples in cold water. Peel the apple, if desired. Remove all bruised and soft parts. Cut the apples into slices ⅛-inch thick.

2. If using a food hydrator, follow the manufacturer's directions. If your hydrator has a thermostat, set it for 40°F. It will take at least twelve hours to dry your apples.

3. If using an oven, preheat the oven to 150°F. Arrange the sliced apples not touching each other on cake racks or cookie sheets. If desired, sprinkle the apples with cinnamon, allspice, or nutmeg. Place the apples in the preheated oven. It will take at least ten hours to dry your apples.

4. When done, the apple slices will be flexible, not brittle, and deep red in color. Allow the apple slices to cool to room temperature. Store the slices in zipper-type plastic bags. Do not overfill the bags, and squeeze out excess air before sealing the bags tight. Vacuum seal the bags if you have a vacuum sealer.

5. Store the tightly sealed bags in a cool, dark location where they will keep for six to nine months. They will keep even longer if stored in a freezer.

A Motto to Live By

"Life is short. . . eat dessert first" is the motto for dessert lovers everywhere. And desserts made with the bountiful fruits from an orchard are among the best to have as your first (or last) course.

For a couple of basic fresh fruit desserts, we turn to two orchards in Massachusetts. Russell Orchards in Ipswich shows how easy it is to poach pears, and Smolak Farms in North Andover teaches us how to stew peaches.

Poached Pears

6 firm pears

1½ cups sugar

2 cups strawberry fruit wine (or your choice)

Juice and zest of 2 lemons

2 cups water

2 teaspoons vanilla

Whipped cream (optional)

6 sprigs fresh mint (optional)

Peel the pears, leaving the stems intact.

In a medium saucepan, combine all the other ingredients and bring to a simmer. Drop the pears into the liquid and let barely simmer for 45 minutes or so.

Serve in elegant dishes with the liquid and a dollop of whipped cream. Garnish with fresh mint if desired.

Makes 6 servings.

Stewed Peaches

6 freestone peaches

3 tablespoons unsalted butter

2 tablespoons brown sugar

Pinch of kosher salt

Pinch of black pepper

Pinch of cinnamon

¼ cup water

Coconut gelato, as needed

12 shortbread cookies

Preheat oven to 350°F. Drop the peaches into a pot of boiling water for 30 seconds, and then immediately drop them into an ice bath. Remove the skins. Cut peaches in half and remove the pit. Place the peaches cut side up in an oven-proof pan.

In a bowl, combine the butter, brown sugar, salt, pepper, and cinnamon. Evenly distribute the butter mixture into the center of each of the peach halves (pit area).

Put the water in the bottom of the pan. Place the pan in the 350°F oven for 20–25 minutes. Remove the pan from the oven. Serve the peaches warm or let cool to room temperature.

To elevate this simple dish, place 2 peach halves in a shallow bowl with a scoop of coconut gelato and 2 shortbread cookies per serving.

Makes 6 servings.

Note: This dish can be made ahead of time and reheated in a microwave.

Smolak Farms

Smolak Farms in North Andover, Massachusetts, offers evidence that the American dream still comes true. English settlers once colonized the area, which is now farmed by the descendants of European immigrants: Martin and Magdalenna Smolak and their son, Henry, and his wife Helen. Their grandson, H. Michael Smolak, has overseen the growth of the family dairy to one of the most progressive farms in the hills of northern Massachusetts during the past thirty-five-plus years.

Parts of the Smolak homestead are 300 years old. In 1982, the Smolak family preserved 107 of its 160 acres in cooperation with the state's Agricultural Preservation Restriction Program. This ensures that the acreage will remain open land forever. It will never be developed.

In 1985, the Smolak Farm Stand opened in an old chicken coop that had been converted to a garage for trucks and storage. The wood used in this and all other buildings came from local trees. If you could go back in time, you would see a pasture out back and an attached shelter for cows pregnant with calves. A flower garden bloomed on one side of the farm stand.

With customers requesting pies and muffins, the bakery was soon added. People from all over started going to the Smolak Farm just for the apple cider doughnuts. A greenhouse was added in 1992, followed by an ice cream stand in 2004. Throughout the decades the Smolaks strove to improve their property and at the same time renew their agricultural heritage.

The Smolak Farms of today offers pick-your-own fruit when in season as well as hayrides and animals, including llamas, alpacas, golden pheasants, fallow deer, goats, and more. Families from metropolitan Boston come for the festivals and classic car shows. Private parties, even farm-to-table weddings, can be scheduled.

Dog lovers especially like Smolak Farms for it is one of very few locations that permits dogs in the apple orchard. The dogs must be on leashes at all times. On top of that, Smolak Farms offers dog agility classes, which is fun for all breeds and their humans.

From Smolak Farms, we have here a classic French dessert—the challenging Apple Galette. A galette can also be called a *crostata* or free-form apple pie made without any pie pan.

My mother rarely baked, but when she did, she usually made a big baking pan of apple-flavored bars. They go great with a cold glass of cider or a hot cup of coffee. Here's how they do it at Smolak Farms, followed by my recipe for Drunken Peach Bars.

Apple Galette

1½ cups all-purpose flour

1 tablespoon granulated sugar

¼ teaspoon salt

½ cup (¼ pound) plus 2 tablespoons cold butter

1 large egg yolk, lightly beaten

Cold water, as needed

½ cup walnuts

2 pounds tart apples (3–5), such as Pink Lady or Granny Smith

½ cup firmly packed brown sugar

¼ teaspoon ground nutmeg

1 large egg, beaten to blend with

1 tablespoon water

Preheat oven to 375°F.

In a food processor or large bowl, combine flour, granulated sugar, and salt. Cut the ½ cup of butter into pieces, and add to the flour mixture. Pulse the motor, cut in with a pastry blender, or rub in with your fingers until the mixture resembles coarse meal. With the motor running (or stirring with a fork after each addition), add the egg yolk and 3–4 tablespoons of cold water, 1 tablespoon at a time. Process or stir just until the mixture comes together in a ball. Form the dough into a flat disk, wrap in plastic wrap, and chill until firm but still pliable, about 1 hour.

Meanwhile, spread the walnuts in a baking pan and bake in the 375°F oven until barely golden under their skins, 6–8 minutes. (Leave the oven on.) Coarsely chop the walnuts.

Peel and core the apples. Cut each apple into 8 wedges. In a 10- to 12-inch nonstick frying pan over medium heat, melt the remaining 2 tablespoons of butter. When foamy, add the apple wedges and stir often until slightly softened and brown at the edges, 10–12 minutes. Sprinkle the brown sugar and nutmeg over the fruit, and stir until the liquid is syrupy and bubbling, about 5 minutes. Stir in the walnuts. Remove the pan from the heat.

Unwrap the dough. On a lightly floured surface, with a lightly floured rolling pin, roll the dough into a round shape about 15 inches in diameter. Line a 12 x 15-inch baking sheet with cooking parchment (or butter the baking sheet well), and carefully transfer the rolled-out dough to the baking sheet (the edges will hang over).

Pour the apple mixture onto the center of the rolled-out dough, mounding the apple wedges in a circle about 8 inches wide and 2 inches high. Gently fold the edges of the dough inward over the apples, pleating the dough as you go, leaving an opening about 4 inches wide in the center. Brush the dough all over with the beaten egg.

Bake in the 375°F oven until the pastry is golden brown and the apples are tender when pierced, 40–45 minutes (or 35–40 minutes in a convection oven). Transfer your galette (with the parchment paper, if using) to a wire rack to cool.

To serve, transfer the galette to a large plate, gently pulling the parchment paper from under the galette. Cut into wedges and serve slightly warm or at room temperature.

Makes 6 servings.

Note: If you're pressed for time, you can make this dessert with ready-to-bake pastry dough available in most supermarkets.

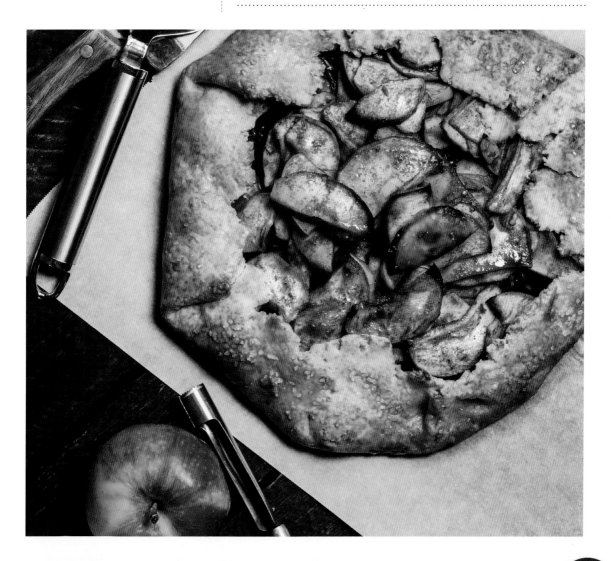

Chunky Apple Bars

FOR THE FILLING:

4 cups cored and coarsely chopped apples (about 2 large apples)

¼ cup water

1 tablespoon honey

1 teaspoon cinnamon

FOR THE CRUST:

¾ cup butter, softened

2 tablespoons cane sugar

2 cups oats (regular or quick cooking)

1½ cups white flour

½ cup whole wheat flour

1 teaspoon baking powder

1 teaspoon cinnamon

Preheat oven to 350°F. Grease a 9 x 13-inch pan.

To make the filling, combine the chopped apples, water, honey, and cinnamon in a medium saucepan. Bring to a boil. Reduce the heat and simmer uncovered for about 5 minutes, or until the apples are slightly soft. Remove from the heat.

For the crust, cream the butter and sugar in a large mixing bowl. Reserving 2 cups for the topping, add the oats, flours, baking powder, and cinnamon. Mix well. Press the crust into the bottom of the prepared pan, and bake in the 350°F oven for 12 minutes.

Spread the cooked apple filling over the baked crust. Sprinkle the reserved oat mixture over the top of the filling.

Bake in the 350°F oven for 15–20 minutes, or until the top is nicely browned. Cool. Cut into bars.

Makes 12 servings.

Drunken Peach Bars

3 small peaches, not quite ripe, peeled and sliced

2 tablespoons whiskey

1 tablespoon brown sugar

7 tablespoons unsalted butter, softened

⅓ cup sugar

⅔ cup flour

½ teaspoon cinnamon

1 tablespoon cornstarch

Preheat oven to 350°F. Grease and flour a standard loaf pan.

In a bowl, combine the sliced peaches with the whiskey and brown sugar. Set aside.

In another bowl, combine the butter, sugar, flour, and cinnamon. Mix well. Set aside ¼ cup of the dough mixture. Press the remaining dough mixture evenly into the loaf pan.

Add the cornstarch to the peach-whiskey mixture. Mix well. Pour the mixture into the loaf pan. Crumble the ¼ cup of dough that was set aside over the top.

Bake in the 350°F oven for 40 minutes, or until golden brown. Allow the pan to cool completely before cutting into bars.

Makes 8 servings.

Fairmount Fruit Farm

For everyone who can't bear getting through almost an entire year before they can bake a fresh fruit pie, here's a way to capture perfectly ripe fruit for any time you get a craving. This technique is recommended by Fairmount Fruit Farm in Franklin, Massachusetts.

Fairmount Fruit Farm has a rich history going back to 1920 when James Koshivas emigrated from Greece to America. He purchased the farm and envisioned plenty of apple trees on the land, enough to support his growing family. Almost a century later, the third, fourth, and fifth generations of the Koshivas family are working toward keeping that vision alive. This small family business still farms more than twenty acres of apple, nectarine, peach, and pear trees.

They grow about ten varieties of apple, with Macoun and Honey Crisp being the favorites. In addition, the farm grows strawberries, raspberries, and blueberries. Interestingly, they grow their strawberries in a greenhouse. They are "ever bearers" and produce fruit throughout the summer. Most of their vegetables are grown hydroponically.

The farm store at Fairmount is brimming with baskets of apples, plenty of produce, jams, jellies, and local honey. Open year-round, this is where the locals go to purchase their free-range eggs, dairy products, and baked goods, both fresh and frozen. The frozen pies can be taken home and baked in your own kitchen. Wonderful aromas will fill the air.

Freezing Apples For Pies

10 cups water

4½ cups sugar

1 cup cornstarch

2 teaspoons cinnamon

¼ teaspoon nutmeg

1 teaspoon salt

3 teaspoons lemon juice

5½ pounds apples, peeled, cored, and sliced

In a large stockpot, combine all the ingredients except the apples. Bring to a boil and allow to thicken a bit. Remove the pot from the heat, and allow to cool a little. Drop the sliced apples into the mixture and coat well. Divide up evenly and place in containers to freeze. (Can freeze for six months.)

Makes enough for 2 pies.

George Hill Orchards

First come the Ginger Gold, Gala, and Earl Mac apples in late August. Then in September the selection expands to Royal Gala, McIntosh, Cortland, Jonathan, and Macoun. And so it goes at George Hill Orchards in Lancaster, Massachusetts, until the end of October when the pick-your-own season draws to a close with the Red Delicious and Empire apples finally ripe.

From its beginning in 1974, George Hill Orchards has been farmed by the Siver family, starting with Don and Frieda, now known to all as Poppy and Grammy. This small family operation grew through the years, thanks to the hard work of their children, grandchildren, friends, and loyal customers. It's Poppy's recipe for apple cider dough-nuts that draws the crowd on any weekend in the fall. So does the aroma of freshly baked pies. But it's the gorgeous fresh fruit that seals the deal at George Hill Orchards.

The Farm House Grille opens in late September, offering basic fare as well as lots of baked goodies, plus live entertainment with a panoramic view of the historic town of Lancaster. Make sure you look for the growing number of rescued animals being cared for at this farm. From the kitchen at George Hill Orchards comes this cookie recipe—simply pure, old-fashioned comfort food.

Apple Cinnamon Oatmeal Cookies

¾ cup butter, softened

1 cup packed light brown sugar

1 egg

1 tablespoon apple juice

½ teaspoon vanilla

1½ cups all-purpose flour

1 teaspoon baking powder

1 teaspoon baking soda

¼ teaspoon salt

1½ cups quick-cooking oats

1 (10-ounce) package Hershey's cinnamon baking chips

1 cup peeled, cored, and chopped apple

½ cup raisins

Preheat oven to 350°F. Lightly grease a cookie sheet.

In a large bowl, beat the butter, brown sugar, egg, apple juice, and vanilla until creamy.

In another bowl, stir together the flour, baking powder, baking soda, and salt. Add to the butter mixture, and beat until blended. Stir in the oats. Add the cinnamon chips, apple, and raisins. Stir until blended.

Drop by teaspoons onto the prepared cookie sheet. Bake in the 350°F oven for 10 minutes, or until the edges are lightly browned.

Makes about 48 cookies.

Blueberry Nectarine Buckle

1½ sticks (¾ cup) unsalted butter, softened

¾ cup sugar

1 teaspoon vanilla

1⅓ cups all-purpose flour

¼ teaspoon double-acting baking powder

½ teaspoon salt

3 large eggs

2 cups blueberries, picked over and rinsed

2 nectarines, pitted and cut into 1-inch wedges

FOR THE TOPPING:

½ stick (¼ cup) cold unsalted butter, cut into small pieces

½ cup sugar

⅓ cup all-purpose flour

½ teaspoon cinnamon

½ teaspoon freshly grated nutmeg

Whipped cream or vanilla ice cream, as needed

Preheat oven to 350°F. In a small bowl with an electric mixer, cream together the butter and sugar, and beat in the vanilla.

In another small bowl, stir together the flour, baking powder, and salt. Mix the flour mixture into the butter mixture alternately with the eggs, one at a time, beating well after each addition. Fold in the blueberries and the nectarines. Set aside.

To make the topping, in a small bowl, blend together the butter, sugar, flour, cinnamon, and nutmeg until the mixture resembles coarse meal. Chill the topping.

Spread the batter in a well-buttered 10 x 2-inch round cake pan or a 2-quart baking pan. Sprinkle the topping evenly over the batter.

Bake in the middle of the 350°F oven for 45–50 minutes, or until a tester comes out clean and the topping is crisp and golden. Serve with whipped cream or vanilla ice cream.

Makes 8 servings.

Cider Hill Farm

Cider Hill Farm sits on 145 golden acres in Amesbury, Massachusetts, that corner of the state that leads travelers into New Hampshire and then onto Maine. Seventy of those acres are planted with fruits and vegetables, all of which are sold in the farm store, the heart of Cider Hill.

The weathered barn with its big red doors is open from May to December 24. Its wood-hewn interior holds the farm's fresh produce, a bakery (yes, they have cider doughnuts) and

prepared foods (they are known for their chicken pot pies). Items unique to Cider Hill include fresh eggs from their own chickens, local cheeses, their own jams (try the plum jam), and all-natural meats.

You can also pick your own fruit at Cider Hill Farm starting with the berries of early summer and then the nectarines, peaches, plums, apples, and pumpkins during the annual growing season.

Ed and Eleanor Cook established Cider Hill Farm in 1978, when they purchased an old dairy farm with plans to operate an apple farm. Soon after that, their son Glenn and his wife Karen bought an adjacent poultry farm. Today, three generations of the Cook family work on the diverse farm operation, including the Cook boys, Chad and Greg. The extended Cook family includes students and families from all over Europe and Australia, who come to Cider Hill to learn more about American agriculture.

The latest addition to the farm is the cidery run by Glenn and Chad, which is already on its way to winning awards. Cider Hill Farm is finally in the cider business.

BEST TIME TO MAKE CIDER

So many people ask when is the best time for cider? At Cider Hill Farm, they begin pressing for Labor Day weekend. That early in the season the cider is a bit on the tart side. The October and November ciders offer the fruitiest, deepest, and most complex flavors.

Rhode Island

Rhode Island is known for many "firsts." It was the first of the original thirteen colonies to declare independence from English rule, and the first colony to prohibit slavery in 1652. On the food side of life, the first lunch wagon in America—the forerunner of the classic diner—appeared in Providence in 1872. The first North American apple variety was developed in Rhode Island by William Blackstone in the 1600s. The Rhode Island Greening apple—crisp, juicy, and quite tart—is the official state fruit. That apple originated around 1650. Today Rhode Island is called the Ocean State.

When it comes to superlatives, Rhode Island can claim many, including the highest number and highest density of doughnut shops per capita in the United States, with about 350 coffee shops selling their doughnuts throughout the smallest state in the nation. Could that explain this quirky state's obsession with apple cider doughnuts? Once available only at orchard farm stands, the beloved apple cider doughnut can now be found at chain coffee shops and major supermarkets.

But the best way to get an authentic apple cider doughnut is at an apple orchard, cider mill, or farm stand. Often you can watch them being made, and their sweet, yeasty aroma wafts over you. This is just one more reason to visit the orchards and farm stands that are scattered throughout the state, but mostly in the northern area known as Apple Valley.

As a child, one of my favorite things to do in the summer was to take a ride into the country with my father at the wheel in search of fresh produce. As my generation grew older, many of us got away from such simple traditions, but we are now making a strong return. Once again I'm visiting local farm stands and orchards. In the fall, a day spent at a pick-your-own orchard is a day well spent, and there's plenty to pick beyond apples—all kinds of berries, peaches, pears, plums, nectarines, pumpkins, and even quince—and all so much more desirable than fruit trucked in from California or Mexico. People who understand the importance of fresh local food are willing to pay more, but surprisingly local produce is not always more expensive than what is found in supermarkets.

Many of us have come to appreciate the hard work of local farmers and the challenges they must meet on a regular basis. Keeping our farms viable ensures that the rural character of Rhode Island will continue on. And for the first time in decades, the children of farmers are confident that they can carry on the family business.

Rhode Island's renewed love and respect for farm stands and orchards may also be rooted in the state's climate. Known for having warm rainy summers and raw snowy winters, Rhode Island has average temperatures that range from a high of 83°F to a low of 20°F, making the shoulder seasons of spring and fall a favorite time of year for many residents. In the spring, every orchard sees its fruit trees blossom, and in the fall, much of that fruit is ready to pick.

We hope the following down-home recipes will tempt you to head to your kitchen, and when the season is right, go in search of orchards, cider mills, and farm stands.

THE VERY FIRST

William Blackstone developed the first North American apple variety in Rhode Island in the 1600s.

Historic Steere Orchard

On the last day of summer in 2015, we went to the first of many orchards we would visit as I wrote this book. The Steere family orchard is not far from our home in Lincoln, yet we had never been there before. It was a perfect day, not too warm, and the trip to the Steere Orchard led us down roads we'd never before traveled. The residential section of Greenville, which is a village in Smithfield, morphed into rural countryside. I spotted an orchard and a long line of sunflowers to my left. I knew the retail operation would be "up the road a piece," as they say around here. And there it was, not the prettiest of barns, simply a large, obviously old, cement building, but still appealing, with its doors open wide, piles of colorful pumpkins on display, and plenty of Indian corn decorating the rustic interior.

One of the largest apple orchards in Rhode Island, the Steere family orchard is also one of the oldest, established in 1930 by Arthur W. Steere. The fourth generation of the Steere family now runs the business.

In late September, apple season is in full swing in this part of the state, which is known as Apple Valley. At the Steere stand, large wooden bins overflow with about a dozen varieties, including Macoun, Cortland, Red and Golden Delicious, McIntosh, and Rhode Island Greening. You can also pick your own apples every day from 9 a.m. to 5 p.m.

Applefest is the annual fall harvest celebration held in mid-October at Steere Orchard. Free apple samples are offered along with a farmers' market, vendor, live music, and pumpkin painting.

Late summer also means peaches are available at Steere Orchard as well as pumpkins, squash, gourds, jams, jellies, apple butter, honey, and apple cider. Free hayrides are also offered on weekends from August through October.

As I was checking out, I spotted a small display case containing apple cider doughnuts near the register. When I asked about them, I was told they were a day old. I still wanted a couple to take home for my late afternoon coffee break. After the young man at the register tallied up my purchases, he threw in the doughnuts for free, informing me they are made fresh only on the weekends. He then helped me carry all my purchases, including an assortment of pumpkins, out to my car. All in all, this was a fine way to say goodbye to summer and hello to fall.

Here is Steere Farm's recipe for Apple Harvest Cake.

Apple Harvest Cake

FOR THE APPLE CAKE:

1½ cups all-purpose flour

⅔ cup sugar, divided

¾ teaspoon salt

½ cup butter, at room temperature

4 cups peeled, sliced apples

2 tablespoons lemon juice

1 teaspoon cinnamon

FOR THE TOPPING:

1 egg

⅓ cup evaporated milk

1 teaspoon vanilla

¾ cup chopped nuts

1 cup flaked coconut

FOR THE GARNISH:

1 apple, cut into slices

....

Note: Keep the apple slices in a bowl of water mixed with the juice of a lemon to prevent them from turning brown.

....

In a large bowl, sift together the flour, ⅓ cup of sugar, and salt. Blend in the butter to make a crumb mixture. Press mixture into the bottom of a 9 x 13-inch baking pan.

Place the sliced apples over the crumb mixture. Sprinkle the lemon juice over the apples.

Preheat oven to 375°F.

In a small bowl, combine the remaining ⅓ cup of sugar and cinnamon. Mix well. Sprinkle over the apples. Bake the cake in the 375°F oven for 25 minutes.

To make the topping, whisk the egg in a bowl. Add the remaining ingredients and mix together. When the cake is done baking, spoon the topping over the cake. Continue to bake at 375°F for 20–25 minutes, or until the top is golden brown. Top each serving with an apple slice. Serve warm.

Makes 12 servings.

A Tale of Three Orchards

Orchard hopping is a wonderful afternoon activity in northern Rhode Island. Motoring along Route 116, you will find Appleland in Smithfield, and then Knight Farm and Elwood Orchard just over the town line in North Scituate, all within one mile of one another in the Apple Valley section of the state.

Appleland is known for its cider doughnuts, made in an immaculate commercial kitchen at the farm stand. Doughnut samples are offered at the fruit stand so you can try before you buy. Owners Mary Lou and Joe D'Andrea won't share their recipe, but Mary Lou will say it's their apple cider that makes the doughnuts so special. The cider is pressed from fresh apples grown in their orchard. Joe always blends at least two kinds of apples to make his famous cider. Much like a winemaker, Joe looks for the perfect combination of sweet and tart.

Appleland Orchard has been in the family since the 1960s, when Joseph and Louise D'Andrea purchased the land from another farming family. Joseph died, and Louise retired, leaving the business to their son Joe and his wife Mary Lou, who have expanded the line of products to include fruit wine, pies, chocolate-covered apples, and a doughnut-making kit in a mason jar. It's filled with all the ingredients. All you need to do is add the apple cider. The kit, which costs $5.95, makes two- dozen doughnuts.

But as my mother used to say, don't fill up on doughnuts because a stone's throw down the road is Knight Farm, one of the very few orchards to have a restaurant on the premises. The country cafe offers hearty breakfasts and all-American lunch items for before or after a hayride into the forty-acre orchard for apple picking.

Established in 1800, Knight Farm is now owned and operated by the Iaciofano family. As the newest owners of Knight Farm, the Iaciofanos want to continue the standard and tradition that was set before them. They have pledged to provide a place where the entire community can bring family and friends for a wholesome experience and a lifetime of memories.

Further down winding Snake Hill Road is Elwood Orchard, founded in 1998. Al and Jean Fuoroli run the twenty-five-acre farm. This small operation (only 1,000 or so fruit trees) has a short season, open from late August through October. Most of their back orchard is certified organic, rather rare in New England orchards. So their apples and apple cider are organic. Many of the pick-your-own apples are pest-resistant varieties such as Nova Spy with names that are new to many apple lovers. Al and Jean also grow two varieties of nectarines: Red Gold and Ovation, both large, freestone, and deep red in color. Their primary peach is the famed Elberta variety with its buttery flavor. The juicy Asian pears include the mellow Hosui and the sweet Korean Giant. Gourmet cooks will be interested to learn that Elwood Orchard grows organic garlic (six different kinds) and shallots, which quickly sell out.

Mary Lou D'Andrea, co-owner of Appleland Orchards in Smithfield, won't reveal her recipe for their famous apple cider doughnuts, but she is willing to share her recipe for Apple Cider Muffins followed by her recipe for Apple Cider Cake.

Apple Cider Muffins

4 cups flour

4 teaspoons baking powder

4 eggs

1 teaspoon vanilla

1 teaspoon cinnamon

½ cup brown sugar

½ cup canola oil

1 cup apple cider

½ cup walnuts

½ cup raisins

1 cup chopped apples

Preheat oven to 400°F. Prepare a muffin tin with paper liners or grease and flour.

In a large bowl, combine the flour and baking powder. In another bowl, beat the eggs and add the vanilla, cinnamon, sugar, oil, and cider. Mix well and then add to the flour mixture. Fold in the walnuts, raisins, and chopped apples.

Pour an equal amount of batter into each part of the muffin tin. Bake for 20 minutes, or until a muffin tests done with a toothpick.

Makes 12 large muffins.

Apple Cider Cake

4 eggs

1½ cups sugar

1 cup oil

3 cups flour

4 teaspoons baking powder

1 teaspoon nutmeg

1 teaspoon cinnamon

1½ cups chopped, peeled apples or raisins

1 cup apple cider

Whipped cream (optional)

Preheat oven to 350°F. In a large bowl, beat the eggs into the sugar. Add the oil, flour, and baking powder.

In another large bowl, mix the spice into the apples or raisins. Add this mixture to the batter along with the cider. Mix well.

Pour the batter into a greased, lightly floured 9 x 13-inch pan. Bake in the 350°F oven until done, about 40 minutes. Serve plain or with whipped cream.

Makes 12 servings.

Note: I made this with the raisins instead of the chopped apples for a change of pace. We loved the results: it's more of a spice cake than another apple dessert.

Knight Farm

Most people associate doughnuts with breakfast, but when you're talking about apple cider doughnuts, they're good any time of the day—with an afternoon cup of coffee and even with a scoop of ice cream for dessert. Cider doughnut mania has spread throughout New England, especially in Rhode Island, the smallest state in the Union.

One of the newest places to add apple cider doughnuts to their list of offerings is Knight Farm in North Scituate. The Iaciofano family now owns Knight Farm. When it's "time to make the doughnuts," it's likely that you will see Joe Iaciofano manning the cider doughnut machine.

Joe didn't share his recipe for apple cider doughnuts, but he did provide this recipe for Apple Loaf, which calls for Macoun apples or, if you can find them, Roxbury Russets. Joe said the Roxbury Russet apple was brought over by the Pilgrims on the *Mayflower*, and that's what his family uses to make this tasty dessert. But Joe notes that any apple will do. This recipe also calls for reducing apple cider into that elixir known as boiled apple cider syrup, an almost magical ingredient in many New England dishes.

Apple Loaf

2 cups apple cider, divided

½ cup heavy cream

3–4 medium-size Macoun or Roxbury Russet apples

¼ cup melted butter

1 cup extra-fine granulated sugar

2 large eggs

2 cups flour

1½ teaspoons baking powder

½ teaspoon baking soda

¼ teaspoon salt

1 teaspoon sugar

1 teaspoon cinnamon

1¼ cups confectioners' sugar

1 tablespoon milk, or more if needed

Vanilla ice cream, as needed (optional)

Preheat oven to 350°F. Bring 1 cup of the apple cider to a boil and reduce to ¼ cup. Allow to cool. When the cider reduction is cool, add the cream.

Peel, core, and slice the apples.

In a large bowl, combine the butter and sugar until well mixed. Add the eggs and beat until smooth.

In another bowl, combine the flour, baking powder, baking soda, and salt.

In a small bowl, mix the cinnamon and sugar .

With an electric mixer set on low, alternate adding the flour mixture and cider/cream mixture to the butter/sugar/egg mixture until the batter is well combined. Scrape down the sides of the bowl, and mix until smooth.

Grease a 9 x 9-inch baking pan with vegetable shortening. Pour the batter into the pan. Arrange the sliced apples along the outer edges on top of the batter. Sprinkle the sugar-cinnamon mixture on the top of the cake. Bake in the 350°F oven for 50–60 minutes.

While the cake is baking, make the glaze. Reduce the remaining cup of apple cider down to 2 tablespoons. In a small bowl, combine the cider reduction with the confectioners' sugar and 1 tablespoon of milk. Mix well. Add more milk if needed to get the desired consistency.

Remove the cake from the oven, and cool to room temperature. Cut the cake into 9 squares. Drizzle each square with the glaze. For an added treat, serve with a scoop of vanilla ice cream.

Makes 9 servings.

The Grande Dame of Rhode Island Orchards

Last fall we headed over to Dame Farm and Orchard in Johnston, Rhode Island, right after our Sunday breakfast, hoping to avoid the crowds. We were surprised to see, on this crisp October morning, cars were already winding along rural Brown Avenue and streaming into the orchard's large parking area.

The motto here is "Our Family Serving Your Family Since 1840." That's seven generations, with four generations of the Dame family found on the farm today.

The Dame family land did lay fallow for several years, but farming resumed on the premises in the 1970s. The Dame family was raising large amounts of corn and apples, most of which was sold on the wholesale level. The Dames eventually shifted from wholesale to retail, developing a well-respected farm that offers a wide variety of fresh local produce.

Their pick-your-own apple season usually starts on Labor Day weekend. The seven-acre orchard offers McIntosh, Cortland, Gala, Honeycrisp, Macoun, Jonagold, Brayburn, Ida Red, Red Delicious, and pears. Customers are provided with picking bags. The fruit trees are tagged so you know what you are picking. Each tag provides information on what that type of apple is good for, from baking to making preserves. For example, Gala and Honeycrisp are excellent for making applesauce. All the apples are priced the same per pound, with a $10 minimum purchase. At the height of apple picking season, there is no shortage of low-hanging fruit for youngsters to pick. The other motto at Dame Farm is: "You can be sure it's American grown when you pick your own."

It's always wise to call ahead or check the website (www.damefarmorchards.com) to learn what is ready for picking and to check on the seasonal hours. Here is Darlene Dame's appetizer recipe for those with a sweet tooth.

Fruit Ambrosia Dip

1 (8-ounce) package cream cheese, softened

1 cup sour cream

½ cup cream of coconut

¼ cup shredded coconut

1 (8-ounce) can crushed pineapple

1 cup fresh strawberries, cut in half

1 (8-ounce) container vanilla yogurt

In a large bowl, combine all the ingredients. Using an electric mixer, blend well. Serve chilled with plain crackers or cut-up pieces of apples, peaches, and pears.

Makes about 6 cups.

Rocky Brook Orchard

This unusual appetizer recipe is courtesy of Greg and Katy Ostheimer, owners of Rocky Brook Orchard in Middletown, Rhode Island, and they credit the original recipe to Barbara Ghazarian. The pick-your-own orchard offers more than sixty apple varieties, as well as peaches, pears, and quince. Many of the trees have low-hanging fruit that even toddlers can pick. It's always a good idea to check their Facebook page to see what's ripe for picking before visiting this Newport-area orchard.

Rocky Brook is one of the very few orchards to be growing quince, which can be used to make jelly, or added to apple pie and chicken, pork, or lamb stew for a unique flavor. Here it is combined with traditional salsa ingredients to make a very untraditional appetizer.

Quince Salsa

¾ pound (about 2 cups) fresh quince, peeled, cored, and shredded

1 cup water

1 (14-ounce) can diced tomatoes, drained and mashed

¼ cup grated yellow onion

2 teaspoons grated fresh jalapeno

¼ cup finely chopped fresh cilantro

2-3 tablespoons fresh lime juice

¾ teaspoon salt

In a saucepan, combine the shredded quince and water. Bring to a boil, and then reduce the heat. Simmer until almost all the liquid is gone, 20–25 minutes. The quince will be a yellow-gold color.

Transfer the cooked quince to a large bowl. Add the tomatoes, onion, jalapeno, cilantro, lime juice, and salt. Cover and chill before serving. Serve with tortilla chips.

Makes about 4 cups.

Goodwin Brothers Farm Stand

This quintessential fall recipe is from Goodwin Brothers Farm Stand in North Smithfield, Rhode Island. What could be more autumnal than a stuffed sugar pumpkin? It makes for a spectacular presentation and can even serve as a centerpiece for your holiday table. This recipe makes good use of those smaller pumpkins that were part of your outdoor fall decorations. Mother Nature acted as a refrigerator for those pumpkins as the weather turned cold in November—at least that's what happens in New England.

No one can say for sure when farming operations started at the Goodwin Brothers property, but it may go back as far as the American Civil War. The typical New England farmhouse on the original property was actually a home and a schoolhouse joined together. The schoolhouse was moved onto the farmhouse property by slowly sliding it over the snow during the winter months. Now that's Yankee ingenuity!

What started out as a dairy in the early days evolved into the production of fruits and vegetables in the 1950s. It became known as Goodwin Brothers in the 1960s when Fred Goodwin retired from General Mills and joined his brother Warren on the family farm. The business was passed on down to Fred's youngest son, Robert, on a full-time basis in 1989. It was Robert who added apple trees to the farm's list of crops.

In 2007, a new farm stand was constructed, a handsome post-and-beam building, to better fit the needs of the flourishing business. Throughout their many years, Goodwin Brothers has continued to grow with the help of wives, children, grandchildren, and other family members. The Goodwins are dedicated to providing fresh fruits and vegetables to their customers for many years to come. Don't put off a visit to this multi-generational operation for it's open only from June through October.

Stuffed Sugar Pumpkin

1 sugar pumpkin

1 tablespoon melted butter

1 tablespoon honey or brown sugar

3 pounds bulk Italian sausage

1 cup chopped green onion

16 slices Italian or French bread, cut into 1-inch cubes

2 eggs, beaten

¼ cup Chablis or dry wine

½ teaspoon salt

½ teaspoon pepper

1½ cups chopped apples

Preheat oven to 350°F. Prepare the pumpkin by cutting the top off so you can remove all the seeds and strings. Rinse the pumpkin with cold water.

In a small saucepan (or the microwave), melt the butter. Add the honey or brown sugar to the butter. Mix well and spread on the interior of the pumpkin.

In a large skillet, combine the sausage and onions over medium heat. Cook until the sausage is browned and the onions are tender. Drain off the fat from the skillet.

In a large mixing bowl, combine the remaining ingredients and then add the cooked sausage-onion mixture. Mix well. Fill the pumpkin with this stuffing mixture. Place the pumpkin in a shallow pan. Place the pan in the 350°F oven, and bake for 1½ hours, or until you can easily puncture the pumpkin with a fork.

Remove the pan from the oven, and very carefully transfer the cooked pumpkin to a serving platter.

Makes 4–8 servings, depending on the size of the sugar pumpkin.

Narrow Lane Orchard

Aptly named, Narrow Lane Orchard in North Kingstown, Rhode Island, is well off the beaten path, but a prettier ride on a sunny fall day would be hard to find. Zipping along the country road, we missed the turnoff, but my eye caught a glimpse of the rustic red apple sign and we soon were back on track. Narrow Lane is narrow, and the turnoff to the orchard is even narrower. We slowly made our way down the bumpy cart path and came upon a large clearing with rows of parked cars and streams of people, young and old, heading to and from the modest farm stand. They were there for the pick-your-own apples, peaches, and nectarines.

The seven-plus acres are owned and managed by Steven and Sharon Grenier. They have diversified the orchard and now offer fourteen kinds of peaches and a dozen types of apples, including heirloom varieties, which are available at different times in the picking season. This calls for more than one visit to the orchard. What you will pick in August will be totally different from what's available in October. The dwarf trees with low-hanging fruit (great for the kids) and picnic spots make Narrow Lane a lovely spot to spend a few hours on a weekend afternoon. Their Chocolate Zucchini Bread really hits the spot with a cup of coffee.

Chocolate Zucchini Bread

3 squares unsweetened chocolate

4 eggs

3 cups sugar

1½ cups oil

3 cups flour

1½ teaspoons baking powder

1 teaspoon baking soda

1 teaspoon salt

3 cups grated zucchini

1 cup chopped nuts (optional)

Preheat oven to 350°F. Grease and flour three loaf pans.

In a glass bowl in the microwave, carefully melt the chocolate. Allow to cool.

In another bowl, beat the eggs until light and fluffy. Add the sugar, oil, and melted chocolate. Beat well.

In a third bowl, combine the dry ingredients and mix well. Add the dry ingredients to the egg mixture, alternating with the grated zucchini. Add the nuts, if desired, and blend well.

Pour the batter evenly into the prepared loaf pans. Bake in the 350°F oven for 1 hour.

Makes 3 loaves.

More Orchard-Hopping in Rhode Island

On an absolutely perfect November afternoon, we headed out to North Scituate, Rhode Island, to visit three orchards clustered within the state's official apple country. In mid-autumn, the drive down Snake Hill Road is as pretty as the proverbial postcard. Bright yellow leaves flutter down, and impressive stone walls mark property lines between country homes and acres of orchards. Piles of pumpkins and dried cornstalks complete nature's seasonal decor.

Macouns abound at the Barden Family Orchard on Elmdale Road. So many apples, so little time, from Granny Smith and Fuji to Rome Beauty and Crispin, to name just a few of the varieties offered. Earlier in the season, yellow and white peaches are ripe for the picking. This being a farm, more than fruit trees are on the premises. You can pick your own luscious berries in the summer and plump pumpkins in the fall. Hayrides circle down to the pumpkin patch to help visitors tote their choice pumpkins back to the farm stand, where you can find everything from nectarines and plums to corn on the cob and tomatoes, depending on the month. The rustic farm market also offers jams, jellies, salsa, local honey, and local cheese.

The Barden Family Orchard was founded in 1931 by John and Hazel Barden. Their grandson Gilbert helped to replant the orchard and diversify its produce. Today Gilbert, Sandra, Andrew, Stacey, and Luke Barden actively work during the growing season at the farm. They are full-time farmers dedicated to growing quality fruits and vegetables for a public increasingly interested in locally grown produce.

Barden Family Orchard closes for the season when cold weather dictates they must do so. But a summer of excellent weather and a mild fall guarantees an ideal harvest. That means that Barden's apples and apple cider will be for sale at winter farmer's markets throughout the state. Their cider is treated only with ultra-violet light and no preservatives.

Sandra Barden provided the recipe for Frozen Peach Filling so that you can make a peach pie in the dead of winter. For everyone who can't bear getting through almost an entire year before they can bake a pie, here's how to capture perfectly ripe fruit for any time you get that craving.

Frozen Peach Filling for a Peach Pie

4 cups sliced peaches

1 tablespoon tapioca

1 cup sugar

2 tablespoons cornstarch

1 teaspoon almond flavoring

1 unbaked pie shell

2½ tablespoons butter, cut into cubes

Combine the sliced peaches, tapioca, sugar, and cornstarch. Mix well. Place mixture in a plastic bag and freeze.

When you are ready to bake a peach pie, remove the frozen peaches from the freezer and allow them to thaw. Add the almond flavoring to the peaches. Mix well.

Preheat oven to 425°F.

Pour the peach mixture into an unbaked pie shell. Dot the top of the pie with the cubes of butter. Bake in the 425°F oven for 15 minutes. Reduce the oven temperature to 375°F, and bake for another 30 minutes. (Can feeze for six months.)

Makes 6 servings.

White Oak Farm

Continuing down Elmdale Road just a bit, I came upon White Oak Farm, as rural a property you will ever find. A long gravel road leads down to a farmhouse and farm stand, open only from August through October. The corn is sweet, pumpkins are piled high for your consideration, and apple trees are loaded with heavy fruit.

This farm was established in 1909, and five generations of the Phillips family have tended the seventy-eight acres. Henry and Laura Phillips ran it as a dairy farm. Their son Newell and wife Myra turned the property into an orchard. In the 1980s, the family began to offer pick-your-own apples, which has been a very successful move. School and church groups as well as families flock to this farm every fall.

Today White Oak Farm is owned by Roger and Pat Phillips and their son, Paul, and his wife Jessica. The busy foursome is assisted by the next generation: Shelby, Jackson, and Lily, who help out by picking blueberries and watering the crops. The family is especially proud of their yellow and white peaches, which they claim to be the sweetest in New England. In addition to seven different types of apples, the farm also now offers corn, cucumber, tomatoes, eggplant, and green beans, and their produce can be found at local farmer's markets in season.

Harmony Farms

And down the main road a piece, Harmony Farms can trace its roots back to 1796 when the Windsor brothers built a house with six fireplaces and a beehive oven. The house still stands today, owned by Bernard and Mary Ellen Smith, who have made major renovations to the property. They planted 1,700 apple trees and more than 5,000 blueberry bushes in an orchard that meanders in a circle back to the original farmhouse.

The twenty-eight-acre farm has three ponds, which help with the irrigation of the apples, peaches, blueberries, blackberries, and raspberries grown there. Fresh herbs, pumpkins, gourds, and pre-picked fruit are sold in the rustic farm stand along with home-made jam and honey harvested on the premises. The folks at Harmony Farms provided the following recipe for an easy-to-prepare Apple Cake.

Apple Cake

1 cup sugar

¼ cup shortening

1 egg, beaten

3 cups peeled, diced apples

¼ cup chopped nuts (optional)

1 teaspoon vanilla

½ teaspoon baking powder

½ teaspoon baking soda

½ teaspoon salt

½ teaspoon cinnamon

½ teaspoon nutmeg

1 cup flour

Whipped cream or ice cream (optional)

Preheat oven to 350°F. In a mixing bowl, cream the sugar and shortening. Add the beaten egg. Add the apples, nuts, and vanilla. Sift the baking powder, baking soda, salt, cinnamon, nutmeg, and flour. Add and mix well.

Pour the batter into a greased 8-inch square pan. Bake in the 350°F oven for 45 minutes.

Serve warm or at room temperature, with or without whipped cream or ice cream.

Makes 8 servings.

Jaswell's Farm

In the heart of Rhode Island's Apple Valley is the historic town of Smithfield, home to Jaswell's Farm now run by the fourth generation of the Jaswell family. The farm was started in 1899 by Nicholas Jaswell, the Americanized name of Nicola Gesualdi who emigrated from Italy.

Nicholas passed the farm to his son Joe in the 1930s, and Joe's son Richard took over in 1967 with his wife, Pat. That was the beginning of the Jaswell's Farm that so many families have come to know and love. Richard and Pat built the first farm stand and started offering "pick-your-own" fruits to the public. They diversified the business, and that included adding a cider mill, a pasteurizer for the cider, and an on-site bakery.

In 1999, on the one-hundred-year anniversary of the founding of the farm, Richard and Pat turned Jaswell's over to their two children, Chris and Allison, who are hopeful the next generation will someday be ready to continue the family tradition.

The farm stand is now a large open building crammed with huge bags of apples and a wide variety of baked goods that are impossible to resist. The apple cider doughnuts are outstanding. All things local are on sale, including milk from Wright's Dairy Farm, eggs from Stamp Farm, and fresh honey. Antique farm tools hang on the walls as well as old newspaper articles about the farm from decades gone by. Just about the friendliest people on earth work at Jaswell's, which makes for a very pleasant experience. Hayrides are offered on Sundays, weather permitting, from September into October. A donation is requested to benefit the Rhode Island Community Food Bank.

One of Jaswell's famous recipes is for Apple Nut Coffee Cake, which goes so well with a cup of the farm stand's gourmet coffee. These amiable folks are eager to share their recipes and invite customers to submit their favorites. This one would be pretty hard to top.

Apple Nut Coffee Cake

½ cup butter, at room temperature

1 cup sugar

2 eggs

1 teaspoon vanilla

2 cups flour

1 teaspoon baking powder

1 teaspoon baking soda

¼ teaspoon salt

1 cup sour cream

2 cups finely chopped apples

½ cup chopped walnuts (optional)

½ cup brown sugar

1 teaspoon cinnamon

2 tablespoons flour

Preheat oven to 350°F. In a large bowl, cream together the butter and sugar. Add the eggs and vanilla, and beat well.

In a separate bowl, stir together the 2 cups of flour, baking powder, baking soda, and salt. Slowly add the dry mixture to the creamed mixture alternating with the sour cream. Fold in the apples. Spread the batter into a greased 13 x 9-inch pan.

In another bowl, combine the nuts, brown sugar, cinnamon, and the 2 tablespoons of flour. Mix well and sprinkle over the batter.

Bake in the 350°F oven for 35–40 minutes, or until it tests done when a wooden toothpick is inserted into the coffee cake and comes out clean.

Makes 10–12 servings.

Rhode Island Fruit Growers

Many thanks go out to Heather Faubert from the Rhode Island Fruit Growers Association. When she heard that I was writing this book, she enthusiastically helped me obtain recipes from the best orchards in Rhode Island. Made up of more than forty local farmers, the Rhode Island Fruit Growers Association has grown high-quality fresh fruits and vegetables for one hundred years. This particular dessert is from the association itself, and it's clearly a winner.

Peach-Blueberry Upside Down Cake

FOR THE FRUIT TOPPING:

2 tablespoons butter or margarine

½ cup packed brown sugar, divided

2 peaches, skinned and sliced

1½ cups fresh blueberries

1 tablespoon cornstarch

FOR THE CAKE:

⅓ cup butter or margarine

¾ cup granulated sugar

½ teaspoon vanilla

1 egg

1⅓ cups sifted flour

2 teaspoons baking powder

½ cup milk

Whipped cream or ice cream (optional)

To make the fruit topping, melt the butter in the bottom of an 8-inch-square baking pan. Stir in ¼ cup of the brown sugar. Arrange the peach slices on top of the butter-sugar mixture.

Heat the blueberries in a saucepan until they are juicy. Combine the remaining ¼ cup of brown sugar with the cornstarch, and add to the hot blueberries. Cook over medium heat, stirring constantly, until the mixture thickens, 3 minutes. Spread the blueberries over the peach slices.

To make the cake, cream the butter, sugar, and vanilla in a large bowl until light and fluffy. Beat in the egg.

In another bowl, sift together the flour and baking powder. Add to the creamed mixture alternately with the milk, beginning and ending with the sifted flour mixture.

Preheat oven to 375°F. Spoon this batter over the topping mixture in the baking pan. Bake in the 375°F oven for 40 minutes.

Turn the baking pan upside down on a serving platter and allow cake to fall out. Serve warm or at room temperature with whipped cream or ice cream.

Makes 8 servings.

Sweet Berry Farm

If there is a heaven, it just may look a lot like Sweet Berry Farm in Middletown, Rhode Island. Off the beaten path, yet close to downtown Newport and beautiful beaches, Sweet Berry Farm was founded in 1980. The one hundred-acre farm is run by Jan and Michelle Eckhart, who partnered with Aquidneck Land Trust to preserve most of their land. Instead of rows of new homes, a charming farm market was constructed in the traditional post-and-beam style. The rambling structure begs to be explored.

Surrounding the marketplace are acres of apple and peach orchards and berries. In the fall, you can pick your own apples or select the perfect pumpkin. Certified for its good agricultural practices (GAP) and its use of integrated pest management (IPM), Sweet Berry Farm even has its own honey bees that pollinate the crops and then make honey that is sold in the market.

The market is filled with items that tempt the senses of sight and smell, from brightly colored kitchenware to the aromas emanating from the self-serve cafe. What a concept! The cafe is open for breakfast, lunch, and afternoon pick-me-ups. Customers grill their own gourmet sandwiches, including an amazing over-sized ham and Brie with caramelized onion jam on sourdough. For dessert, I recommend any of the extraordinary ice creams available, from the apple-cinnamon ice cream in the fall to the spiced chocolate orange ice cream during the winter holidays. All this can be enjoyed inside by the oversized fireplace or in warm weather out on the porch. Heat-and-serve gourmet dinners and pure comfort food, as in creamy mac and cheese, are available to take home.

But this just scratches the surface of the Sweet Berry Farm market. House-made jams and jellies, artisan cheeses, fresh eggs, local meats and seafood, and seasonal produce from local fields fill the shelves. The many local products are from Helger's Turkey Farm and Arruda's Dairy, both in nearby Tiverton. The work of local artists and craftsmen is on display, and free concerts are offered every Tuesday night in the summer. Everything from reggae to American folk music fills the air, when weather permits. The farm is available for private events such as intimate weddings in the orchard and land trust fundraisers under huge white tents.

One of the most basic apple recipes is for apple crisp, and just about every orchard in New England has their version of this perfect dessert. This is how they make it at Sweet Berry Farm. If you're too busy to bake, you can always stop by the market and pick up some of their apple crisp to go.

Apple Crisp

1½ cups sugar

3 tablespoons cornstarch

1 tablespoon cinnamon

1 teaspoon nutmeg

8 apples, peeled, cored, and sliced

Juice and zest from 1 large lemon

FOR THE TOPPING:

2 cups brown sugar

Oats, if desired

1 cup flour

1 stick cold butter, cut into cubes

Whipped cream or ice cream (optional)

Note: I try to avoid wheat so I left out the flour when I made this apple crisp, and it turned out just fine.

Preheat oven to 350°F. Grease a baking pan or casserole dish (9 x 12-inch or the equivalent).

In a large bowl, sift the dry ingredients together. Toss the apples and lemon into the bowl with the dry ingredients. Mix well. Place the apple mixture into the prepared baking dish.

In another bowl, gently mix together all the topping ingredients. Sprinkle the topping evenly over the apple mixture.

Bake in the 350°F oven for 30–40 minutes, or until golden brown. Serve with ice cream or whipped cream, if desired.

Makes 8–10 servings.

Hill Orchards

Founded in 1949, Hill Orchards is a fifty-acre farm run by Allan Hill. This Rhode Island orchard has two locations. The pick-your-own orchard is at 25 Emerald Lane in Johnston, and the farm stand is less than two miles away at 25 Sanderson Road in Smithfield. The original orchard was planted in the 1920s, and some of the old fruit trees still stand today, despite harsh New England winters.

Hill Orchards is usually open from Labor Day weekend to Christmas with a gradually changing array of fruit and vegetables grown on the farm and from their neighbors' farms. Hill specializes in apples, nectarines, peaches, pears, plums, and cider made from their own apples. Hill Orchards products, including apple butter, applesauce, and cider vinegar, are regular features at local farmer's markets.

The pick-your-own orchard is open on weekends in September and October. As the weeks progress, the various apples become ready for picking: McIntosh, Cortland, Gala, Macoun, Empire, and so on, including heirloom varieties and new flavors. A pair of handsome horses pulls a rustic wagon for hayrides through the groves of fruit trees. Pumpkins, fall decorations, and Christmas trees round out the seasonal offerings.

Hill Orchards makes it possible for Rhode Islanders to eat local apples year-round by working with Buell Orchard in Connecticut, whose controlled atmosphere storage keeps farm fresh apples crisp into the following spring and summer, until the next crop of delicious apples arrives. And with those apples you can make this traditional Swedish apple pie. Hill Orchards provided the recipe.

Swedish Apple Pie

FOR THE PIE:

8–10 apples, peeled, cored, and sliced

1 teaspoon brown sugar

1 teaspoon pumpkin pie spice

½ cups chopped nuts or raisins (optional)

Pinch of salt

FOR THE CRUST:

1 cup brown sugar

1 stick butter, melted

1 cup wheat or white flour

1 egg

Pinch of salt

FOR THE GARNISH:

1 apple, sliced very thin (optional)

Preheat oven to 350°F. Grease a 9-inch pie dish.

In a large bowl, combine the sliced apples, brown sugar, spice, nuts or raisins (if desired), and salt. Mix well and pour into the pie dish.

In a medium bowl, combine the brown sugar and melted butter. Stir in the flour, egg, and salt. Mix well. Spread this crust over the apple mixture.

Bake in the 350°F oven for 45–55 minutes, or until golden brown. Garnish with very thin slices of apple if desired. Allow to cool a bit before serving.

Makes 6 servings.

The Legend of Phantom Farms

No one knows for sure the origin of this legend. It's simply something to ponder and enjoy. A long time ago, Rebecca, the daughter of a Rhode Island farmer, was picking apples in the orchard at what is now called Phantom Farms in Cumberland, Rhode Island. On this beautiful day, she met Bo, a Native American boy. Even as small children, they were forbidden to see each other because of unrest between the farm family and the local tribe. Somehow the youngsters managed to meet secretly beneath the branches of one particular apple tree. Like that tree, their undying love started to blossom.

Fearing a major attack by the tribe, Rebecca's family fled the farm only to return many years later. During all that time Rebecca never forgot Bo. As she grew into a young lady, so did her love for Bo grow. When the family returned, Rebecca went in search of her beloved. Day after day she would walk through the orchard and wait for her Bo beneath their secret apple tree. He never returned. For the rest of her life Rebecca was heartbroken.

Sometimes, when the moon is full, a white cotton pinafore—much like the one that Rebecca wore—can be seen floating through the orchard. Some romantics believe that is Rebecca, still searching for her lost love. The folks at Phantom Farms invite everyone to see if they can catch a glimpse of the hazy gossamer on full moon nights.

But this legend is not why Phantom Farms has such an eerie name. The farm dates back to the 1930s and was the site of secret meetings during Prohibition. Either way, Phantom Farms is aptly named. The fourteen-acre orchard has been in business for more than sixty years, and some of its trees are said to be more than a century old. More than fifteen varieties of apples are grown on the property, now owned by Kerri Stenovich. Like other modern-day farmers, Kerri and her staff realized their small farm needed to diversify in order to survive. They now grow various berries, vegetables, and giant pumpkins. A once-simple farm stand was expanded and now houses a bakery, country cafe, garden center, and gift shop. They also now ship in-season apples, jams, jellies, dips, and their award-winning Eccles Cakes throughout the United States. The pick-your-own orchard with its quaint hayrides is seasonal, but the farm stand is open year-round. Rocking chairs line the rustic front porch. It's a favorite spot for locals to stop in for coffee or tea with select pastries. This is country charm at its best.

Phantom Farms is especially known for its twenty varieties of muffins (I recommend the Fruits of the Forest) and for its Pumpkin Mousse Roll, which was featured on the Food Network. Here is that recipe for you to make at home.

Pumpkin Mousse Roll

FOR THE PUMPKIN SPONGE CAKE:

6 eggs

1¼ cups granulated sugar

¾ cup pumpkin puree

1¼ cups all-purpose flour

¾ teaspoon salt

1½ teaspoons baking powder

1 tablespoon cinnamon

¼ teaspoon nutmeg

¼ teaspoon ginger

¼ teaspoon cloves

FOR THE MOUSSE FILLING:

20 ounces cream cheese, at room temperature

¾ ounce pure vanilla extract

7 ounces heavy cream

1½ cups powdered sugar, plus more for dusting

Preheat oven to 350°F. In a bowl with an electric mixer, beat the eggs until yellow and foamy, about 5 minutes. Add the sugar and pumpkin puree, and continue to beat for 2 minutes.

In a separate bowl, combine the dry ingredients, and add them to the egg mixture. Beat on low speed for 1 minute.

Grease a 13 x 18-inch sheet pan. Line the sheet pan with parchment paper, and grease the paper.

Pour the batter onto the sheet pan, and smooth evenly into a rectangle shape. Bake in the 350°F oven for 12–15 minutes.

When finished, flip the cake onto a clean towel. Remove the parchment paper from the bottom of the cake. Roll up the cake (like a jelly roll). Allow the cake to cool completely before filling.

To make the filling, beat the softened cream cheese until smooth in a bowl with an electric mixer on high speed. Scrape down the sides of the bowl. With the mixer on low speed, slowly add the vanilla and heavy cream. When blended, beat on high speed until smooth. Scrape down the sides of the bowl once again. Add the powdered sugar with the mixer on low speed. When combined, beat on high speed until smooth.

Carefully unroll the sponge cake. Evenly spread the mousse filling on the inside of the cake. Re-roll the sponge cake. For a finished look, dust the top of the roll with powdered sugar.

Makes 8 servings.

Young Family Farm

Their mission, as stewards of the land, is to grow safe, fresh, and healthy food for the community. The Young family—Tyler, Karla, and their three daughters, Emma, Hattie, and Sarah—are locavores. That is, they are dedicated to the local food movement for locally grown produce because "fresh is best."

The Young Family Farm delivers its fresh produce to grocery stores throughout New England and sells the fruits of their labor at a farm stand/greenhouse operation in beautiful Little Compton, Rhode Island. They also donate an extraordinary amount of potatoes, turnips, and squash to the Rhode Island Community Food Bank (241,000 pounds in fiscal year 2013).

Ever since he was five years old, Tyler Young knew he wanted to be a farmer. With generations of farming in his blood, Tyler jumped at the chance to buy the Little Compton farmland with his wife Karla in 1997. They sold their first crop of strawberries at a picnic table on their front lawn. They eventually developed a small wholesale potato business, which blossomed into the diversified operation it is today. Their retail farm stand—very popular with their locavore customers—is open from May through Thanksgiving. A five-acre orchard with ten varieties of apples is open for pick-your-own enthusiasts from September through October. The annual Apple Festival is held every Columbus Day weekend.

Things quiet down in the winter, but come March, the farm is again in full operation. The doors to the Young Family Farm retail stand open in May, much to the delight of die-hard fans. And so, the circle of farm life continues.

From the Young Family Farm comes this surprisingly simple recipe that has spectacular results. The addition of blueberries to these peach tarts sends this dessert into the stratosphere.

Peach Tarts

FOR THE CRUMBLE TOPPING:

¼ cup brown sugar

¼ cup white sugar

¾ cup equal parts oats and flour

½ teaspoon cinnamon

½ teaspoon salt

1 stick cold butter, cut into cubes

1 cup chopped nuts (optional)

FOR THE FILLING:

6–7 cups sliced peaches

1 cup blueberries (optional)

¼ cup brown sugar

¼–½ cup white sugar

1 teaspoon cinnamon

1-inch piece fresh ginger, grated

Lemon zest

2 tablespoons flour

2 tablespoons cornstarch

TO SERVE:

4 ready-made tart shells, or
1 large tart shell

Ice cream or whipped cream, as
needed

Preheat oven to 400°F. For the topping, combine the brown sugar, white sugar, oats-flour mixture, cinnamon, and salt in a bowl. Cut in the butter until the mixture is crumbly. Add the nuts, if desired.

In another bowl, gently mix together all the filling ingredients. Fill the ready-made tart shells with the filling mixture. Top with the crumble topping mixture.

Bake the tarts in the 400°F oven for 15 minutes. Reduce the oven temperature to 350°F, and bake for an additional 30 minutes, or until the tarts are bubbling. Serve with ice cream or whipped cream.

Makes 4 servings.

Pippin Orchards

Move over, apple cider doughnuts. Pippin Orchards in Cranston, Rhode Island, goes one step further with their pumpkin doughnuts. Don't dawdle because on most days, the pumpkin doughnuts are sold out by mid-afternoon. They go well with Rhode Island's famous coffee milk, the official state drink.

They tend to get pretty creative at this roadside orchard and farm store. You never know what the kitchen will come up with—granola apple brittle, caramel apple ice cream, and peach-cherry pies are just some of the unique items in the store.

The logo for Pippin Orchards is one artist's rendering of Johnny Appleseed, the American pioneer nurseryman who introduced apple trees to large parts of the country. His real name was John Chapman (1774-1845). He became an American legend while still alive because of his kind and generous ways.

The owner of Pippin Orchards is a modern-day Johnny Appleseed. Joe Polsena now runs the business started more than a half century ago by his father. Joe is dedicated to educating his customers on how food is grown and brought to market. September is their busiest month, and the orchard closes in December for the winter. The Polsena family would like to share with you this recipe for Apple Torte.

Apple Torte

FOR THE CRUST:

½ cup softened butter

⅓ cup sugar (or Splenda)

½ teaspoon vanilla

1 cup flour

¼ cup raspberry jam

FOR THE FILLING:

2 (8-ounce) packages cream cheese, softened

½ cup sugar (or Splenda)

½ teaspoon vanilla

2 eggs

FOR THE TOPPING:

⅔ cup sugar (or Splenda)

1 teaspoon cinnamon

4 cups peeled and sliced apples

1 cup sliced almonds

Preheat oven to 350°F.

For the crust, cream the butter, sugar, and vanilla in a bowl. Add the flour and mix well. Press the mixture into the bottom of a 10-inch springform pan. Spread the crust with the jam.

For the filling, beat the cream cheese, sugar, and vanilla in a bowl until smooth. Add the eggs once at a time, and beat well. Pour the mixture over the jam layer.

For the topping, combine the sugar and cinnamon in a large bowl. Toss in the sliced apples to coat with the sugar mixture. Spoon the apples over the cream cheese layer. Sprinkle with the almonds.

Bake in the 350°F oven for 75 minutes, or until golden. Chill 8 hours before serving.

Makes 8 servings.

Where to Get Apple Cider Doughnuts in Rhode Island

People (like me), who seriously love apple cider doughnuts, will spend their free time every autumn making the rounds, visiting every local orchard to sample their sugar-coated offerings. Rhode Island may be small, but there's no shortage of orchards that sell apple cider doughnuts, usually made with their own apple cider. It's always a good idea to call before you go because these sweet beauties disappear quickly.

- Appleland Orchard, 135 Smith Avenue, Greenville, 401-949-3690, www.applelandorchard.com

- Barden Orchards, 56 Elmdale Road, North Scituate, 401-934-1413, www.bardenfamilyyorchard.com

- Knight Farm, 1 Snake Hill Road, North Scituate, 401-349-4408, www.knightfarm.com

- Pippin Orchard, 751 Pippin Orchard Road, Cranston, 401-943-7096

- Sunset Orchard Farm, 244 Gleaner Road, North Scituate, 401-934-1900, www.sunsetorchards.freeservers.com

- Sweet Berry Farm, 913 Mitchell's Lane, Middletown, 401-847-3912, www.sweetberryfarmri.com

- Young Family Farm, 260 West Main Road, Little Compton, 401-635-0110, www.youngfamilyfarm.com

- And my favorite, Jaswell's Farm, 50 Swan Road, Smithfield, 401-231-9043, www.jaswellsfarm.com. In my honest opinion, they make the best apple cider doughnuts in Rhode Island.

A Spicy Hot, Deliciously Sweet Vinegar Tonic

Fire cider is a new concept to me. I heard about it at the Food for Thought natural food store I frequent in Narragansett, and I was intrigued. Looking into fire cider, the story became more and more interesting.

According to Rosemary Gladstar, fire cider was first concocted in the early 1980s in the kitchen at the California School of Herbal Studies. Rosemary taught hundreds of people how to make fire cider, a spicy hot, deliciously sweet vinegar tonic. Her aim was to bring medicinal herbalism back into people's kitchens. Fire cider was a crossover recipe, part medicine, and part food. Small shot glasses of fire cider daily serves as an excellent pick-me-up, or take it by the teaspoon if you feel a cold coming on. Take it more frequently if necessary to help strengthen your immune system.

Rosemary says there were no other fire cider recipes available and no commercial products specifically named Fire Cider when it was first produced. Since then several private companies trademarked the herbal product and name, Fire Cider, which has caused a contentious uproar. Rosemary is urging people to boycott pirated versions of fire cider, and she urges everyone to make their own, which is very simple to do. For details on this controversy, visit www.freefirecidercom. In the meantime, you can make your own with Rosemary's recipe. There are other fire cider recipes online, but this is the original.

The Original Fire Cider Recipe

½ cup grated fresh horseradish root

½ cup or more fresh chopped onions

¼ cup or more chopped garlic

¼ cup or more grated ginger

Chopped fresh or dried cayenne pepper, to taste (whole or powdered)

Apple cider vinegar, raw and unpasteurized, as needed

Honey, to taste

Optional ingredients: turmeric, echinacea, and cinnamon

Place the herbs in a half-gallon canning jar, and add enough raw unpasteurized apple cider vinegar to cover the herbs by at least 3–4 inches. Cover with a tight-fitting lid.

Place the jar in a warm place, and let it sit for 3–4 weeks. Shake the jar every day to help in the maceration process.

After 3–4 weeks, strain out the herbs, and reserve the liquid. Add honey to taste. Warm the honey first so it mixes in well. Your fire cider should taste hot, spicy, and sweet.

Transfer the strained fire cider into bottles. Fire cider will keep for several months unrefrigerated if stored in a cool pantry. But it's better to store in the refrigerator if you have the room.

Makes 1 large jar.

Note: Pepper "to taste" means it should be hot, but not so hot you can't tolerate it. Better to make it a little milder than too hot. You can always add more pepper later if necessary.

Connecticut

Connecticut is unofficially known as The Nutmeg State, and no one is sure why. It may have come from sailors returning from far-off voyages with nutmeg in hand—a very valuable spice back in 1788, when Connecticut became a state. It seems to be a fitting nickname because Connecticut is well known for certain residents (Jacques Pepin and Martha Stewart, to name just two) from the upper echelons of the culinary world.

The state's name comes from the Mohegan word "quonehtacut," which means "beside the long tidal river." The Connecticut River is indeed long, cutting through much of the state and flowing into Long Island Sound. The 406-mile river starts at the U.S.–Canada border and runs through Vermont, New Hampshire, and Massachusetts, making it the longest river in New England. In 1614, the Dutch were the first to chart the river. In the following decades, Puritans from Massachusetts relocated to Connecticut.

Weather wise, there are two main seasons in Connecticut—a warm to hot season from April to late October, and a cool to cold season from November through March.

Connecticut is home to the venerable Yale University in New Haven, and to the oldest U.S. newspaper still being published, *The Hartford Courant*, established in 1764. Other "firsts" include the hamburger (1895) and the lollipop-making machine (1908). That sweet treat was named after a popular racehorse of the time. New Haven was the site of the first PEZ® Candy, which is made in Orange. B.F. Clyde's Cider Mill, built in 1881 in Old Mystic, is the only steam-powered cider mill still operating in the United States. (See page 112 for details.)

In the Colonial era, pumpkins were cut open, cleaned out, and used as guides for haircuts to ensure a uniform cut. Because of this look, New Englanders were called "pumpkin heads," especially in the New Haven area.

Connecticut's most important crops are dairy, poultry, forest and nursery, tobacco, vegetables, and fruit. According to Agriculture Commissioner Steven K. Reviczky, apples are one of the state's largest and important agricultural crops, with an average yearly harvest of about a half-million bushels worth $12 million.

Every New England state seems to have its own Apple Valley. In Connecticut, it's Southington, located between Hartford and Waterbury. This small town is known for its many orchards with an incredible variety and supply. The area celebrates this staple crop with the Harvest Festival every October. Folks traveling through this beautiful state in the fall are urged to stop in Southington for a bag of apple fritters and other foods made from the town's famous apples.

B.F. Clyde's Cider Mill

What a treat it is to visit B.F. Clyde's Cider Mill in Old Mystic, Connecticut, where the oldest steam-powered cider mill in the United States is still operating. This cider mill is off the beaten path, a bit challenging to find. You'll need a good map or a navigation system to find this out-of-the-way compound consisting of several quaint buildings, but it's well worth the trip.

Thousands of tourists visit Mystic every year, drawn to the old seaport village and the bustling downtown with its charming shops and trendy restaurants. But only those who look for B.F. Clyde's Cider Mill in nearby Old Mystic get a taste of what the historic area used to be like.

People are often amazed at how that area looks the same as it did more than a century ago. The quiet hamlet of Old Mystic is known for its country roads with many stone walls that defined property lines between homesteads and fields, still intact after hundreds of years.

At B.F. Clyde's, some say it's like stepping back in time as you roam about, starting with the general store that's packed to the rafters with all kinds of deliciousness. The colorful site is a National Historic Landmark, and over at the cider mill you will see them making a mighty fine apple cider just like Clyde did in 1881. The adults will enjoy stopping at Clyde's tasting room for free sips of apple wine and hard cider, while the youngsters will be happy with some of Clyde's famous kettle corn and an apple cider slushie.

B.F. Clyde's is the only steam-powered cider mill in the United States. Open only September through November, the old white mill with its dark, aromatic interior is the quintessential place to visit on a crisp fall day. Antique jugs hang from the ceiling. An old cashier's

bench even has a turn-of-the-century phone that you almost expect to ring.

Their season begins in September with the making of cider, wine, jams, jellies, and all kinds of fruit pies and breads, and the general store remains open until late December. We were on the hunt for their famed apple cider doughnuts, but they had run out the day we were there. Fans say those doughnuts are "amazing," so maybe next time we'll have better luck. Instead we bought some apple butter, which I used to make a number of recipes in this book.

The quaint general store houses all things old-fashioned: jams, jellies, honey, maple syrup, and fudge. Outdoors, there are rustic wooden bins of apples and pumpkins, and the indoor shelves are well stocked with cider, apple pies, and candy apples.

This is one of those rare places where you can purchase a pocket pie. They are hand-held pies, or pie you can eat with your fingers, a lot like empanadas or turnovers. Pocket pies can be made with any fruit filling, and they can be baked, fried, or toasted. At B.F. Clyde's, they are soft pillows of filled piecrust that are baked until golden. The history of the pocket pie, also known as a pasty in the Midwest, is lost to time but more than likely it originated in England and was brought over to New England by early settlers. Or it could have come from the Irish, known for their beef hand pies. Whatever their origin, these small pies with the tasty contents sealed inside are truly "handy" and affordable to boot.

Cider making is demonstrated by the sixth generation of the Clyde family every week-end. The process begins with an old dump truck filled with apples delivering its load into a hopper under watchful eyes. Damaged apples are pulled out while the rest bounce their way onto an antique conveyor belt into the cider mill. There the apples are crushed and pressed, just as it was done more than a century ago. Today the mill is owned and operated by Clyde's grandson, John Bucklyn.

B.F. Clyde's also now has a winery that produces hard ciders and apple wines. Tastings are scheduled on the weekends. Hard cider in plastic jugs is sold in the cider mill's cellar. Fans rave about the 28-proof "Black Out" cider.

On fall weekends, B.F. Clyde's is jam packed with families and young couples. We went there on a Thursday and didn't have to wait in any lines. If it's cold, I recommend the hot mulled cider with caramel.

Holmberg Orchards

Holmberg Orchards in Gales Ferry, Connecticut, is a family-owned farm now in its fourth generation. Adolph and Hulda Holmberg, arrivals from Sweden, purchased the farm in 1896. Sons Harry and Henry took over in 1931 and began planting fruit trees. Harold's son, Richard, with his wife, Diane, returned home after college, and purchased the farm from Harold in the 1980s. Richard offered fresh ideas that led to successful expansion into retail and pick-your-own markets. Don't be surprised to see Diane on the weekend helping out in the orchard's bakery, especially during the busy fall season.

Richard and Diane now work cooperatively with two of their children, Amy and Russell. The two college graduates have added new dimensions to the business. Amy developed a specialty foods market that retains its agricultural roots and charms. Russell created a winery that has already won awards for its fruit wines and hard ciders.

Apples aren't the only tree fruit that can be used to make your morning breakfast or afternoon brunch special. Peaches are perfect for making moist muffins. The following recipe from Holmberg Orchards recommends using fresh peaches, but frozen will have to do in the dead of winter. They also offer two more breakfast suggestions, also made with peaches.

Peach Praline Muffins

FOR THE MUFFINS:

1⅔ cups all-purpose flour

2 teaspoons baking powder

¼ teaspoon salt

½ cup packed brown sugar

½ cup milk

⅓ cup vegetable oil

1 egg

1 teaspoon vanilla extract

1 cup chopped fresh or frozen peaches, thawed and drained

½ cup chopped pecans

FOR THE PRALINE TOPPING:

¼ cup packed brown sugar

¼ cup chopped pecans

1 tablespoon cold butter or margarine

Preheat oven to 400°F.

In a large bowl, combine the flour, baking powder, and salt. In another bowl, combine the brown sugar, milk, oil, egg, and vanilla. Stir the wet ingredients into the dry ingredients just until moistened. Fold in the peaches and pecans. Fill greased or paper-lined muffin cups two-thirds full.

Combine the topping ingredients until crumbly; sprinkle over batter.

Bake in the 400°F oven for 15–18 minutes, or until a toothpick comes out clean when inserted into a muffin. Cool for 5 minutes before removing from the muffin pan to a wire rack.

Makes 12 muffins.

Cinnamon-Peach Cottage Cheese Pancakes

4 eggs

1 cup cottage cheese

½ cup milk

1 teaspoon vanilla extract

2 tablespoons butter, melted

1 peach, shredded

1 cup all-purpose flour

2 tablespoons white sugar

1 pinch salt

¾ teaspoon baking soda

1 teaspoon ground cinnamon

In a large bowl, mix the eggs, cottage cheese, milk, vanilla, butter, and shredded peach.

In a small bowl, combine the flour, sugar, salt, baking soda, and cinnamon. Stir the flour mixture into the cottage cheese mixture until just combined.

Prepare a lightly oiled griddle over medium-high heat. Drop large spoonfuls of batter onto the griddle, and cook until bubbles form and the edges are dry. Flip, and cook until browned on the other side. Repeat with remaining batter.

Makes 4 servings.

Mascarpone Stuffed French Toast with Peaches

8 fresh peaches

½ cup sugar

4 pinches ground nutmeg

½ teaspoon ground cinnamon

4 Mexican bolillo rolls*

1 cup mascarpone cheese

6 tablespoons confectioners' sugar

1 lemon, zested

6 eggs

¾ cup milk

½ teaspoon vanilla extract

2 teaspoons butter, or as needed

2 teaspoons vegetable oil, or as needed

Peel the peaches, remove the pits, and cut slices into a heavy saucepan, catching all the juices. Stir in the sugar, nutmeg, and cinnamon, and cook over medium heat until bubbly. Continue cooking, stirring occasionally, until the sauce reaches a syrupy consistency, about 10 minutes. Remove from heat.

Meanwhile, cut off and discard the ends of the bolillo rolls. Slice the rolls into 1¼-inch-thick slices. Lay each slice of bread on a board, and with a sharp knife held parallel to the board, cut a pocket into each slice, leaving three sides intact. Set aside.

In a bowl, stir together the mascarpone, confectioners' sugar, and lemon zest until smooth. Scoop this mixture into a small plastic bag. Cut off one corner of the bag, and pipe as much filling into the pocket in each slice of bread as will fit without overflowing.

In a shallow bowl, whisk together the eggs, milk, and vanilla. Melt the butter with the oil over medium heat in a large non-stick skillet. Dip each stuffed piece of bread into the batter, add to the skillet, and cook until browned on both sides.

Makes 4 servings.

....

Bolillo is a type of bread made in Mexico, and it is similar to a French baguette. If you can't find bolillo rolls, you can substitute a French baguette in this recipe.

....

Sandwiches Minus the Bread

Lettuce wraps are wonderful "sandwiches" any time of the year, but especially in warm weather when you want to eat light. Eliminating the bread is ideal for those wanting to reduce the number of carbs in their diet. Both of the following lettuce wrap recipes are absolutely delicious. The peach version is a favorite of mine, a combination of sweet and spicy. Fresh peaches are essential to this recipe, cubed and paired with beef, then wrapped in a simple lettuce leaf. You can dip the wrap in one of two sauces.

Vietnamese Peach Lettuce Wraps

3 fresh peaches, divided

1 pound lean ground beef (or pork)

1 garlic clove, minced

2 tablespoons soy sauce

½ teaspoon freshly grated ginger root

Lettuce, washed and separated into leaves, as needed

⅔ cup fresh mint

½ cup chopped green onion

2 cups hot cooked rice

Peach-Ginger or Peach-Hoisin Sauce (recipes follow)

Cut 2½ peaches into large cubes. Reserve the remaining half peach for the sauce.

In a bowl, combine the beef, garlic, soy sauce, and ginger. Mix well. Shape into 16 equal-size balls. Alternate the peach cubes and beef balls on 4 metal skewers. Prepare your grill.

Grill the skewers 4–5 inches above the hot coals for 5–6 minutes per side, or until cooked through. Remove the cooked beef balls and peaches from each skewer.

To serve, wrap the grilled beef balls and peaches in the lettuce leaves, adding some of the mint, green onions, and rice, as desired. Roll up each lettuce leaf to make a bundle. Dip the bundle into the sauce of your choice (see recipes below).

Makes 4 servings.

Peach-Ginger Sauce: In a blender, combine the reserved ½ peach, 3 tablespoons of soy sauce, 2 or 3 slices of fresh ginger root, 1 large garlic clove, and 1 tablespoon of sugar. Blend until smooth. Pour into 4 small dipping bowls. Makes ¾ cup.

Peach-Hoisin Sauce: In a blender, combine the reserved ½ peach, ¼ cup hoisin sauce, and ¼ cup water. Blend until smooth. Makes ¾ cup.

Fresh Ideas

It always amazes me how home cooks (and orchard owners) come up with creative variations on classic dishes, such as this Chicken Peach Salad recipe from Holmberg Orchards in Gales Ferry, Connecticut. They also provided the following formulas for a wonderful salad of fruit and cheese and a modern soup that combines the flavors of apple and fennel.

Peach Chicken Salad

FOR THE SALAD:

3 medium fresh peaches, peeled and cubed

2 cups cubed cooked chicken breast

1 medium cucumber, seeded and chopped

3 tablespoons finely chopped red onion

FOR THE MINT VINAIGRETTE:

¼ cup white wine vinegar

1 tablespoon lemon juice

⅓ cup sugar

¼ cup minced fresh mint

¼ teaspoon salt

⅛ teaspoon pepper

4 lettuce leaves

In a large bowl, combine the peaches, chicken, cucumber, and onion. Set aside.

In a blender, combine the vinegar, lemon juice, sugar, mint, salt and pepper. Cover and process until smooth. Drizzle over the chicken mixture. Toss to coat. Cover and refrigerate until chilled. Use a slotted spoon to serve on lettuce-lined plates.

Makes 4 servings.

Apple, Cheese, and Walnut Salad

FOR THE VINAIGRETTE:

3 tablespoons olive oil

2 tablespoons balsamic vinegar

2 teaspoons Dijon-style mustard

1 clove garlic, crushed

Fresh ground black pepper, to taste

FOR THE SALAD:

8 cups torn mixed salad greens

2 medium Fuji apples, halved, cored, and sliced ⅛-inch thick

⅓ cup crumbled blue cheese

¼ cup coarsely chopped toasted walnuts

Combine the vinaigrette ingredients in a bowl, and mix well.

In a large bowl, combine salad greens and apple slices. Add the vinaigrette to the salad. Toss gently to coat.

Arrange the salad on a large platter; sprinkle with the cheese and walnuts.

Makes 4 servings.

Apple Fennel Soup

1 (14½-ounce) can low-sodium chicken broth

2 cups water

½ cup white wine

2 Golden Delicious apples, peeled, cored, and chopped

1 cup thinly sliced carrots

1 small onion, thinly sliced

½ cup chopped fresh fennel

1 bay leaf

¼ teaspoon dried thyme leaves

6 black peppercorns

Plain low-fat yogurt (optional)

In a large pot, combine the broth, water, wine, apples, carrots, onion, fennel, bay leaf, thyme, and peppercorns. Bring to a boil. Reduce the heat to simmer, cover, and cook for 20 minutes.

Strain the soup, reserving the liquid. Remove the bay leaf from apple-vegetable mixture. In a blender or food processor, puree mixture. Add the reserved liquid and blend well. Reheat the soup if necessary.

To serve, ladle into warm soup bowls, and top with a dollop of yogurt, if desired.

Makes 4–6 servings.

Appetizing Apps

Next is a different take on that classic French dish ratatouille. The traditional eggplant is replaced with apple, and you'll have enough "apps" for a crowd. This ratatouille recipe and the following recipe for mini burgers (or sliders) are from Holmberg Orchards in Gales Ferry, Connecticut.

Apple Ratatouille on Crostini

½ cup (4 ounces) walnut oil

¼ cup (2 ounces) vegetable oil

2½ cups diced celery

2 cups diced red onions

4 cups cored, peeled and diced apples (about 1 pound)

2 tablespoons minced garlic

4 cups diced zucchini (about 1 pound)

2 cups diced yellow squash (about ½ pound)

1½ cups canned diced tomatoes, drained

¾ cup walnuts, coarsely chopped

1 tablespoon salt

1½ teaspoons pepper

1 teaspoon ground nutmeg

1 teaspoon turmeric

¼ cup thinly sliced fresh basil leaves

48 (3-inch) bread rounds or slices, grilled or toasted

Blend the oils in a large measuring cup. In a large heavy skillet, heat ¼ cup of the blended oils. Add the celery and red onions. Sauté over medium heat until soft and browned. Remove the vegetables to a bowl.

Heat ¼ cup of the blended oil in the same skillet, and add the apples. Sauté until the apples are soft and golden. Add the apples to the bowl.

Heat the remaining ¼ cup oil in the same skillet. Add the garlic, zucchini, and yellow squash. Sauté until soft.

Return the vegetable-apple mixture to the skillet. Stir in the tomatoes, walnuts, salt, pepper, nutmeg, and turmeric. Continue cooking over medium heat for 5–10 minutes, or until the mixture is thickened.

Stir in the basil and cook for an additional 1–2 minutes.

To serve, portion 2 tablespoons of the ratatouille on each grilled bread slice.

Makes 48 servings.

Plan on 2 crostini servings per person—unless your guests fall in love with this party offering, and then you'll watch it quickly disappear.

Pork Apple Mini Burgers

1 tablespoon olive oil

1 cup minced onions

2 garlic cloves, minced

1 pound extra lean ground pork

1 cup grated Cameo apples

½ cup seasoned bread crumbs

¼ cup spicy plum sauce

½ teaspoon each salt, pepper, and ground ginger

Slider rolls, as needed

In a skillet, heat oil over medium high heat. Cook the onions, stirring often, until tender, about 5 minutes. Add the garlic and cook 1 minute more. Remove the skillet from the heat and let cool.

In a bowl, combine the pork, grated apple, bread crumbs, plum sauce, salt, pepper, ginger, and the cooked onion and garlic mixture. Mix until well combined. Using a ¼-cup measure, form into ½-inch-thick patties.

In a non-stick skillet, brown the patties on both sides until no longer pink in the center, about 5 minutes per side. Serve immediately on slider rolls.

Makes about 12 sliders (depending on their size).

More From The Holmbergs

Here are five more wonderful recipes from the Holmberg family—appetizers that will dazzle your family and friends. Thanks go out to Harold, Richard and Diane, Amy and Russell—three generations now working together at Holmberg Orchards in Gales Ferry, Connecticut. Three of the dishes call for perfectly ripe pears. The fourth recipe for Zippy Pear Cheese Bites is from my files. Surprise friends and family with this creative appetizer that combines luscious pears with sharp cheeses. The best pears to use in this recipe would be Bosc, Anjou, or Bartlett. Be sure to have small plates and lots of napkins on hand for your guests. Then try two more appetizing dishes that are peachy keen and sure to "wow" your guests with their appetite-whetting flavors.

Balsamic Glazed Pear and Goat Cheese Crostini

½ cup slivered almonds

2 pears

3 tablespoons balsamic vinegar

1 tablespoon butter

1 teaspoon honey

24 baguette rounds, toasted

½ cup spreadable goat cheese

Ground black pepper, if desired

Toast the almonds, placing them in a heavy frying pan and toasting over medium heat, stirring constantly, for 1–2 minutes, or until you can detect a toasted aroma.

Slice the pears stem side up into 12 quarter-inch-wide vertical planks. Cut large slices in half lengthwise for a total of 48 slices.

In a large frying pan, heat the vinegar, butter, and honey over medium heat for 2–3 minutes, stirring constantly, until reduced by half, or about 2 tablespoons. Add the pear slices, and continue cooking for 1 minute, turning the pears over once.

Place 2 pear slices on each baguette round, and top with 1 teaspoon goat cheese. Sprinkle almonds over the cheese, and garnish with black pepper, if desired.

Makes 24 servings.

Pear and Squash Bruschetta

1 butternut squash (about 1½ pounds)

2 yellow onions (about 1 pound), coarsely chopped

2 medium carrots, coarsely chopped

1 tablespoon extra virgin olive oil

1 tablespoon butter

4 sage leaves

3 ripe pears, cored and cut into half-inch cubes

Salt and pepper, to taste

½ loaf sourdough bread

¼ pound smoked ricotta or smoked mozzarella cheese

Pumpkin seed oil or extra virgin olive oil, as needed

Peel the squash. Combine the squash trimmings, onions, and carrots in a large saucepan. Add enough water to cover the vegetables. Bring to a boil and simmer for 45 minutes or until the liquid is flavorful, adding additional water as needed to keep about 3 cups liquid in the pan. Strain. Reserve the liquid and discard the solids.

Cut the peeled squash in half. Scrape all the seeds from the squash and discard the seeds. Cut the squash into ½-inch cubes.

In a large shallow pan, heat the olive oil and butter. Add the sage and fry for 30 seconds, or until crisp and fragrant. Remove the sage with a slotted spoon, drain on paper towels, and reserve for garnish.

Add the cut-up squash and pears to the pan. Cook over medium heat, stirring frequently, until just starting to brown. Add 1 cup of the squash stock and cook until reduced. Repeat, using about 3 cups of stock. The pears and squash should be soft but still hold their shape. Season with salt and pepper.

Preheat oven to 350°F.

Meanwhile, cut the bread into ½-inch slices. Toast in the 350°F oven until golden brown, about 10 minutes.

Spoon about ¼ cup of the warm pear-squash mixture onto each slice of bread. Using a vegetable peeler, create ribbons of cheese to place on top of bruschetta. Drizzle with pumpkin seed or olive oil, if desired. Garnish with the fried sage leaves.

Makes 8 servings.

Grilled Asian Shrimp Skewers with Pears

½ cup honey

½ cup soy sauce

2 tablespoons sesame oil

1 tablespoon ground ginger

2 teaspoons minced garlic

½ teaspoon red pepper flakes

2 pears, cored, cut into 1-inch cubes

36 medium-size shrimp, peeled and deveined

1 green bell pepper, cored, seeded, cut into 12 (1-inch) squares

12 cherry tomatoes

In a bowl, whisk together the honey, soy sauce, sesame oil, ground ginger, garlic, and red pepper flakes until blended. Set aside.

Thread 12 skewers each with 3 cubes of pear, 3 shrimp, 1 pepper square, and 1 cherry tomato.

Place the skewers in a large shallow pan. Pour the marinade over the kabobs and refrigerate for 1 hour.

Brush a grill with oil. Preheat the grill.

Grill the kabobs over medium heat for 3–5 minutes on each side, or until the shrimp is cooked. Serve with your favorite dipping sauce, if desired.

Makes 12 servings.

Zippy Pear Cheese Bites

2 pears, cored and cut into slices

Lemon juice, as needed

½ cup shredded sharp cheddar cheese

¼ cup shredded hot pepper cheese

Dip the pear slices in the lemon juice to prevent discoloration. Place the pear slices in a baking dish.

Combine the cheeses in a bowl. Sprinkle the cheeses over the pear slices.

Place the baking dish 6 inches under the oven broiler. Broil until the pears are heated and the cheese is bubbly. Serve with a sturdy cracker, such as Triscuit.

Makes 4 servings.

Pancetta-Wrapped Peaches

16 thin slices pancetta

2 medium freestone peaches, halved, pitted, and each cut into 8 wedges

Salt and freshly ground pepper, to taste

16 basil leaves

Balsamic vinegar, for drizzling

Lay the pancetta slices out on a work surface. Set a peach wedge at the edge of each slice, season with salt and pepper, and top with a basil leaf. Roll up the slices of pancetta to enclose the peaches, and secure each bundle with a toothpick.

Prepare your grill. Place the peaches on the grill over medium heat, and grill until the pancetta is crisp and the peaches are soft, 20-25 minutes. Turn the bundles so each side is cooked.

Transfer the grilled peaches to a platter, and lightly drizzle with aged balsamic vinegar.

Makes 16 servings.

Peach and Brie Quesadillas with Lime-Honey Dipping Sauce

FOR THE SAUCE:

2 tablespoons honey

2 teaspoons fresh lime juice

½ teaspoon grated lime rind

FOR THE QUESADILLAS:

1 cup peeled, thinly sliced, firm ripe peaches (about 2 large)

1 tablespoon chopped fresh chives

1 teaspoon brown sugar

3 ounces Brie cheese, thinly sliced

4 (8-inch) fat-free flour tortillas

Fresh chives (optional)

To prepare the sauce: Combine the honey, limejuice, and rind in a bowl, stirring with a whisk. Set aside.

To prepare the quesadillas: Combine the peaches, chives, and sugar in a bowl, tossing gently to coat. Heat a large nonstick skillet over medium-high heat. Arrange one-fourth of the cheese and one-fourth of the peach mixture over half of each tortilla. Fold the tortillas in half.

Place 2 quesadillas in the pan. Cook for 2 minutes on each side, or until the tortillas are lightly browned and crisp. Remove the quesadillas from the pan, and keep warm. Repeat this procedure with the remaining quesadillas.

Cut each quesadilla into 3 wedges, and serve with the sauce. Garnish with fresh chives, if desired.

Makes 4 servings.

Food From Faraway

This sounds so exotic, but it could not be much easier to accomplish. The unique aromas in your kitchen will transport you to faraway places. We thank Holmberg Orchards in Gales Ferry, Connecticut, for sharing this wonderful Moroccan dish with us. They also provided the following recipes for Balsamic Fig-Glazed Chicken Breast with Pears, Brined Pork Chops with Spicy Pear Chutney, and Spicy Fish Tacos with Pear Mango Salsa, three more delicious dishes.

Moroccan Peach Roasted Chicken

¼ cup margarine or butter

¼ cup honey

1 teaspoon rose water*

1 teaspoon salt

Ground black pepper, to taste

4 pounds bone-in chicken pieces, with skin

1 pound fresh peaches, pitted and sliced

1 tablespoon white sugar

½ cup toasted slivered almonds (optional)

Preheat oven to 425°F. In a glass measuring cup, combine the margarine, honey, rose water, salt and pepper. Heat in the microwave until the margarine has melted, about 30 seconds.

Place the chicken in a baking dish and pour the margarine mixture over it. Coat the chicken completely. Place the baking dish in the oven.

Cook uncovered in the 425°F oven until the chicken pieces have browned, about 15 minutes. Reduce the oven temperature to 350°F. Add the peaches to the dish and sprinkle with the sugar. Continue to roast until the chicken is cooked through, about 20 more minutes.

Remove the chicken pieces to a serving dish, and pour the pan juices over the chicken. Garnish with slivered almonds, if desired.

Makes 4 servings.

Rose water is used in Moroccan cooking and baking to flavor savory dishes, soups, pastries, desserts, and beverages. Orange flower water may be used in place of rose water. You will find either in large supermarkets and Middle Eastern markets.

Balsamic Fig Glazed Pear-Topped Chicken Breast

4 ounces goat cheese

¾ teaspoon dried thyme

¼ teaspoon fresh minced garlic

3 pears, cored and cut in half

1⅓ cups low-sodium chicken broth

1½ cups dried figs

¾ cup balsamic vinegar

¼ cup sugar

6 boneless, skinless chicken breast halves

2 teaspoons salt

1 teaspoon ground black pepper

Fresh thyme sprigs, for garnish (optional)

Mix goat cheese, thyme, and garlic until blended. Place 1 rounded tablespoon of the goat cheese mixture into the center of each pear half.

Puree the chicken broth, figs, vinegar, and sugar in batches in a blender until smooth. Pour this mixture into a strainer set over a bowl. With the back of a spoon, press the fig sauce into the bowl and discard the solids. Pour half of the fig sauce into 13 x 9-inch pan.

Preheat oven to 375°F. Place the chicken breasts over the fig sauce in the pan. Season with salt and pepper. Place the filled pear halves cut side down over each chicken breast and drizzle with the remaining fig sauce. Cover pan with foil and bake in the 375°F oven for 20 minutes. Remove the foil and continue to bake, basting occasionally, for 30–40 minutes, or until the chicken breasts reach an internal temperature of 160°F.

Cut the chicken breasts and pears in half to serve. Spoon the sauce over the pears. Garnish with a thyme sprig, if desired.

Makes 6 servings.

CHEESE SELECTION GUIDE FOR PEARS

It's a perfect marriage: Fresh New England pears go well with a variety of cheeses, such as:

BLUE CHEESE: Blue-veined, semi-soft, crumbly, with a spicy flavor that will pique your taste buds.

BRIE: Soft, ripened cheese with a straw-colored interior and an edible rind. Usually mild in flavor.

CHEDDAR: A hard cheese, light yellow to orange in color, with a wide range of flavor, from mild to extra sharp.

GOUDA: A hard cheese with a creamy interior and a mild, slightly nutty flavor. Always coated with wax.

SWISS: A hard cheese with large holes. Pale yellow in color. A mild, nutty flavor.

Brined Pork Chops with Spicy Pear Chutney

FOR THE BRINED PORK CHOPS:

4 cups water, divided

¼ cup kosher salt

¼ cup brown sugar, packed

1 teaspoon black pepper

1 tablespoon apple cider vinegar

4 pork chops, about ¾ inch thick

½ white onion, sliced

2 or 3 fresh sage leaves

Olive oil, as needed for brushing the pork chops

FOR THE SPICY PEAR CHUTNEY:

1 tablespoon olive oil

½ medium-sized red onion, minced

½ cup dried cranberries

¼ cup granulated sugar

1 tablespoon apple cider vinegar

1 tablespoon freshly squeezed lemon juice

1 teaspoon kosher or sea salt

½ teaspoon black pepper

¼–½ teaspoon red pepper flakes (depending on how spicy you want it)

3 fresh pears, chopped

In a small saucepan, combine 1 cup of water with the salt, brown sugar, and pepper. Heat, stirring until the salt and sugar dissolve. Add the remaining cold water and let the mixture cool. Stir in the apple cider vinegar. Pour the mixture into a glass baking dish or large freezer weight plastic storage bag. Add the pork chops, onions, and sage. Refrigerate for at least 1 hour and up to 12 hours.

Take the pork chops out of the refrigerator, and rinse them well with cold water. Pat dry with paper towels. Let rest for about 5 minutes before cooking.

Heat a grill pan or skillet over medium high heat. Brush the pork chops with the olive oil, and cook for 4 minutes per side (more or less depending on the thickness of the pork chops). Remove from the pan, brush the tops with a little more olive oil, and let rest for 5 minutes before serving.

To make the chutney, heat a large saucepan over medium heat. Add the olive oil and minced red onion. Cook for 2–3 minutes until the onions start to soften. Add the dried cranberries and cook for 5 more minutes. Stir in the sugar, vinegar, lemon juice, salt, pepper, red pepper flakes, and chopped pears. Combine well. Simmer on low heat for 5–10 minutes or until the pears and cranberries have softened but the pears still retain their shape. If the mixture is too liquid, turn the heat up and cook until most of the liquid has evaporated. Serve warm with the pork chops.

Makes 4 servings.

....

Note: I used the leftover pear chutney with boneless chicken breasts baked in the oven, and it was excellent.

....

Spicy Fish Tacos with Pear Mango Salsa

TO PREPARE THE FISH:

¼ cup vegetable oil

¼ cup lime juice

1 teaspoon minced garlic

1 teaspoon ground cumin

½ teaspoon salt

½ teaspoon ground cayenne
pepper

6 (4 ounce) fish fillets fresh or
frozen (thawed)

FOR THE SALSA:

⅔ cup pears, cored, cut into
¼-inch cubes

½ cup mango, peeled, pitted, cut
into ¼-inch cubes

½ cup sliced red grapes

1 tablespoon minced red onion

1 tablespoon minced jalapeno
pepper, seeded

1 tablespoon chopped cilantro

½ teaspoon salt

TO SERVE:

12 (6-inch) flour tortillas

Preheat oven to 350°F. In a small bowl, whisk the oil, lime juice, garlic, cumin, salt, and cayenne pepper. Set aside.

Place the fish in a single layer in 13 x 9-inch baking pan. Pour oil and lime juice mixture over the fish, and refrigerate for 30 minutes.

After the fish has marinated, place the baking pan in the 350°F oven. Bake for 20–25 minutes, or until the fish is opaque and flakes with a fork.

In another small bowl, mix the cubed pears, mango, grapes, onions, jalapeno, cilantro, and salt to make the salsa.

Serve the fish in warm tortillas topped with some of the salsa.

Makes 6 servings.

Fruit and Cheese

New Englanders like a thick slice of cheddar cheese with their apple pie. Here we have a similar fruit and cheese pairing with apples entering a traditional Italian dish called risotto, flavored with grated Parmigiano cheese. Risotto is a creamy rice dish that absorbs a great deal of broth to make it tender and flavorful. This is a creation from Holmberg Orchard in Gales Ferry, Connecticut.

Golden Delicious Risotto

4-5 cups low-sodium chicken or vegetable broth

4 tablespoons (½ stick) butter, divided

2 tablespoons minced onion

1 cup arborio rice or short grain rice

2 cups diced, peeled Golden Delicious apples, divided

⅓ cup dry white wine

2 tablespoons grated Parmigiano cheese, plus more for garnish

¼ teaspoon salt

Freshly grated nutmeg, to taste

In a medium saucepan, heat the broth to boiling. Reduce the heat to maintain a steady simmer and cover the saucepan with a lid.

In a large saucepan, melt 2 tablespoons butter over low heat. Add the onions and sauté for 3 minutes. Add the rice and 1 cup of the diced apple. Sauté, stirring constantly, for 3 minutes. Stir in the wine, and stir until the wine evaporates.

Constantly stirring, add enough hot broth (about ¾ cup) to just cover the rice. Adjust the heat to maintain a steady simmer, and cook the rice, stirring constantly, until almost all broth has been absorbed, about 4 minutes.

Remove the saucepan from the heat. Stir in the grated Parmigiano cheese, salt, and nutmeg. Garnish each serving with additional grated cheese.

Makes 4 servings

Note: Always be careful with nutmeg—too much of a good thing can ruin a dish.

Not So Distant Relations

These fall and winter dishes from Connecticut are related yet very different from one another. The first is from Holmberg Orchards in Gales Ferry, and the second is from Belltown Hill Orchards in South Glastonbury.

Acorn Squash Stuffed with Wild Rice, Pears, Cranberries, and Walnuts

FOR THE SQUASH:

3 acorn or dumpling squash

Salt and freshly ground pepper, as needed

Freshly ground nutmeg, to taste

4 tablespoons (½ stick) unsalted butter, at room temperature, divided

FOR THE RICE:

¾ cup wild rice

1½ cups low-sodium chicken or vegetable broth

¼ teaspoon salt, plus extra to taste

2 cups water

2 tablespoons olive oil

1 medium yellow onion, finely chopped

1 large garlic clove, minced

1 large celery stalk, finely chopped

1 large carrot, peeled and finely chopped

2 firm Bosc or Anjou pears, peeled, halved lengthwise, cored, and cut into ½-inch dice

2 teaspoons minced fresh sage

2 teaspoons minced fresh thyme leaves

⅓ cup minced fresh parsley

⅓ cup chopped walnuts, toasted

⅓ cup sweetened dried cranberries

Preheat oven to 350°F.

Cut each squash in half crosswise. Scoop out and discard the seeds and strings. If necessary, trim the top and bottom so that the squash will sit level. Place the squash on a rimmed baking sheet, cut side up. Sprinkle each half with a little salt, pepper, and nutmeg. Using 3 tablespoons of the butter, dot each half with butter. Cover the pan tightly with foil. Bake the squash just until moist and tender, about 45 minutes.

Meanwhile, combine the rice, chicken broth, ¼ teaspoon salt, and 2 cups of water in a medium saucepan. Bring to a boil over medium-high heat. Reduce the heat to a low simmer, partially cover, and cook, stirring occasionally, until the rice is tender, about 40 minutes. When the rice is done, most of the water should be evaporated. Set aside.

In a 10-inch sauté pan, heat the olive oil over medium heat. Swirl to coat the pan, and sauté the onions, garlic, celery, and carrots until slightly softened, about 3 minutes. Add the pears and sauté 2 minutes longer. Cover the pan, adjust the heat to medium-low, and cook the vegetables until crisp-tender, 3 minutes longer. Add the sage, thyme, and parsley, and sauté for 1 minute more. Remove from the heat.

In a large bowl, combine the cooked rice, sautéed vegetables and pears, walnuts, and dried cranberries. Taste and add salt and pepper, if desired.

Mound the rice mixture into the squash halves, dividing it evenly. Cut the remaining tablespoon of butter into small pieces. Dot each stuffed squash with butter. Cover with foil. Bake until heated through, about 20 minutes.

Makes 6 servings.

Apple Butternut Squash Casserole

1½ pounds butternut squash

1¼ pounds fresh apples (your choice), peeled and cut into 2-inch chunks

½ teaspoon ground ginger

½ cup apple cider

¼ teaspoon nutmeg

2 tablespoons butter

½ cup chopped pecans

Preheat oven to 350°F. Grease a 2-quart casserole dish.

In a large saucepan, combine the first 4 ingredients. Simmer over medium heat for 15 minutes, or until the squash and apples are tender.

Turn the into the prepared casserole dish. Sprinkle with nutmeg, dot with butter, and top with pecans. Bake in the 350°F oven for 20 minutes.

Makes 4–6 servings.

Belltown Hill Orchards

Located in South Glastonbury, Connecticut, Belltown Hill Orchards can trace its roots back to 1904 when Louis Preli emigrated from Italy to find work and the American dream. He eventually purchased seven acres of land, a parcel that grew over the years to 155 acres. The retail farm market was added, as well as wholesale accounts, a pick-your-own operation, a vineyard, and a bakery, with friendly old-time service. Louis Preli's American dream was realized.

Things change over time, but the Preli family's commitment to the orchard never waivered. The orchard was passed on from son to sons. The present owners are brothers Don and Michael with wives, sisters, and other family members all working to ensure the orchard's continued success.

For pick-your-own enthusiasts, the informative website (www.belltownhillorchards.com) provides detailed information as to when the apples, sweet and tart cherries, nectarines, white and yellow peaches, pears, and plums are ripe. The orchard closes in February, and regular customers can't wait for Belltown Hill to reopen at the end of every May.

Even when all the fresh fruit is gone, customers are drawn back again and again for the goodies in Grandma's Pantry and the bakery. The pies are extraordinary, from the overstuffed apple to the wild berry. Apple cider doughnuts are made fresh daily from June through January. Fruit squares, crisps, tea breads, and muffins are just some of the tempting items for which Belltown Hill Orchards is so well known.

Dessert Time in The Nutmeg State

Cobbler is a deep-dish pie with a thick crust and a fruit filling. It's sometimes called bird's nest pudding or crow's nest pudding in other parts of New England. Here we have a tart cherry cobbler from Belltown Hill Orchards in South Glastonbury, Connecticut.

And then it's on to a couple of crisps, also from Belltown Hill. A crisp consists of chopped fruit, topped with a streusel crust, then baked. This dessert has also been called a crumble. Culinary historians believe it is the modern version of the pandowdy of yesteryear. The first crisp recipe demonstrates how nectarines and blueberries have appealing flavors and colors that go well together. For the second crisp, fresh cranberries will give you a tart dessert, and dried cranberries will yield sweeter results. It's your choice.

Lastly, we have a true crumble, also from Belltown Hill. Crumble pies are a breeze to make. Instead of topping the pie with a full pastry crust, you combine a few essential ingredients and sprinkle this topping over the pie. Once baked, the crumb topping offers a slight crunch when you bite into the juicy fruit pie.

Tart Cherry Cobbler

FOR THE FILLING:

6 cups tart red cherries, pitted

1¼ cups sugar

¼ cup water

4 teaspoons cornstarch

FOR THE TOPPING:

1 cup flour

¼ cup sugar

2 tablespoons brown sugar

1 teaspoon baking powder

½ teaspoon cinnamon

3 tablespoons butter

1 egg, beaten

3 tablespoons milk

Preheat oven to 400°F.

In a saucepan, combine the filling ingredients and cook until bubbling and thickened, stirring often. Pour into an 8-inch square baking dish.

In a bowl, stir together the flour, sugars, baking powder, and cinnamon. Cut in the butter until crumbly.

In another bowl, mix together the egg and milk. Add to the flour mixture and stir with a fork just until combined. Drop the topping by the tablespoonful onto the filling.

Bake for 25 minutes in the 400°F oven until browned and bubbly.

Makes 4–6 servings.

Nectarine and Blueberry Crisp

⅓ cup firmly packed brown sugar

⅓ cup sifted all-purpose flour

⅓ cup rolled oats

1 teaspoon ground cinnamon

⅓ cup (5⅓ tablespoons) butter, sliced and chilled

⅓ cup chopped pecans

2 pounds (5 or 6) nectarines, pitted, sliced, and cut into chunks

2 cups blueberries

½ cup granulated sugar

Preheat oven to 375°F.

In a large bowl, mix the brown sugar, flour, oats, and cinnamon. Cut in the butter with a pastry cutter or knife until the mixture forms large crumbs. Stir in the pecans.

In a 2-quart baking dish, combine the nectarines, blueberries, and granulated sugar, and spoon the flour mixture evenly over the top of the fruits.

Bake in the middle of the 375°F oven for 40 minutes, or until golden.

Makes 6–8 servings.

Pear Cranberry Crisp

½ cup unbleached all-purpose flour

½ cup light brown sugar, packed

½ cup rolled oats

1 cup fresh or dried cranberries

1 teaspoon ground cinnamon

½ teaspoon ground cloves

¼ teaspoon ground nutmeg

2 pounds Bosc pears, cored, peeled and chopped (about 4 cups)

¼ cup cranberry juice

¼ cup cold butter, chopped into bits

Whipped cream or vanilla ice cream, as needed for serving

Preheat oven to 400°F. Coat a 9-inch square baking dish with cooking spray and set aside.

In a medium bowl, combine the flour, brown sugar, and oats. Mix well. Set aside.

In a small bowl, toss the dried cranberries with the cinnamon, cloves, and nutmeg. Mix well. Add the chopped pears, and mix well. Arrange the fruit mixture on the bottom of the baking dish.

Pour the cranberry juice over the top.

Cut the butter into the flour mixture to make coarse crumbs. Sprinkle the butter and flour mixture over the fruit.

Bake on the middle rack of the 400°F oven for 35–45 minutes, until bubbly and brown. Remove and let cool for 20 minutes. Serve warm in bowls with whipped cream or vanilla ice cream.

Makes 6 servings.

Pear Cranberry Crumble Pie

FOR THE PIE:

1 cup sugar, divided

2 tablespoons cornstarch

1 teaspoon lemon peel

7 cups peeled, cored and sliced pears

3 tablespoons lemon juice

1 cup chopped cranberries

Single 9-inch unbaked pie shell

FOR THE TOPPING:

½ cup flour

½ teaspoon ground ginger

½ teaspoon cinnamon

¼ teaspoon nutmeg

¼ cup butter

FOR THE GARNISH:

6 sprigs fresh mint (optional)

Preheat oven to 375°F. In a bowl, combine ½ cup sugar, cornstarch, and lemon peel.

In a large bowl, sprinkle the sliced pears with lemon juice. Add the sugar mixture and cranberries to the pears, and toss to coat. Fill the pie shell with the mixture.

To make the topping, combine the flour, remaining ½ cup sugar, and all the spices. Cut in the butter until the mixture resembles coarse crumbs. Sprinkle the topping over the pear filling.

Cover the outer edge of the pie with foil to prevent over baking. Bake for 40-50 minutes, or until filling is bubbling and the crust is golden brown.

Garnish with fresh mint if desired.

Makes 6 servings.

Similar Yet Different

Many New England restaurants offer sautéed apples as a side dish, which is pretty hard to pass up especially when they are so much better for you than the usual side dish of home fries. This is how they make warm cinnamon apples at Belltown Hills Orchard in South Glastonbury, Connecticut. This dish should not be confused with Scalloped Apples, the recipe for which follows, provided by the New England Apple Growers Association.

Sautéed Apples

¼ cup butter

4 large tart apples, peeled, cored and sliced ¼-inch thick

2 teaspoons cornstarch

½ cup cold water

½ cup brown sugar

½ teaspoon ground cinnamon

In a large skillet or saucepan, melt the butter over medium heat. Add the sliced apples. Cook, stirring constantly, until the apples are almost tender, 6–7 minutes.

Dissolve the cornstarch in water, and add to the skillet. Stir in the brown sugar and cinnamon. Bring to a boil for 2 minutes, stirring occasionally. Remove from the heat and serve warm.

Makes 4 servings.

Scalloped Apples

6 baking apples, peeled, cored, and quartered

2½ cups water

½ cup sugar

3 tablespoons butter or margarine, cut into tiny cubes

⅓ cup fresh lemon juice

½–1 cup maple syrup

Preheat oven to 350°F. Butter a 9 x 13-inch baking dish.

In a large saucepan, combine the apples, water, and sugar. Bring to a boil, and cook for 1 minute. Place the apples, rounded side up, in the prepared baking dish. Pour one half of the cooking liquid over them. Dot with the butter. Pour the lemon juice and then the maple syrup over all.

Bake in the 350°F oven for 1 hour, or until the apples are tender. Use the remaining cooking liquid to baste, if needed.

Makes 6 servings.

Fruit on the Grill

In the summer, we are avid grillers. We like to grill all sorts of things over charwood, and sometimes we even add some of winter's leftover firewood to the flames. One of our favorite side dishes is carefully grilled summer fruit that goes especially well with grilled chicken. The amounts aren't crucial—simply use whatever summer fruit you have on hand. It's a delicious way to use up peaches, plums, and nectarines that are a little too ripe. Peaches especially are delicious with a brief stay over a medium-hot fire. The grilled nectarine recipe is from Belltown Hill Orchards in South Glastonbury, Connecticut. As summer begins to fade, we turn to apples on the grill. I also offer a colorful fruit kabab. Here are the recipes.

Grilled Peaches and Plums

Peaches

Plums

Lemon or lime juice, as needed

OPTIONAL:

Honey butter

A fruity vinaigrette

Your own mixture of lime juice, lime zest, honey, and mint leaves

Cut the peaches, plums, and nectarines into slices, and remove the pits. If they will be sitting out for a while, pour a little lemon or lime juice on them to prevent discoloration.

Place the cut-up fruit on heavy-duty foil on the grill for 3 minutes, or until they brown. You can also thread the fruit pieces on skewers, if desired. Allow 1 skewer per serving.

Drizzle the fruit with one of the following: honey butter, a fruity vinaigrette, or your own mixture of 2–3 tablespoons of lime juice mixed with lime zest, honey to taste, and mint leaves. Continue to brown the fruit for 1–2 minutes, to allow the sugars to caramelize.

> **WHEN GRILLING PEACHES...**
>
> The skin on a grilled peach half will slip right off after just a few minutes on a hot grill. Just use your fingers to push the skin away from the flesh.

Grilled Nectarines with Blueberries

3 nectarines, quartered and pitted

2 tablespoons sugar

½ pint blueberries

In a medium bowl, toss together the nectarine slices and sugar. Set aside to macerate for 15 minutes.

While the nectarines are macerating, heat the grill to medium. Stack 2 pieces of 10 x 12-inch heavy-duty aluminum foil, and place on the grill.

With a slotted spoon, transfer the nectarines to the foil, reserving any juice in the bowl. Cover the grill and cook the nectarines until charred and softened, turning occasionally, 10–15 minutes.

Return the nectarines to the bowl. Add the blueberries, and toss to combine. Serve as a side dish to any grilled meat. (This can also be served as a dessert, topped with ice cream or whipped cream, if desired.)

Makes 6 servings.

Grilled Apples

½ cup water

¼ cup lemon juice

2 apples, cored and cut into ¼-inch slices

1 teaspoon cinnamon

2 tablespoons brown sugar

Prepare your grill. It's best to grill the apples toward the end of your cooking so they will be grilled over medium heat. (Or preheat your gas grill for medium heat.)

In a large bowl, combine the water and lemon juice. Add the apple slices to the bowl. This will prevent discoloration.

In a small bowl, combine the cinnamon and sugar.

Place the apples directly on the grill rack, and allow them to cook for 5–6 minutes on each side, turning them once.

Place the cooked apples in a large serving dish, and sprinkle with the cinnamon-sugar mixture. Cover the dish with foil to allow the cinnamon and sugar to melt into the apples. Toss gently and serve.

Makes 4 servings.

Curry Cherry Kebabs

2 cups sweet cherries, fresh or frozen

2 cups pineapple chunks

¼ cup red wine vinegar

2 tablespoons olive oil

1 tablespoon honey

½ teaspoon curry powder, more or less to taste

If frozen, thaw the cherries. Thread the cherries alternately with the pineapple on skewers. If using bamboo skewers, pre-soak them in water to prevent burning during cooking.

In a small bowl, combine the vinegar, oil, honey, and curry powder. Mix well.

Grill the kebabs over medium-hot coals. Brush with the vinegar mixture. Or you can broil them. Place the kebabs on a broiler pan. Broil the kebabs 4–6 inches from the heat source.

Cook for 4–5 minutes, turning and basting with additional sauce after each turn.

Makes 6 servings.

Time to Get Stuffed

Stuffing can be traced back to 1538, according to culinary historians. Interestingly, the ever-so-proper Victorians in America found "dressing" to be a more acceptable word in the late 1800s. To this day, the two words are still in our vocabulary. My family always uses the word stuffing while my husband's kin prefer the word dressing—and we all live in New England. No matter what you call it, here are a bunch of stuffing/dressing recipes to whet your appetite. The Apple Stuffing comes from the New England Apple Growers Association. The tart cherry recipe is one of my personal favorites, and my family loves it. The chestnut, leek, and apple combination is the creation of Belltown Hill Orchards in South Glastonbury, Connecticut.

Apple Stuffing

2 apples, chopped

2 tablespoons butter

¼ cup raisins

⅛ teaspoon nutmeg

¼ teaspoon cinnamon

1 teaspoon parsley

¼ teaspoon rosemary

¼ teaspoon thyme

1 cup whole-grain bread, crumbled

2 teaspoons brown sugar

In a small microwave-safe bowl, mix together all but the last two ingredients. Microwave on high for 2 minutes.

Add the crumbled bread and brown sugar. Microwave on high for 1 more minute, or until apples are tender. Allow the stuffing to cool completely before stuffing a turkey or any other kind of meat.

Makes 4 servings.

Tart Cherry Stuffing

2 tablespoons butter

1 cup chopped celery

½ cup chopped onion

1 (7-ounce) package dried, herb-seasoned stuffing cubes

1 teaspoon dried thyme leaves

¼ teaspoon poultry seasoning

½ cup chicken broth

2 cups pitted tart cherries, rinsed and drained (fresh or frozen)

In a 1½-quart microwave-safe casserole dish, microwave the butter on high for 1 minute, or until melted. Add the celery and onions to the melted butter. Mix well. Cover the dish and microwave on high for 3 minutes, stirring once, or until the vegetables are tender.

In a large bowl, combine the cooked celery and onions with the stuffing cubes, thyme, poultry seasoning, and chicken broth. Mix well. Stir in the cherries. Return this mixture to the casserole dish. Cover and microwave on high for 4–5 minutes, stirring once or twice, or until the stuffing is hot. Serve as a side dish with turkey, chicken, or pork chops.

Makes 6–8 servings.

Note: I like to finish this stuffing in a conventional oven, especially at Thanksgiving. When I take the turkey out of the oven to let it rest before carving, I put the Tart Cherry Stuffing into the hot oven without a cover for about 20 minutes, and it comes out perfect every time.

Chestnut, Leek, and Apple Stuffing

6 cups white bread cubes (½ inch), preferably from a pullman loaf with crusts discarded

3 large leeks (white and pale green parts only), cut into 1-inch pieces (about 4 cups)

1 stick unsalted butter

2 celery ribs, sliced ¼-inch thick

1 teaspoon chopped thyme

2 Granny Smith apples, peeled and cut into ½-inch cubes

Salt and pepper, as needed

3 cups (14–16 ounces) bottled peeled roasted chestnuts, halved

1 cup heavy cream

½ cup chopped flat-leaf parsley

Preheat oven to 350°F with racks in the upper and lower third sections of the oven.

Bake the bread cubes on a large sheet pan in the upper third of the oven until dried slightly, about 15 minutes. (Alternatively, leave the bread cubes out to dry at room temperature for 8–24 hours.)

Increase the oven temperature to 450°F.

Meanwhile, wash the leeks. Melt the butter in a 12-inch heavy skillet over medium heat. Cook the leeks and celery, covered, stirring occasionally, until softened, about 10 minutes. Add the thyme, apples, 1 teaspoon salt, and ½ teaspoon pepper. Cover and cook, stirring occasionally, until the apples are just tender, about 5 minutes.

Transfer the apple mixture to a large bowl, and toss with the bread, chestnuts, cream, parsley, ½ teaspoon salt, and ¼ teaspoon pepper. Spread the stuffing in a 2½- to 3-quart shallow baking dish. Bake, uncovered, in lower third of oven until heated through and top is golden, about 30 minutes.

Makes 8 servings.

For The Last Time

Here is the Connecticut version of a famous dessert recipe, from Belltown Hill Orchards in South Glastonbury. Plum torte recipes are amazingly popular because of the torte's old-fashioned taste and its ease of preparation. Back in the 1990s, a food editor at *The New York Times* was so tired of readers requesting that the plum torte recipe be reprinted, she recommended that they cut the recipe out of the paper, laminate it, and stick it on their refrigerator door.

Italian Plum Torte

1 cup all-purpose flour

1 teaspoon baking powder

¼ teaspoon salt

½ cup unsalted butter, at room temperature

¾ cup plus 1½ tablespoons granulated sugar, divided

2 large eggs

8–10 Italian prune plums, halved and pitted

¾ teaspoon ground cinnamon

Freshly whipped cream or vanilla ice cream, as needed

Position a rack in the oven to the center position, and preheat the oven to 350°F. Butter and flour an 8-inch springform pan. Set aside.

In a medium bowl, whisk together the flour, baking powder, and salt.

In another bowl, using an electric mixer, cream together the butter and ¾ cup sugar until light and fluffy. Beat in the eggs one at a time.

Add the dry ingredients, and mix on medium speed for 1 minute, scraping down the sides of the bowl. Pour this batter into the prepared pan. Arrange the plum halves on top. In a small bowl, combine the remaining 1½ tablespoons of sugar and cinnamon, and sprinkle on top of the plums.

Bake in the 350°F oven for 45 minutes, or until a toothpick inserted comes out clean. Cool on a rack for 20 minutes.

Run a sharp knife around the edge of the torte, and remove the springform pan. Serve warm or at room temperature with freshly whipped cream or vanilla ice cream.

Makes 6 servings.

Beardsley's Cider Mill and Orchard

The Beardsley family has been farming in the White Hills of Shelton, Connecticut, since 1849. They may still be in the dairy business had not a school bus crashed into the barn, burning it to the ground, in 1973.

These days the main crop is apples. Peaches, plums, and nectarines are also available as well as local raw honey. Did you know that a bee visits an apple blossom eighteen times before the blossom is pollinated? Once pollinated, the blossom becomes an apple. Think about that the next time you bite into a Ginger Gold (usually the first to ripen) or a Braeburn (among the last to ripen).

Visitors can pick their own apples weekends only in September and October. More than 10,000 dwarf and semi-dwarf trees are in the orchard for easy picking. Some of the trees date back to the 1920s. But it's cider that rules at Beardsley's—this is a cider mill, first and foremost.

They make their cider with ripe apples that have blemishes or are too small for retail sales. Their press is a state-of-the-art system that is kept clean and sanitary. Instead of being pasteurized, Beardsley's cider is treated with ultraviolet light, which reduces pathogens without the cider losing any of its unique flavor. They also make cider in small batches for maximum freshness. It takes about twenty-five apples to make one gallon of cider, according to the folks at Beardsley's.

They also offer untreated cider for making hard (alcoholic) cider. Aficionados can bring in their own containers for filling. According to the experts, the best apples for making hard cider are the late ripeners: Golden Russet, Northern Spy, Winesap, and Yellow Delicious. Just ask Dave or Dan Beardsley for their advice on how to make your own hard cider.

A visit to Beardsley's is not complete without a stop at the Farm Bakery, where a dozen different pies, pumpkin cheesecake, cider doughnuts, and cookies are there for your consideration. The Fruit and Berry Pie contains apple, blackberry, raspberry, rhubarb, and strawberry. Deciding which fruit bread to buy won't be easy, so buy one of each: Apple Caramel, Orange Cranberry Nut, and Pumpkin Bread.

Open daily from August 1 to Christmas Eve, Beardsley's Cider Mill and Orchard is especially known for its country singer strumming the guitar at the checkout.

Apples as a Side Dish

One of the most basic recipes involving apples is for applesauce, which makes a nice accompaniment (especially the chunky variety) to roasted meats. And from that simple, basic recipe there are all kinds of variations, from how to make it in a microwave oven or a slow cooker to how to get creative by adding other fruits to the mix. Beardsley's Cider Mill in Shelton, Connecticut, opts for that last option, adding cranberries to the usual mix.

Next, apples and sweet potatoes seem to be made for one another. Paired in a hot casserole, they make a perfect side dish for all kinds of meat and chicken. This super easy recipe is another keeper from Beardsley's. Last Thanksgiving, I cut this recipe in half, and it turned out just fine. It's followed by another unusual combination of apples with baked potatoes, which can serve as a side dish. That recipe is from Belltown Hill Orchards in South Glastonbury, Connecticut.

No-Headache Apple-Cranberry Sauce

12 ounces fresh cranberries

½ cup water

4 tablespoons sugar

3 Gala or Rome apples, peeled and chopped coarsely

2 pears, peeled and chopped coarsely

4 teaspoons cinnamon

Combine all the ingredients in a saucepan. Cover and simmer over medium heat, stirring occasionally, until the cranberries pop, 25–30 minutes.

Cool to room temperature and then store in the refrigerator.

Makes 2 cups.

Apple-Sweet Potato Bake

6 Rome apples, peeled and thinly sliced

2 medium-size sweet potatoes, peeled, halved, and thinly sliced

1 cup oatmeal

½ cup packed brown sugar

¼ teaspoon each cinnamon, ginger, and nutmeg

½ cup maple syrup

2 tablespoons butter or margarine, melted

Preheat the oven to 350°F.

In a greased 3-quart shallow baking dish, combine the sliced apples and sweet potatoes.

In a bowl, combine the remaining ingredients. Sprinkle over the apple-potato mixture. Cover and bake in the 350°F oven for 40 minutes. Uncover and bake another 15–20 minutes.

Makes 6–8 servings.

Baked Potatoes with Apples

2 pounds potatoes (any variety), scrubbed

2 medium onions, cut into 1-inch wedges

2 tablespoons olive oil

3 Ida Red apples

1¼ cups beef broth

¾ cup apple cider

2 tablespoons cornstarch

¾ teaspoon allspice

Preheat oven to 400°F.

Place the potatoes in a greased 9 x 13-inch baking dish. Break apart the onion wedges and sprinkle over the potatoes. Add the oil and mix well. Bake uncovered in the 400°F oven for 25 minutes, stirring occasionally.

While the potatoes are baking, rinse the apples, core, and cut into ¾-inch wedges.

In a large bowl, whisk together the broth, apple cider, cornstarch, and allspice.

Remove the potatoes from the oven, and mix in the apples and broth mixture. Return the baking dish to the oven for another 25 minutes, or until potatoes are tender and the liquid is bubbly and thick. Baste any uncovered potatoes or apples with the broth throughout the second baking.

Makes 8 servings.

Fall Soups

Here we have two soups from Connecticut orchards, starting with the Carrot and Apple Soup offered by Belltown Hill Orchards in South Glastonbury. The Pumpkin Apple Soup is a creation from Ellsworth Hill Orchard & Berry Farm in Sharon.

Carrot and Apple Soup

2 tablespoons butter

1 large onion, roughly chopped

3 medium Golden Delicious apples

2 pounds carrots

14–15 ounces chicken or vegetable broth

1 tablespoon sugar

1 teaspoon salt

1 teaspoon peeled and grated fresh ginger

2 cups water

Half & half or heavy cream, as desired

Fresh chives, for garnish

In a 5-quart Dutch oven, melt the butter over medium heat. Add the onions, and cook for 12 minutes or until tender and golden, stirring occasionally.

Meanwhile, peel the apples and carrots. Cut each apple in half, and use a melon baller to remove the core. Cut the apples and carrots into 1-inch chunks.

Add the apples and carrots to the onions. Add the broth, sugar, salt, ginger, and water. Bring to a boil over high heat. Reduce the heal to low, cover, and simmer for 20 minutes or until the carrots are very tender. Remove the Dutch oven from the heat.

Using a hand blender, puree the mixture right in the Dutch oven until very smooth. Serve this soup with a swirl of half-and-half or cream, if you like, and garnish with fresh chives.

Makes 4–6 servings.

Pumpkin Apple Soup

1 large onion, diced

3 tablespoons olive oil

1 apple, washed, cored, diced

1 tablespoon curry powder

5 cups stock (vegetable or chicken)

3 cups pumpkin puree

½ cup apple juice concentrate

1 cup evaporated milk or half & half

Paprika, for garnish

In a large skillet, sauté the onions in the olive oil for about 3 minutes. Add the diced apple, and sauté for 2 more minutes. Sprinkle with curry powder, and sauté for 1 minute more. Remove from the heat and set aside.

In a large stockpot, combine half of the onion/apple mixture. Add the stock and pumpkin puree. Bring to a boil, lower the heat, and simmer gently for 10 minutes, stirring occasionally.

In the meantime, put the remaining half of the onion/apple mixture and the apple juice concentrate in a food processor or blender. Process until smooth. Add this mixture to the stockpot. Add the evaporated milk (or half & half), and continue cooking until the soup is piping hot. Do not bring to a boil.

Serve in warm soup bowls garnished with a dash of paprika.

Makes about 6 servings.

Note: At Ellsworth Hill Orchard, they make this soup with their own pumpkin apple stock. See the recipe below.

Pumpkin Apple Stock

Seeds and strings from any size pumpkin

3 crisp apples, quartered

3 cups pumpkin puree (fresh or frozen is recommended)

1 head garlic, unpeeled

1 large onion, quartered

Zest of ½ orange

1½ teaspoons salt

6 cups water

Place all the ingredients in a large stockpot. Bring to a boil. Lower the heat and simmer for 45 minutes.

Allow the stock to cool for about 30 minutes. Strain and discard the solids.

Ellsworth Hill Orchard and Berry Farm

They call their land "Mother Nature's Candy Store" for all of its sweet bounty, from cherries and plums to peaches and pears. Located in Sharon in the northwest hills of Connecticut, Ellsworth Hill Orchard and Berry Farm is a family-owned and -operated farm that has a cider mill on the premises.

A well-organized operation, Ellsworth Hill kicks off the pick-your-own season in June when cherries and strawberries are the first fruit to ripen. In the following months, regular customers return again and again as other berries, plums, peaches, pumpkins, apples, and pears become ready for picking. This is one of those rare orchards that grows figs, available mid-September into October. Around that same time, the apple cider is pressed on site without pasteurization or preservatives, using five or six different varieties of apples for that unique Ellsworth Hill taste. After all the fresh corn is picked, the massive cornfield is turned into an ornate maze for endless wandering. They really try to entertain all their visitors—they even have a vintage Lionel model train display.

Not to be missed is the weekend hayride with "Farmer Mike" as your tour guide. He shows visitors the beautiful hills of western Connecticut while describing all the fruit varieties grown at Ellsworth Hill.

The folks at Ellsworth Hill offer the following apple tips:

- One pound of apples generally consists of four small apples, three medium apples, or two large apples.

- Allow two pounds of apples for one (nine-inch) pie.

- Two medium apples are needed to yield one cup of grated apples.

- One bushel of apples weighs about forty-two pounds and will yield eighteen to twenty quarts of canned apple slices.

- Apples keep best in a cool, dry place (33°F to 44°F).

- When freezing apple cider, take three inches off the top to allow for expansion. When ready to serve, simply put in the refrigerator a few days a head of time to thaw.

Say It Ain't So

The saddest words for fans of Ellsworth Hill Orchard in Sharon, Connecticut, are: "The farm is now closed for the season." Regular customers must wait six months for the farm to reopen, just in time for the strawberry picking season in June. The cherries will start coming in at the end of June, followed by the plums in July, apples in September, and pears in October. These two recipes from Ellsworth Hill celebrate ripe pears and plums.

Fresh Pear Pie

½ cup white sugar

3 tablespoons all-purpose flour

¼ teaspoon salt

1 teaspoon ground cinnamon

1 teaspoon lemon zest

5 cups peeled and sliced pears

Pastry dough for a 9-inch double crust pie

1 tablespoon butter, cut into small pieces

1 tablespoon lemon juice

Preheat oven to 450°F. In a mixing bowl, combine the sugar, flour, salt, cinnamon, and lemon zest.

Arrange the pears in layers in a 9-inch pie pan lined with pastry dough, sprinkling the sugar mixture over each layer. Dot with butter. Sprinkle with lemon juice.

Roll out the remaining pastry dough to cover the pie. Cut slits in the top of the pie for the escape of steam. Moisten the rim of the bottom crust. Place the top crust over the filling. Fold the edges under the bottom crust, pressing to seal. Flute the edges.

Bake in the 450°F oven for 10 minutes. Reduce the oven temperature to 350°F, and bake for an additional 35–40 minutes.

Makes 6 servings.

Plum Pie

FOR THE CRUST:

3 cups all-purpose flour

3/4 cup white sugar

2½ teaspoons baking powder

⅛ teaspoon salt

⅔ cup butter

2 eggs

1 teaspoon vanilla extract

3 tablespoons milk

½ teaspoon lemon zest

FOR THE STREUSEL TOPPING:

½ cup all-purpose flour

¼ cup packed brown sugar

½ teaspoon ground cinnamon

¼ teaspoon salt

⅓ cup chopped hazelnuts

1 teaspoon lemon zest

3 tablespoons butter

FOR THE FRUIT FILLING:

5 cups plums, pitted and sliced

1 cup white sugar

¼ cup all-purpose flour

1 teaspoon ground cinnamon

½ teaspoon ground nutmeg

Preheat oven to 375°F.

FOR THE CRUST:

Combine the flour, white sugar, baking powder, and salt in a large bowl. Mix thoroughly. Cut in the butter with a pastry blender until the pieces are the size of small peas. Stir in the eggs, vanilla extract, milk, and lemon zest. Mix just until all the dough ingredients are combined. Cover the dough with plastic wrap. Allow the dough to rest in the refrigerator.

FOR THE TOPPING:

Combine the flour, brown sugar, cinnamon, salt, chopped nuts, and lemon zest in a medium bowl. Mix well. Work in the butter with your fingers until all the ingredients are well combined. Set aside.

Place the sliced fruit in a large bowl. In a small bowl, mix the remaining sugar, flour, cinnamon, and nutmeg until thoroughly combined. Pour the sugar mixture over the fruit, and stir gently until all the fruit is evenly covered.

Roll out the pie dough, and place in a 9-inch pie pan. Trim and flute the edges, then pour in the fruit filling. Evenly cover the fruit with the streusel topping. Bake in the 375°F oven for 45–55 minutes.

Serve warm or at room temperature.

Makes 6 servings.

Bishop's Orchards

Its full name is Bishop's Orchards, Farm Market & Winery, located near the shore line in Guilford, Connecticut. Established in 1871, Bishop's has seen seven generations of the Bishop family growing up and working on the farm. And there's no end in sight with extensive plans for the future in the works and the family committed to carry on.

The 313 acres include a thriving pick-your-own (PYO) business that begins with strawberries in June, blueberries in July and August, and raspberries from August into October. Peaches and pears can be picked in August and September, while apples—the primary fruit of the orchards—are available for picking through October. The PYO season wraps up in the fall with pumpkins.

Beyond the PYO side of things, Bishop's Orchards is a well-known Connecticut landmark, drawing thousands of consumers to one of the largest farm markets in New England. Open year-round, the market has an excellent bakery and kitchen where you can find traditional and contemporary goodies, from apple cider doughnuts to rustic breads and rolls. Soups, salads, sandwiches, entrees, and side dishes are also available for take-home lunch and dinner. The kitchen staff is always creating new seasonal offerings that utilize the farm's fresh ingredients.

When it comes to beverages, Bishop's Orchards offers pasteurized sweet apple cider, hard cider, and fruit wines. The sweet cider business began in the 1930s. The winery opened in 2005 and has already produced award-winning fruit wines and hard ciders. Seven days a week, visitors can experience tastings at a wine bar that is part of the original 1928 barn. The wines include a mix of dry, semi-dry, semi-sweet, and sparkling varieties. As a designated Connecticut Farm Winery, Bishop's also produces a diverse array of dry to sweet wines, from Chardonnay and Pinot Gris to Merlot and Cabernet Sauvignon. All the wines are well described on the website (www.bishopsorchards.com). That site also has a bevy of wine recipes, including many summer sangrias. Tours of the winery are offered on weekends.

The annual Shoreline Wine Festival at Bishop's Orchards is not to be missed by wine enthusiasts. Held in mid-August in a beautiful orchard setting, the festival celebrates the wines from wineries and vineyards from all over Connecticut, paired with fine food and music.

Blue Jay Orchards

With 140 acres and thirty-seven varieties of apples, Blue Jay Orchards in Bethel, Connecticut, dates back to 1934. Today a farm market and modern-day bakery are on the premises, but if you close your eyes and take in the sweet aromas, you'll think you are back in your grandma's kitchen. People come from miles away especially for the apple cider and cider doughnuts, the two biggest-selling items.

Late summer means there's no shortage of zucchini whether you have a small home garden or a large farm. In some parts of New England, there is an unofficial day in August when home gardeners leave zucchini on the porches of all their neighbors who don't have gardens.

It seems everyone who loves to cook is always looking for new recipes that utilize all that zucchini. Here's one from Blue Jay Orchards. What's different about this easy recipe is that it makes three loaves of Zucchini-Apple Bread—one for you, one for a friend, and one for the freezer. This bread freezes beautifully. But first, Blue Jay Orchards offers one more soup recipe that you can whip up in less than a minute.

Summer Cider Soup

3 cups roughly chopped cucumbers

½ cup chopped shallots

1 cup sour cream

1 cup cider

½ teaspoon salt

Freshly ground pepper, to taste

Toasted croutons, as needed

Place all the ingredients in a blender, and mix at the highest speed for 30 seconds. Serve this cold creamy soup in chilled cups garnished with toasted croutons.

Makes 4 servings.

Note: All the ingredients should be very cold.

Zucchini-Apple Bread

4 cups all-purpose flour

1 tablespoon baking soda

¼ teaspoon baking powder

1½ tablespoons ground cinnamon

½ teaspoon ground nutmeg

5 eggs

2 cups sugar

1 cup firmly packed brown sugar

1½ cups vegetable oil

1 tablespoon vanilla extract

2 cups shredded zucchini (3 medium)

1 cup shredded apple (1 medium)

1½ cups chopped pecans

In a large bowl, combine the first 5 ingredients. Set aside.

In another large bowl, combine the eggs, sugars, oil, and vanilla in a large bowl. With an electric mixer, beat at medium speed until well blended. Stir in the zucchini, apple, and pecans. Add dry ingredients, stirring just until moistened.

Preheat oven to 350°F.

Spoon the batter into 3 greased and floured 8 x 4-inch loaf pans (approximately 3 inches deep). Bake in the 350°F oven for 50–55 minutes, or until a wooden pick inserted into the center comes out clean.

Allow the breads to cool in their pans for 10 minutes. Transfer the pans to a wire rack to cool completely.

Makes 3 loaves.

Drazen Orchards

Like so many New England orchards, Drazen Orchards in Cheshire, Connecticut, has a rich history. In the early 1800s, it began as a farm, orchard, and wood mill. David Drazen purchased the property in 1951. His son Gordon replanted the entire orchard, utilizing a trellis support system that provides maximum sunshine for the growing fruit.

The orchard is now operated by Gordon's children, Eli and Lisa Drazen. They grow apples, nectarines, peaches, pears, and plums, all available in a pick-your-own system that runs from August into October. Most people come for the apples, from the Macoun (nature's candy apple) to the juicy Mutsu. Wagon rides are available on weekends. Picnic tables in a shady area complete the outdoor scene. Make sure you say hello to the farm dog, Honeycrisp.

The Drazen farm stand is open daily in August through November. In addition to their fresh fruit, they carry locally grown vegetables, apple cider from Buell's Orchard in nearby Eastford, cider doughnuts, honey, artisan pies, and much more.

What makes Drazen Orchards unique is that Korean is spoken there, thanks to the on-site farmer Won Hee. An entire section of their website (www.drazenorchards.com) is written in Korean.

Silverman's Farm

The story behind Silverman's Farm in Easton, Connecticut, is another tale of the American dream. Born in 1898, Ben Silverman worked on cow farms for $1 a day. When World War I broke out, Ben worked in a munitions factory and was able to save enough money to buy his first parcel of land on Sport Hill Road in Easton. His first venture was building a cider mill, the only one in the area, and local families would bring their apples to be pressed into sweet and hard cider. Ben lived in one room in the cider mill building until he married Rose Hartz and built a home next to what is now Silverman's Farm Market. Rose baked bread and canned preserves for their roadside stand, and Ben cleared the land for their growing farm.

Ben pressed apple cider for more than sixty years. His old mill was retired in 2004 because of new processing standards. But the cider mill is still on display at the farm market. Ben raised everything—tomatoes, potatoes, onions, cabbage, cauliflower beet, eggplants, berries, and tree fruits such as apples, peaches, and plums. Ben and Rose had eight children. All helped out on the farm, but eventually they pursued other careers—that is all but Irv, their youngest, who graduated from college while working on the farm.

Today Irv is the owner and operator of Silverman's Farm, with much help from the family. Irv and his wife Nancy have three daughters and three grandchildren. It has become an annual tradition that the immediate and extended family comes together to help out at harvest time.

Silverman's started to evolve into a pick-your-own fruit farm back in the 1970s. The family likes to say that they offer a total farm experience to the public. The farm market is

open year-round. In the fall, there are scenic tractor rides even after the fruit-picking season is over. Children especially enjoy a visit to Bunnytown and the chance to pet and feed some of the barnyard animals. The menagerie includes buffalo, llamas, alpacas, sheep, goats, deer, long horn cattle, and exotic birds such as emus.

Silverman's Farm gives away thousands of pumpkins every year. Before making their purchase, customers may guess the weight of the pumpkin they have selected. If the customers can guess the correct weight of their pumpkins within 2 ounces over or under, the pumpkin is free, regardless of its size.

Throughout the fall there are all kinds of old-fashioned events, from nostalgic live music to freshly made kettle corn for munching. And a visit to Silverman's would not be complete without a stop at the farm market, where there are no less than sixteen varieties of pie available along with cookies, baked goods, preserves, jams, jellies, sauces, condiments, syrups, and local honey. A visit to their informative website is a good idea before heading over to Silverman's. The recipe is courtesy of the New England Apple Association.

Grilled Chicken with Crunchy Apple Salsa

FOR THE SALSA:

2 apples, halved, cored, and chopped

1 (6-inch, mild, green) Anaheim chile pepper, seeded and chopped

½ cup chopped onion

¼ cup lime juice

Salt and pepper, to taste

FOR THE MARINADE AND CHICKEN:

¼ cup dry white wine

¼ cup cider or apple juice

1 teaspoon lime zest

½ teaspoon salt

Dash of pepper

4 boneless, skinless chicken breasts

To prepare the salsa: In a bowl, combine the salsa ingredients and mix well. Allow the flavors to blend for 30 minutes. Makes 3 cups.

To prepare the marinade and chicken: In another bowl, combine the marinade ingredients and pour over the chicken breasts. Marinate for 20–30 minutes.

Drain the chicken breasts, and cook on a medium-hot grill, turning once, until the chicken tests done.

Serve the salsa over or alongside the grilled chicken.

Makes 4 servings.

Lyman Orchards

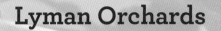

Lyman Orchards is not just another wonderful orchard with home-grown fruits and an amazing market. It's also home to three championship golf courses ranked among the best in the Northeast. No wonder people say Lyman Orchards is Connecticut's sweet spot!

Located in centrally located Middlefield, Lyman Orchards is a well-known destination for people from all over New England and beyond. The entire operation shuts down on Christmas Day for the winter, and loyal customers wait the reopening on the first day of spring in March.

Established in 1741, Lyman Orchards has been growing fruit commercially for more than a century on land overlooking the Connecticut River. Nearly one hundred varieties of fruit are available for picking from June through October, starting with berries and moving on to nectarines, peaches, pears, apples, and pumpkins. Recipes are given out at every pick-your-own station.

If you prefer someone else to do the picking, the Apple Barrel is just for you with its locally grown fruits and vegetables. Aromas from the Farm Kitchen Bakery will have you off your diet in minutes as you shop for freshly baked goodies. More than twenty types of handcrafted pies, including the Hi-Top Apple Pie, will tempt you.

The stately Lyman Homestead and the Golf Club Pavilion are available for special events. Spring, summer, or fall—orchard weddings are simply beautiful.

"No other fruit unites the fine qualities of all fruits as does the apple. For one thing, its skin is so clean when you touch it that instead of staining the hands it perfumes them. Its taste is sweet and it is extremely delightful both to smell and to look at. Thus by charming all the senses at once, it deserves the praise that it receives."

—Plutarch (around 100 A.D.)

Southington Orchards

You can find orchards throughout the state of Connecticut, but if you're looking for apple country, head to Southington where an apple harvest festival to beat all others has been held annually for going on fifty years.

The lively festival takes place around the beautiful Southington Town Green in early October, attracting about 100,000 visitors annually. With its food, family fun, and fireworks, this is a real slice of Americana. There's so much going on, from an apple pie baking contest to a red, white, and blue parade, the festival is now conducted over two consecutive weekends.

Two of the popular orchards in this part of Connecticut are Roger Orchards, established in 1809, and Karabin Farms, started in 1972, with two very different stories to tell.

In 1809, Chauncey Merriman purchased a small farm near Shuttle Meadow Lake and planted some apple trees. His son Anson planted 1,000 more. Anson's son Josiah planted some peaches. And so it has gone for eight generations. Today the farm grows twenty varieties of apples, ten varieties of peaches, as well as apricots, pears, plums, and nectarines under the direction of John Rogers, Chauncey's great, great, great, great grandson. Details on this devoted family effort can be seen on their excellent website (www.rogersorchards.com).

Their farm store is well stocked with seasonal fresh produce and an extensive line of products with the Rogers Orchards label—jams, fruit butters, pickles, relishes, and all kinds of mixes to make your own apple muffins, tarts, and slumps. Apples of many varieties are almost always available in the store, while the pick-your-own season is limited to September and October. The on-site bakery offers ten-inch pies piled high with fresh fruit (apple, peach, cherry, and a dozen other flavors) and topped with golden crusts. According to online reviews, the cider doughnuts here are "to die for."

A much more modern tale can be told over at Karabin Farms, which began as a hobby to instill a sense of responsibility in their children when Michael and Diane Karabin moved to Southington in 1972. It started with the family selling produce at the end of their driveway. Eventually the family planted 2,000 fruit trees and more than 10,000 Christmas trees. The children grew up, went to college, and returned home with various skills that help the business to flourish.

The Karabin country store has everything one would expect plus meat from animals grown humanely on the farm. Home-baked pies are available August through December. Wagon rides are offered to folks wanting to pick their own apples, peaches, and pumpkins.

Southington is known for its many orchards and especially for its apple fritters. This fritter recipe comes from Karabin Farms.

Southington Apple Fritters

6 Cortland apples

2 eggs

2 tablespoons sugar

½ teaspoon salt

2⅔ cups flour

4 teaspoons baking powder

1½ cups milk

¼ cup cinnamon sugar

Crisco, as needed for deep frying

Peel and core the apples. Cut each apple into 8 sections.

In a bowl, combine the eggs, sugar, salt, flour, baking powder, and milk to the consistency of thick pancake batter.

In a deep fryer or cast iron fry pan, heat enough shortening for frying (about 2 inches). Dip the apples into the batter until well coated, and fry to a golden brown.

Fry only a few at a time so that the oil stays hot.

Drain the fritters on paper towels. Drop into a paper bag filled with the cinnamon sugar to coat.

Makes 48 fritters.

Buell's Orchard

Five generations of Henry Buell's family have worked the land since Buell's Orchard was founded in 1889 in Eastford, Connecticut—six generations if you count the new baby born into the family in 2015 although she's a bit too young to work right now.

Henry passed the orchard on to his sons, Herbert and Linus. Linus' daughter Barbara and her husband Orrin Sandness took over the business, which evolved from a small orchard, sawmill, and dairy/turkey farm into a 100-acre orchard with about 12,000 trees. Jeff, Patty, and Jonathan Sandness now run Buell's Orchard with the help of their extended family, harvesting some 30,000 bushels of fruit each year.

The pick-your-own season starts in June with strawberries, the demand for which is so great that the family planted 20,000 new strawberry plants in 2015. In addition to the blueberries, peaches, pears, and plums, Buell's is especially known for its apples and pumpkins. The Macs and Galas are the first apples to ripen, usually around Labor Day. In October, the staff will open up other parts of the orchard as the Cameo, Ida Red, and Empire apples are ready for picking. Free hayrides transport visitors to the orchard and pumpkin patch.

Regular customers at the orchard's store still consider Buell's to be a small business but with a big selection of fruits and vegetables. The little store stocks jams, honey, fudge, caramel apples, cider doughnuts, cheese, freshly baked breads, and pies (baked and ready to bake). Around Thanksgiving they offer ten different pie varieties and a half-dozen nut breads, from apple-caramel to peach. This was the only orchard we found in our travels that sold native cranberries. Hot cider and coffee are available as well as jugs of their famous cold sweet cider. (Buell's cider can also be found at some Rhode Island farm stands—I discovered it at Pippin's Orchard in Cranston.)

Regular customers say the staff is friendly and helpful, and that Buell's is definitely "kid friendly." Their hours of operation fluctuate with the seasons so it's wise to call ahead or check their website (www.buellsorchard.com).

Columbus Day weekend in October means one thing in Eastford—it's time for the Fall Harvest Festival at Buell's with live music, an impressive chicken barbecue, and much more.

A short drive from the capital city of Hartford, but a world away from that gritty city, Buell's Orchard is located in The Quiet Corner of Connecticut, a slogan that was recently updated by tourism officials to the more romantic, The Last Green Valley. The federally recognized valley consists of thirty-five towns in eastern Connecticut and south-central Massachusetts. By day, this area is a noticeably deep green. By night, it is so dark that airline pilots use this patch of darkness as a point of reference. Within one of the most densely populated parts of the United States, it is the last unspoiled area of substantial size on the East Coast, more than 1,000-square-miles of precious field, farmland, and forest.

Vermont

With a population of less than 650,000, Vermont is the second least-populated state following the much larger state of Wyoming. The capital, Montpelier, is the smallest state capital with fewer than 9,000 people. Vermont is considered the most rural state in America because a large percentage of its residents live in communities of less than 2,500. Some interesting facts:

- Vermont is the leading producer of maple syrup in the United States.
- The state fruit is the apple, and the state dessert is apple pie.
- Vermont is the home of the popular Ben & Jerry's ice cream.
- Dairying is the primary farm industry, in the state

With forests covering 75 percent of its total land area, it's no wonder that Vermont is called The Green Mountain State. That nickname comes from the French words "verd mont" for green mountain.

Yet when one thinks of Vermont, snow-white fields and deep red barns come to mind. Every season brings about colorful changes. Springtime is often called the mud season. The early part of summer is mild, and August can be surprisingly hot. Vermont is dazzling in the fall with red, orange, and gold foliage. Winter returns with its pure white beauty. Vermont's winters are often "too cold to snow." That is, the air is too cold to hold sufficient moisture to bring about any kind of precipitation.

Vermont was first settled in the early eighteenth century by both the French and English. A century or so later, it attracted French Canadians from neighboring Canada as well as Irish, Scottish, and Italian immigrants, many of whom worked as stonecutters in the state's famous granite quarries. Vermont granite has been used in innumerable public buildings throughout the nation. Today the largest ancestry groups in the state are French or French Canadian, followed by the English and Irish. Their ethnicity is reflected in the food of Vermont.

Interestingly, nearly half of Vermont's current population was born outside of the state. Those newcomers are drawn to the state because of its perceived high quality of life. This has brought about some tension between the transplants and those with multi-generational roots, so much so that a "woodchuck" is someone well established in the state, and a "flatlander" is one of those newcomers. Slightly sarcastic woodchucks are not the least bit interested in aiding any flatlanders, as demonstrated in this oft-told tale:

Newcomer: "Excuse me, sir. Have you lived here all your life?"

Vermonter: "Not yet!"

Doing the Right Thing in Vermont

Here's just a small list of Vermont orchards and fruit farms that use integrated pest management practices and/or are certified organic. You can find more in Vermont at www.pickyourown.org.

Burtt's Apple Orchard
More than forty varieties of apples, pears, and cherries, and apple cider. 283 Cabot Plains Road, Cabot, VT 05647; 802-917-2614.

Chapin Orchard
Pick-your-own apples, pre-picked apples, pumpkins, fresh cider, and honey. 150 Chapin Road, Essex, VT 05452; 802-879-6210.

Dwight Miller Orchards
Apples, cherries, peaches, plums, pears, apricots, honey, maple syrup, and apple cider. 511 Miller Road, East Dummerston, VT 05346; 802-254-9635.

Eagle Peak Farm
Organic, pick-your-own apples, plums, blueberries. 3748 Eagle Peak Road, West Brookfield, VT 05060; 802-505-0080.

Moore's Orchard
Apples, sour cherries, maple syrup, cider mill, fresh cider, U-pick and already picked. Corner of Johnson Road And Pomfret Road, North Pomfret, VT 05053; 802-457-2994.

Scott Farm Orchards
Apples (70 varieties), peaches, pears, plums, berries, grapes, and pumpkins. 107 Kipling Road, Dummerston, VT 05301; 802-254-6868.

Valley Dream Farm
Certified organic, fruit, pumpkins, strawberries, tomatoes, and flowers. 5901 Pleasant Valley Road, Cambridge, VT 05444; 802-644-6598.

Wellwood Orchards
Apples, peaches, plums, strawberries, blueberries, pumpkins, cider, and honey. 529 Wellwood Orchard Road, Springfield, VT 05156; 802-263-5200.

Windswept Farm
Pick-your-own apples, berries, cherries, pears, and maple syrup. 2417 May Pond Road, Barton, VT 05822; 802-525-8849.

Woodman Hill Orchard
Apples, fresh apple cider made on the premises, U-pick and already picked. 175 Plank Road, Vergennes, VT 05491; 802-989-2310.

Wood's Cider Mill

Wood's Cider Mill in Weathersfield, Vermont, has been making boiled cider since 1882. This old-fashioned elixir helps us experience the magic of autumn long after that season has passed us by. For many people, fall is all too fleeting, as are the fragrant fruits of the season. Boiled cider captures the essence of apples in syrup form.

From Colonial times to the 1920s, wherever there were orchards, there were cider mills. Boiled cider is basically reduced apple cider, and jars of boiled cider could be found in every pantry back then. As a basic sweetener, much like modern-day honey, boiled cider was used in the making of baked beans, pies, and fruitcakes. Boiled cider production peaked in the 1930s. By the 1940s, cider presses were closing and orchards gave way to lucrative land development. Today there are just a couple of cider mills still operating in Vermont. One of them is Wood's Cider Mill.

Willis and Tina Wood bought the mill in 1974 from a distant cousin, and over the years they have witnessed a new trend—a younger generation is interested in small-batch food production and the restoration of food traditions. Boiled cider is making a comeback and was even recognized by the Slow Food organization, winning a spot in their catalog of endangered foods.

Boiled cider is easy to make at home. All you need is a heavy stockpot, a wooden spoon, and lots of time. It's not so easy to find boiled cider, especially outside of Vermont, but you can order it online from the Wood's Cider Mill website (www.woodscidermill.com).

Willis and Tina Wood encourage people to use boiled cider when cooking everything from pancakes to pork chops. It adds a sweetly tart tang to cooked dishes such as Boiled Cider Glazed Turkey and Roast Loin of Pork with Boiled Cider, courtesy of Wood's Cider Mill. This is how I cooked our turkey for last Thanksgiving, and it was definitely the best turkey ever—incredibly moist.

BOILED CIDER

To make boiled cider, all you need is a gallon of apple cider, a large stockpot with a heavy bottom, and a wooden spoon. And time, lots of time.

Look for a preservative-free apple cider with high acidity for that will give you the best balance of flavors when reduced. Pour the cider into the stockpot.

Bring the cider to a boil, stirring occasionally. Reduce the heat to medium-low. Cook uncovered for 4 to 5 hours, or until it has been reduced to one-seventh of its original volume, about 2 cups. Stir frequently, especially in the last half-hour of cooking to avoid scorching. The boiled cider is done when it is as thick as molasses and coats the back of a spoon.

Transfer the boiled cider to a sterilized jar. Allow the jar to cool completely. Seal tightly and refrigerate. It will keep indefinitely.

Makes about 1 jar of boiled cider.

Boiled Cider Glazed Turkey

1 (16-pound) fresh turkey, at room temperature

Salt and freshly ground pepper, to taste

2 apples, cored and sliced into ½-inch rings

12 sage leaves

4 tablespoons unsalted butter, melted

1½ cups boiled cider

10 small shallots, peeled

Soak a clay roaster in water according to the manufacturer's instructions.

Rinse the turkey inside and out with cold water. Pat dry with paper towels. Using your fingers, gently loosen the skin on the breast and legs, being careful not to tear the skin. Season the meat under the skin with salt and pepper. Insert 3 apple rings and 3 sage leaves in between the breast meat and skin. Pat the skin back in place. Place the remaining apple rings and sage in the bird's cavity, and season the cavity with more salt and pepper.

Truss the turkey with kitchen twine. Place the turkey, breast side up, in the clay roaster. Pour the melted butter and boiled cider over the turkey, and season with salt and pepper. Arrange the shallots around the turkey, and cover the roaster with its lid. Place the roaster on a lower rack in a cold oven, and set the heat to 400°F.

Roast, basting every 15–20 minutes, until an instant-read thermometer inserted into the thickest part of the thigh away from the bone, registers 180°F, 3–3¼ hours. A half-hour before the turkey is done, remove the lid and continue roasting. Let the turkey rest for 15–20 minutes before carving. Serve with juices and shallots alongside.

Makes 10–12 servings (with leftover turkey for sandwiches).

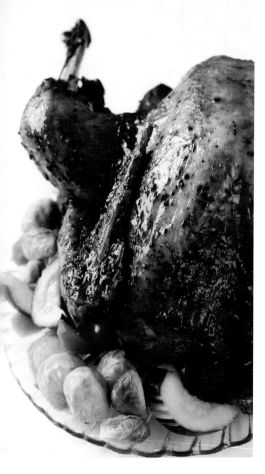

Roast Loin of Pork with Boiled Cider

1 boneless pork loin, about
3 pounds, trimmed

⅔ cup boiled cider

2 teaspoon powdered ginger

½ teaspoon salt

4 tablespoons canola oil

4 garlic cloves, minced

2 teaspoons rosemary, crumbled

2 tablespoons lemon juice

½ cup white wine

Place the pork in a roasting pan. In a small bowl, combine the remaining ingredients, except the wine. Rub the cider mixture over the pork, cover, and marinate for 30 minutes. Pour off and reserve the cider mixture.

Preheat oven to 500°F.

Add the wine to the pan and place in the 500°F oven. Roast for 15 minutes. Reduce the heat to 350°F, and roast for another 30 minutes, basting occasionally with the cider mixture, until a meat thermometer registers 145–150°F. Remove the pan from the oven, and let the pork rest for 10 minutes.

Remove the pork to a cutting board. Place the pan over medium heat. Add ½ cup water and scrape up the caramelized bits, stirring until it reduces slightly. Slice the pork, drizzle with the sauce, and serve immediately.

Makes 6 servings.

An Apple A Day, Or Cider?

Cider was the most popular drink of Colonial America. If you didn't make your own cider, it could be bought by the barrel very cheaply. President John Adams, who lived to be ninety-one, reportedly drank a pitcher of cider every day. Children of that time especially liked cold cider on a hot summer day, and in the fall and winter, cider was used to make all kinds of goodies. Here are three old-time recipes that utilize boiled cider or cider jelly, courtesy of Wood's Cider Mill in Springfield, Vermont. There are several ways to make an authentic cider pie, but we trust the folks at Wood's know how to do it right. Please note that this simple recipe makes two pies.

Boiled Cider Pie

2 cups boiled cider (see recipe on page 167)

4 eggs

1½ cups milk

⅔ cup maple syrup or sugar

6 tablespoons flour

2 prepared piecrust pans

Preheat oven to 350°F.

Put the boiled cider, eggs, milk, maple syrup (or sugar), and flour into a blender, or mix well in a large bowl by hand. Pour the mixture evenly into the two prepared piecrust pans, and bake in the 350°F oven until set, about 50 minutes.

Makes 2 pies or 12 servings.

Thimble Cookies

1½ sticks butter, at room temperature

½ cup sugar

4 egg yolks

1 teaspoon vanilla

2 cups flour

¼ cup cider jelly

Preheat oven to 325°F.

In a large bowl, cream the butter and sugar. Beat in the egg yolks and vanilla. Mix well. Gradually work in the flour. Shape into 1-inch balls.

Place the balls on an ungreased baking sheet. With a floured thimble or your thumb, press a hole into each ball and fill with the cider jelly.

Bake in the 325°F oven for 25 minutes. Remove from the oven and cool on racks.

Makes 48 cookies.

Boiled Cider Cookie Bars

FOR THE CRUST:

½ cup butter

½ cup sugar

1 cup flour

FOR THE FILLING:

2 eggs

½ cup milk

3 tablespoons flour

⅓ cup maple syrup

½ cup boiled cider (see recipe on page 167)

Preheat oven to 400°F. In a large bowl, combine the crust ingredients, mix well, and pat into a greased 8 x 8-inch pan. Bake in the 400°F oven for 10 minutes. Remove the pan from the oven.

Reduce the oven temperature to 350°F.

In another bowl, combine the filling ingredients. Mix well. Pour the filling gently into the prepared crust.

Bake in the 350°F oven for 10 minutes.

Makes 24 cookie bars.

Peaches and Cream

There are more than one hundred online recipes for the classic peach cinnamon tart, and here is one more for you to consider, provided by Wood's Cider Mill in Springfield, Vermont. If rushed for time, you can use a ready-to-use refrigerated piecrust instead of making your pastry crust from scratch.

Peach Cinnamon Tart

FOR THE PASTRY:

1 cup flour

¼ teaspoon salt

¼ cup butter

2-4 tablespoons very cold water

FOR THE FILLING:

4 ounces cream cheese, softened

2 tablespoons sugar

½ teaspoon vanilla

4-5 medium-size peaches, peeled, pitted, and sliced

½ cup boiled cider with cinnamon (see recipe on page 167 and note below)

Preheat oven to 450°F.

To make the pastry, combine the flour and salt in a mixing bowl. Cut in the butter and mix until crumbly. Sprinkle in 1 tablespoon of cold water at a time, mixing well with a fork. Form into a ball.

On a lightly floured surface, roll out the pastry dough into a 12-inch circle. Place carefully into a tart pan. Press the dough ½ inch up on the sides of the pan. Prick the bottom of the crust well with a fork.

Bake in the 450°F oven for 10–12 minutes, or until golden. Cool on a wire rack.

To make the filling, stir together the cream cheese, sugar, and vanilla in a bowl until smooth. Spread this mixture over the prebaked pastry crust, and arrange the peaches in a circle over the cream cheese. Drizzle cinnamon cider syrup over the peaches and chill at least 2 hours.

Makes 8 servings.

Note: To make cinnamon cider syrup, follow the directions on page 167. Simply add a cinnamon stick to the apple cider you are boiling down in the last half hour or so of cooking.

Sweet Success

Sometimes it's the little things that mean a lot—the chutney for roast pork, a jelly glaze for your favorite dessert, a barbecue glaze for that last half hour the chicken is on the grill, or a warm sauce to drizzle over your apple pie. All these recipes come from Wood's Cider Mill in Springfield, Vermont.

Apple Chutney

8 apples, peeled and chopped

1 onion, chopped

2 cups cider vinegar

1 cup raisins

1 cup boiled cider

1 teaspoon ground cloves

1 teaspoon red pepper flakes, optional

1 teaspoon cinnamon

1 teaspoon dry mustard

In a large enameled pan, combine all the ingredients together. Bring to a boil and simmer for 1 hour or until a thick consistency has been reached. Ladle the chutney into hot, pint-size jars. Put into a boiling water bath and process for 5 minutes.

Makes about 4 pints.

Cider Jelly Glaze

4 tablespoons butter

2 tablespoons brown sugar

¼ cup cider jelly

3 tablespoons cream

2 tablespoons orange juice

1 teaspoon orange zest

3 tablespoons brandy, Calvados, or Triple Sec

In a saucepan, melt the butter. Stir in the sugar and jelly. Add the remaining ingredients and bring to a boil. Reduce the heat and cook for 5 minutes. Set aside to cool before spreading over cakes, cheesecakes, or apple tarts.

Makes about ½ cup.

Cider Jelly Barbecue Glaze

8 ounces cider jelly

⅓ cup Dijon mustard

1 or 2 teaspoons horseradish

Splash of soy sauce

In a small saucepan over moderate heat, liquefy the jelly. Add the remaining ingredients and simmer until smooth.

Use this glaze to brush on pork tenderloins, steak, or chicken during the last 10 minutes of cooking on the grill, or use the glaze on lamb, pork, or chicken during the last half hour of roasting.

Makes about 1 cup.

Cinnamon Cider Rum Sauce

½ cup dark rum

1½ tablespoons cornstarch

1¼ cups cinnamon cider syrup

Nutmeg, to taste

Salt, to taste

2 tablespoons butter

In a saucepan, whisk all the ingredients except the butter. Bring to a boil over medium heat. Add the butter. Boil for 2 minutes, and then remove from the heat.

Serve this sauce warm over apple pie, ice cream, or French toast.

Makes about 2 cups.

Apple Cider Doughnuts: Vermont's Secret Ingredient

Apple cider doughnut mania hits New England every September, with orchards claiming their doughnuts are the best but refusing to reveal their recipes. Many assert that their secret ingredient is the apple cider pressed on the premises. The cider adds more than flavor—its acidity makes the doughnuts more tender. And then there are some orchards and cider mills that offer this delicacy year-round, relying on the cider they have in storage.

Most of the orchards I visited deep-fry their doughnuts. A Rube Goldberg-type contraption deposits just the right amount of batter into hot oil and, when the time is right, the floating doughnuts are flipped over so they can cook evenly. At some orchards, the doughnuts fry in oil as they move along on a conveyor belt. The golden brown doughnuts are then lifted out of the cooking oil, allowed to drain, and usually dipped into cinnamon sugar although some of the best cider doughnuts are plain. The key to a good doughnut is the oil temperature. If the oil is too hot, the outside will cook too fast and burn before the inside is done. If the oil is not hot enough, the doughnuts will be greasy.

If you're lucky, these orchard doughnuts are still warm when you purchase them. Fresh from a farm stand, they should have a distinct apple flavor, and their texture is somewhere between that of cake and yeast-style baked goods.

In Vermont, the secret ingredient to their doughnuts is boiled apple cider, which gives these fried treats a rich, slightly tangy flavor. Boiled apple cider, also known as apple cider syrup, is fairly well known in Vermont, New Hampshire, and Maine, but it is unheard of in most of southern New England. If you can't find boiled cider in stores, you can order it online from Wood's Cider Mill in Springfield, Vermont, and from the King Arthur Flour website. Or you can make your own boiled cider. See page 167 for details.

I prefer to bake my apple cider doughnuts, using special non-stick doughnut pans. I've tried every recipe I could find, and I finally developed my own take on this seasonal delight. You can also find apple cider doughnut baking kits in gourmet shops such as Stonewall Kitchens (www.stonewallkitchens.com) in York, Maine.

Baked Apple Cider Doughnuts

2 cups all-purpose flour

1 teaspoon baking powder

1 teaspoon baking soda

¼ teaspoon fine salt

2 eggs

1 cup brown sugar, packed

1 teaspoon apple pie spice

¼ cup oil

½ cup applesauce

½ cup apple cider

4 tablespoons cinnamon sugar

Preheat oven to 350°F. In a large bowl, combine the flour, baking powder, baking soda, and salt. Mix well and set aside.

In a separate bowl, beat the eggs and then add the sugar, apple pie spice, oil, applesauce, and apple cider. Mix well.

Fold the wet ingredients into the dry ingredients.

This recipe makes 12 doughnuts, so you will need two doughnut baking pans, or you can bake them in batches. Spray each pan with baking spray. Fill each doughnut mold half full with batter. Bake in the 350°F oven for 9-10 minutes, or until light brown. Remove the baking pans from the oven and allow to cool.

While still warm, sprinkle the cinnamon sugar on the doughnuts (both sides, if desired).

Makes 12 doughnuts.

Note: You can make your own apple pie spice by combining 4 tablespoons ground cinnamon, 1 tablespoon allspice, 2 teaspoons freshly grated nutmeg, and 1 teaspoon ground ginger. Store unused apple pie spice in a tightly sealed glass jar.

Memories of Vermont

In my thirty-plus years as a food and travel writer, some of my favorite memories are from various trips to Vermont. It seems we always go in winter, when the state is blanketed with unblemished snow.

I remember a romantic weekend at the Governor's Inn in Ludlow near Okemo Mountain. We were given a Victorian suite that just the night before had been occupied by Paul Newman and Joanne Woodward. For our breakfast, we dined on freshly made apple butter smeared on pear bread still warm from the oven.

Another wintry weekend was spent at the beautifully appointed Woodstock Inn in Woodstock, a picturesque village studded with bookstores and art galleries. After an afternoon spent snowshoeing, we dined and shared a perfectly poached pear served with cider sorbet for dessert.

We spent an afternoon touring the Ben & Jerry's Factory and sampling their famous ice cream. Then it was on to Wood's Cider Mill where for the first time I saw cider being made.

Stowe Mountain Lodge provided us more of a resort experience, and I'll never forget the autumn apple salad with asparagus and chèvre (goat cheese) I had there.

But my favorite sensory experience was at a small B&B (the name for which I can't remember). For our breakfast, we were served fluffy pancakes topped with a scoop of cider ice cream. How I wish I had some of that ice cream right now.

I did come home from that trip with the recipe for the Vermont Pear Bread, which I've adapted. Here it is for you to enjoy.

Vermont Pear Bread

9 tablespoons butter, at room temperature

1 cup sugar

2 eggs

2 cups flour

½ teaspoon salt

½ teaspoon baking soda

1 teaspoon baking powder

Pinch of nutmeg

¼ cup buttermilk

1 cup coarsely chopped ripe pears

1 teaspoon vanilla

½ cup chopped walnuts (optional)

Preheat oven to 350°F. Grease a standard loaf pan.

In a large bowl, cream the butter and sugar. Add the eggs one at a time, beating well after each addition.

In another bowl, combine the dry ingredients and mix well. Add to the egg mixture alternately with the buttermilk. Fold in the pears and vanilla. Add the nuts, if desired.

Pour into the prepared loaf pan. Bake in the 350°F oven for 1 hour. Allow to cool slightly before slicing.

Makes 1 loaf (8 servings).

The Roots of the McIntosh Apple Tree

The New England favorite for generations, the McIntosh apple has a special aromatic flavor that makes it perfect for eating and cooking. That flavor is so special that the Mac has been used to develop dozens of other popular varieties. It was discovered as a wild tree in Ontario in 1811. John McIntosh and his wife found the tree as a sapling growing in the woods near their farm. They enjoyed the apples for years. Their son Allen learned how to graft trees, and he propagated the McIntosh tree. The original tree lived until 1910, the year the first McIntosh trees were planted at Shelburne Orchards. More people go to Shelburne looking for Macs than any other variety. During their two-month season (September and October), these apples turn from sour to sweet. Aficionados look for Macs that are sweet and sour at the same time: perfection. Shelburne Orchards holds an annual pie contest, the biggest in the state. Ninety percent of the time it's the pie made with Macs that wins first prize.

Shelburne Orchard

Located on the shores of Lake Champlain in Shelburne, Vermont, Shelburne Orchards is a fascinating place to visit with more than 6,000 apple trees and over thirty varieties of apples, peaches, pears, plums, and sour cherries. Every May the trees go into bloom, and thirty beehives are brought in to pollinate the blossoms.

Shelburne Orchards, as we know it today, was established in the 1950s back when there were only 500 fruit trees on the property. Ninety percent of the apples grown there are sold at the farm rather than on the wholesale market. Many of the apple and pear varieties are heirloom varieties that are grown exclusively to make apple brandy.

Right in the orchard is a distillery where cider is fermented into hard cider, distilled into apple brandy, and aged in used bourbon and port barrels. They also make ginger cider, ginger jack, and cider vinegar. Their farm store is as "country" as country gets with the scent of fresh cider and cider doughnuts in the air.

Flavored with apples, this fall/winter soup recipe is courtesy of Shelburne Orchards.

Roasted Butternut Squash and Apple Soup

4 cups (about 1 of medium size) butternut squash, peeled, cleaned and cubed, or 6 cups frozen squash, cubed

5 garlic cloves, peeled

1 tablespoon minced fresh thyme (or 1 tablespoon dried thyme)

Pinch kosher salt and freshly cracked pepper

Extra virgin olive oil, as needed

2 fall apples such as Braeburn, Gala, or Fuji

1 medium yellow onion, minced

½ tablespoon mild curry powder (or 1 tablespoon if you prefer a spicier soup)

5 cups vegetable or chicken broth

1 cup plain yogurt

1 lemon, zested

Juice of 1 lemon

2 tablespoons shelled pumpkin seeds, for garnish

Preheat oven to 350°F. Spread the cubed butternut squash on a baking sheet with the garlic and sprinkle with some of the thyme, salt, and pepper. Drizzle liberally with extra virgin olive oil. Roast in the 350°F oven for approximately 25 minutes, or until the squash starts to turn golden.

Cut one apple into about 8 chunks; cut the other apple into small pieces, matchsticks, or dice it into small pieces to serve as a garnish just before serving.

Meanwhile, in a large pot heat about 1 tablespoon extra-virgin olive oil, and sauté the onion over medium heat until the onion starts to soften. Add the remaining thyme, curry powder, and apple chunks. Sauté for another few minutes, then add the broth. When squash is done, add it to the pot and simmer for another 10 minutes.

Meanwhile, mix the yogurt with the lemon zest, lemon juice, and a pinch of salt for the soup topping.

Turn off the heat, and puree the soup in a blender a few cups at a time. Remember, when adding hot liquids to a blender, leave the lid slightly off and start with the speed on low. You can also use an immersion blender to puree the soup.

Pour the pureed soup into a large bowl or a different pot. Continue until all the soup is pureed. If it's too thick, add more broth.

Serve with a dollop of the yogurt mix, a sprinkle of the apple, and the shelled pumpkin seeds.

Makes 4 servings.

Note: If you are peeling and cutting a whole butternut squash, stab the entire squash with a fork, and place directly on a rack in the preheated oven for 5 minutes. You can then peel and cut the squash much more easily.

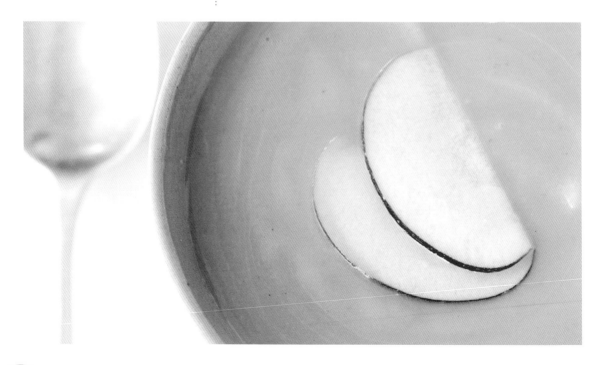

In Perfect Balance

Pork is one of those meats that goes well with just about any fruit. During the summer, you can use peaches or apricots instead of apples in almost any pork dish. Here are a couple of excellent pork recipes from Shelburne Orchards in Shelburne, Vermont.

Pork Tenderloin with Cider Vinegar Reduction

1 pork tenderloin (or 4 boneless pork chops, 1 inch thick)

1 tablespoon butter

1 teaspoon olive oil

2 garlic cloves, chopped

¼ cup cider vinegar

1½ cups apple cider

½ teaspoon high quality mustard

¼ cup maple syrup

Salt and pepper, to taste

Cut the pork tenderloin into 1-inch slices. In a heavy skillet or Dutch oven, cook the meat in a mixture of butter and olive oil until it's done.

Remove the meat from the juices left in the pan. Set aside and keep warm. Add the chopped garlic to the pan, and stir into the drippings over low heat. Add the cider vinegar, apple cider, and mustard. Continue to cook. Reduce this down to a third of its original volume, which takes 15–20 minutes. Let cool.

Finally add the maple syrup and bring to a simmer until it's the consistency of a glaze. Season to taste with salt and pepper. Pour the glaze over the pork tenderloin and serve.

Makes 4 servings.

Pork Tenderloin with Savory Apples

1 pound pork tenderloin

1 tablespoon ground cumin

Salt and pepper, to taste

1 tablespoon extra virgin olive oil

1 large apple, cut into 1-inch slices with skin on

⅓ cup water

2 tablespoons fresh thyme, chopped

Coat the tenderloin with cumin, salt, and pepper.

Heat the extra virgin olive oil in a heavy skillet. When the pan is very hot, add the pork and brown both sides (approximately 2 minutes per side). Remove the pork and add the apples to the pan. Let the apples begin to brown while stirring.

Pour in the water and scrape the bottom of the pan with a wooden spoon. Add the thyme.

Push the apples to the edges of the pan and put the pork back in. Cover with a lid and simmer for 7 minutes. Turn off the heat and let stand for a few minutes. Slice the pork and serve.

Makes 4 servings.

....

Note: You may substitute 1 peach or 2 apricots, when in season, for the apple.

....

Orchards Versus Farms

Do not confuse Shelburne Orchards with Shelburne Farms. Shelburne Orchards is a largely organic apple-growing operation with a distillery on the premises. They make Ginger Jack, a non-alcoholic specialty drink, needed for this luscious lamb recipe. Shelburne Farms is a nonprofit educational organization dedicated to a sustainable future. Both ventures are located in Shelburne, Vermont. If you can't find Ginger Jack where you live, you'll just have to take a ride out to the lovely Shelburne Orchards to make a purchase.

Vermont Lamb Rib Roast with Ginger Jack Glaze

18 baby red potatoes

¼ cup olive oil, divided

2 racks Vermont lamb, frenched*

5 medium shallots, peeled and cut in half

1 medium shallot, chopped

2 rosemary sprigs

Salt and pepper

⅔ cup Shelburne Orchards Ginger Jack

1 tablespoon cornstarch

* If you cannot find frenched lamb racks in your supermarket, you will have to go to a butcher shop and ask the butcher to french the racks for you—that is, unless you are an accomplished chef.

Preheat oven to 400°F. Coat the potatoes with some of the olive oil, and place them in a baking pan. Roast the potatoes in the 400°F oven for 15 minutes.

Remove the roasting pan from the oven. Add to the pan the racks of lamb, 5 of the whole shallots, some of the rosemary sprigs, salt and pepper. Drizzle with more of the olive oil. Roast for 25–30 minutes.

In a medium-size saucepan, sauté the remaining shallot, chopped, and the remaining rosemary in the rest of the olive oil for 3 minutes. Add the Ginger Jack and bring to a boil. Reduce the heat and simmer without a lid for 20 minutes.

In a bowl, combine ¼ cup of the Ginger Jack mixture with the cornstarch. Mix well and add back to the saucepan to thicken the glaze. Cover and set aside.

The lamb is done when the internal temp is 145°F. The racks of lamb should look cooked on the outside, but still be pink in the middle of each rack. Cut the racks into chops, and serve with the roasted potatoes and cooked shallots drizzled with the glaze. Serve immediately.

Makes 6 servings.

Savory and Sweet

Fried onion rings are a popular garnish to the meat dishes served in many American steakhouses. They are generally viewed as a special treat. In reality, they are very easy to make with these basic ingredients—sliced onions, beaten egg, milk, flour mixed with cornmeal, and bread crumbs. This recipe for onion rings from Shelburne Orchards is more specialized with the additional flavors of Ginger Jack and Guinness, the famous Irish beer. If you like exciting new tastes, try Shelburne's fruity ketchup with those onion rings.

Guinness & Ginger Jack Onion Rings

1 cup flour

½ teaspoon salt

2 tablespoons salad oil

1 egg, beaten

⅓ cup Guinness beer

⅓ cup Shelburne Orchards Ginger Jack

1 large Bermuda onion, sliced and separated into rings

Oil, as needed for frying

In a large bowl, make a batter with the flour, salt, oil, egg, beer, and Ginger Jack. Mix well.

Dip the raw onion rings into the batter, and fry them in hot oil until brown. It's recommended you do this in small batches.

Drain the fried onion rings on paper towels. Serve immediately.

Makes 4 servings.

Cherry Ketchup

2 cups pitted cherries

½ cup dried cherries

½ cup cider vinegar

⅓ cup water

2 garlic cloves, crushed

1 tablespoons sugar

¼ teaspoon ginger

⅛ teaspoon ground allspice

⅛ teaspoon cardamom

⅛ teaspoon cinnamon

⅛ teaspoon cayenne pepper (optional)

In a saucepan, combine all the ingredients. Bring to a boil, reduce the heat, and simmer uncovered for about 20 minutes, or until fruit is tender. Let cool slightly and puree in a blender, leaving some chunks (if desired).

Makes about 3 cups.

From Yesteryear

Here are some old-time desserts for you to try in your modern-day kitchen. As old as the hills, the Apple Brown Betty is a layered dessert consisting of apples and buttery crumbs. The origin of this dish is not known. It was first mentioned in a cookbook dating back to 1864. Far more delicious than it sounds, the sour cherry pie recipe is for you if you're tired of apple and berry pies (heaven forbid). Both are from Shelburne Orchards in Shelburne, Vermont, with a definite sense of humor.

Apple Brown Betty

8 Vermont McIntosh apples, peeled, cored, and cut into chunks

¼ cup maple syrup

Cinnamon, nutmeg, and allspice, to taste

1 package graham crackers (there are 3 packages in a box)

1 stick (¼ pound) butter

1 cup brown sugar

Vanilla ice cream, as needed

Preheat oven to 350°F. In a medium casserole dish, combine the apples with the maple syrup and spices. Mix and set aside.

In a large mixing bowl, combine the graham crackers, melted butter, and brown sugar.

Make sure your hands are good and clean. Get right in there with your hands and crumble it all together. It's important to make a sound like a war cry!! Ahhhiiieeee!! It really adds to the taste. You'll know when you're done when people start running into the kitchen, wondering what the heck?

Okay, now pat the crumb mixture over the apples in the casserole dish and slap that baby right in the oven. Cook for 35–40 minutes, or until apples have been perking a while, (bubbling up through) and the crust is golden brown. Best served hot with vanilla ice cream.

Makes 8 servings,

Sour Cherry Pie

⅔ cup sugar, more to taste if desired

4 tablespoons flour

2 teaspoons quick-cooking tapioca

1½ teaspoons lemon juice

2 tablespoons kirsch, if desired

4 cups sour cherries, picked over and pitted

2 (9-inch) prepared piecrusts

1 tablespoon butter, cut into small pieces

Fresh mint leaves (optional)

Preheat oven to 450°F.

In a bowl, combine the sugar, flour, tapioca, lemon juice, and kirsch (if desired).

Sprinkle the sugar mixture over the cherries and stir gently. Pour this filling into a prepared pie pan. Dot with butter. Let stand for 15 minutes.

Cover the pie with a full top crust or a lattice top.

Bake in the 450°F oven for 10 minutes. Then reduce the heat to 350°F and bake until the crust is golden, about 40 minutes in total.

Garnish finished pie with mint leaves if desired.

Makes 6 servings.

Note: For a more jam-like pie, bake at 250°F for an additional 20 minutes.

The Very Surprising Cherry

On one trip to Vermont, I was astonished when the owner of our B&B served us a wonderful egg dish that had a mound of sweet and tart cherries in the center of the plate. It was delicious! I came upon this similar cherry recipe in a microwave owner's manual. I converted the dish to be cooked in a conventional oven. The recipe says it makes 6 servings, but it's so good, I find it's more like a brunch dish for 2 people.

Brunch Pie

2 cups pitted tart cherries, chopped

½ pound bulk pork sausage, crumbled, cooked in advance, and drained

½ cup chopped pecans (optional)

1½ cups shredded Monterey Jack cheese, divided

6 eggs

½ cup milk

1 tablespoon all-purpose flour

Salt and pepper, to taste

Preheat oven to 350°F.

In a saucepan over medium heat, combine the cherries, sausage, and pecans. Mix well, and stir occasionally. Mix in ½ cup of the cheese. Spread this mixture evenly in a lightly greased 9-inch round baking dish.

In a bowl, combine the eggs, milk, flour, salt and pepper. Whisk until well mixed. Pour the egg mixture over the sausage mixture in the baking pan. Top with the remaining cheese.

Bake in the 350°F oven for 30 minutes, or until the eggs are set in the middle. Serve immediately or at room temperature if set on a buffet table.

Makes 4 servings.

Champlain Orchards

Champlain Orchards is located in the heart of Vermont's apple country in the small town of Shoreham. Overlooking Lake Champlain, the orchards consist of more than 220 acres of fruit trees, and that includes over seventy varieties of apples as well as plums, peaches, nectarines, European and Asian Pears, raspberries, cherries, and blueberries. In spring, summer, and fall, a fun way to reach the orchards is to cross the lake via the Ticonderoga Ferry.

The thriving business is owned by Bill Suhr and Andrea Scott, a husband-and-wife team dedicated to sustainability. Bill bought the initial acreage in 1998, a daring move for someone who had never farmed before. But his motivation prevailed, and—with the help of the community and an itinerant picking crew from Jamaica—his orchards produced 20,000 bushels of apples in 1999. Bill delivered those apples, twenty bushels at a time, in his station wagon. Bill's knowledge of farming and his reputation for delivering high-quality fruit grew. Today the orchard harvests 80,000 bushels of ecologically grown apples, and it employs more than thirty locals year-round as well as thirty pickers in season. The Champlain apples are delivered to schools, supermarkets, co-ops, colleges, hospitals, and restaurants.

More than they ever imagined, Bill and Andrea have attained their dream of providing nourishing food to the community—truly the fruits of their labor. Here are the orchard's recipes for delicious muffins and waffles. The waffles get their start on the night before you plan to serve them for breakfast. Quick-cooking oats make for a tender waffle, while old-fashioned oats will result in a more substantial, chewy waffle. Try them both ways to see which version you prefer.

Apple Butter Muffins

½ cup butter

1 cup brown sugar

1 egg

¾ cup buttermilk

2 teaspoons baking soda

2 cups flour

1 teaspoon cinnamon

1 teaspoon nutmeg

1 teaspoon allspice

½ teaspoon ground cloves

1 cup apple butter

½ cup pecans, walnuts, or almonds

Preheat oven to 350°F. In a bowl, cream the butter and sugar until light and fluffy. Beat in the egg.

In a separate bowl, combine the buttermilk and baking soda. Add the flour and spices, combining the flour and buttermilk alternately, beginning and ending with the flour. Stir in the apple butter and nuts.

Prepare a muffin tin with paper liners or grease and flour. Pour an equal amount of batter into each part of the muffin tin. Bake in the 350°F oven for 30 minutes. Make a visual check and test with a wooden toothpick. Continue cooking if necessary until done.

Makes 12 muffins.

Oatmeal Waffles with Apple Butter

2 cups buttermilk

¼ cup orange juice

1 small apple peeled, cored, shredded

⅔ cup quick-cooking rolled oats

½ cup all-purpose flour

½ cup whole wheat flour

1½ teaspoons baking soda

½ teaspoon salt

1 egg

2 tablespoons packed light brown sugar

2 tablespoons melted butter, plus more for cooking

Apple butter (see recipe on page 196), as needed

Whipped cream, as needed, if desired

In a bowl, combine the buttermilk, orange juice, shredded apple, and oats. Mix well, cover, and refrigerate overnight.

In another bowl, combine the flours, baking soda, and salt. Cover and set aside.

When you are ready to prepare the waffles, beat the egg and sugar in a large bowl. Mix in the flour mixture and soaked oats. Stir in the melted butter. The batter should be a bit lumpy.

Prepare your waffle iron. Butter the interior of the iron. Pour ½ cup of batter onto the hot iron, close, and cook until no more steam escapes from the iron, and the waffle is golden on both sides, 5 minutes. Serve immediately with apple butter and whipped cream, if desired.

Makes 8 waffles.

Note: For a variation, serve these waffles with maple syrup or with the Pear Sauce (recipe on page 196). I often use up over-ripe bananas at breakfast by slicing and sautéing them in butter to pour over plain-Jane waffles. You can also do that with pears. The most commonly grown pears in New England are the Bartlett, Bosc, and Asian varieties. There is no shortage of orchards in New England where you can pick your own pears.

Pear Sauce For Waffles

3–4 cups fresh pears, peeled

¾ cup pear or apple juice

¼ cup butter

½ teaspoon each ground cinnamon and grated lemon peel

¼ cup raisins

1 teaspoon cornstarch

1 teaspoon water

Cut the pears into chunks and set aside in a bowl. Combine the juice, butter, cinnamon, and lemon peel in a saucepan. Bring to a boil. Add the pears and raisins. Reduce heat and simmer for 10 minutes.

In a small bowl, combine the cornstarch and water. Stir into pear mixture and cook for 1 minute or until thickened. Serve sauce over waffles.

Makes about 2 cups or 4 servings.

Make Your Own Apple Butter

To make your own apple butter, try this recipe from Wood's Cider Mill in Springfield, Vermont, or make it in your slow cooker. If you're too busy, I recommend purchasing apple butter from your favorite orchard.

Quick Apple Butter

2 cups applesauce, unsweetened
½ cup boiled cider
¼ teaspoon ground allspice
Pinch each of ginger and cloves

Combine all the ingredients in a small saucepan. Bring to a boil and simmer 30 minutes. Makes about 1 cup.

Breakfast Treat

For a slightly healthier take on the classic apple muffin, the folks at Champlain Orchard in Shoreham, Vermont, offer this spicy rendition that's made with yogurt. The recipe starts with an easy-to-make streusel, which can be used on other baked goods.

Streusel Spiced Cider Muffins

FOR THE STREUSEL:

1 tablespoon butter

2 tablespoons brown sugar

4 teaspoons whole wheat flour

½ teaspoon cinnamon

1 tablespoon walnuts, finely chopped

FOR THE MUFFINS:

1 cup whole wheat flour

1 cup all-purpose flour

1½ teaspoons baking powder

½ teaspoon baking soda

¼ teaspoon salt

1 tablespoon cinnamon

½ teaspoon nutmeg

1 large egg

½ cup packed brown sugar

½ cup apple butter or applesauce

⅓ cup maple syrup or honey

⅓ cup apple cider or apple juice

⅓ cup plain yogurt, low fat

¼ cup canola oil

Preheat oven to 400°F.

To make the streusel, in a bowl cut the butter into the sugar, flour, and cinnamon until it resembles coarse crumbs. Stir in the walnuts. Set aside.

In another bowl, mix together the flours, baking powder, baking soda, salt, cinnamon, and nutmeg.

In a separate large bowl, whisk together the egg and brown sugar until the sugar is dissolved. Whisk in the apple butter, maple syrup, cider, yogurt, and oil. Add the dry ingredients to the wet ingredients, using a rubber spatula, just until moistened.

Prepare a muffin tin by spraying the tin with cooking spray or using paper liner cups. Spoon an equal amount of batter into each muffin cup. The cups should be quite full.

Sprinkle with streusel. Bake in the 400°F oven for 15-25 minutes, or until the tops are golden brown and spring back when touched lightly. Allow the muffins to cool for 5 minutes before loosening the edges to remove each muffin from the tin.

Makes 12 muffins.

Breakfast or Dinner?

Pancakes are always a special treat, whether someone makes them at home or they're ordered by the stack at a diner. They are usually considered to be a breakfast item, although I know people who like to have pancakes as their Sunday supper. Champlain Orchards in Shoreham, Vermont, has an excellent selection of recipes on their website (www.champlainorchards.com), including this one for pancakes that are baked in the oven.

Baked Apple or Pear Pancakes

3 eggs

¾ cup milk

¾ cup flour

¼ teaspoon salt

1 teaspoon almond or vanilla extract

2 ripe pears or 2 tart apples, peeled, cored, thinly sliced

2 tablespoons sugar

¾ teaspoon cinnamon

2 tablespoons butter

Confectioners' sugar or maple syrup, as needed

Warm an iron skillet in a 450°F oven.

In a bowl or a blender, whisk together the eggs, milk, flour, salt, and extract until smooth. In a separate bowl, toss together the fruit, sugar, and cinnamon.

Remove the skillet from the oven. Melt the butter in the hot skillet. Arrange the apples or pears, or a combination of the two, in a single layer on the bottom of the skillet. Carefully pour the batter over the fruit.

Bake in the 450°F oven for 25 minutes, or until puffed and golden. Sprinkle with confectioners' sugar, or drizzle with maple syrup before serving.

Makes 1 large pancake, enough for 2 servings.

Note: While this is more like a tart than a pancake, you can use twice as many apples and pack them more solidly in the bottom of the hot skillet. Any leftover apples can be warmed and served alongside the pancake.

Open or Closed

It seems only right that a sandwich from Champlain Orchards in Shoreham, Vermont, would include cheddar cheese because Vermont is so well known for its dairy products. This tasty lunch offering calls for an extra-sharp white cheddar, and it can be served as a regular sandwich or open faced.

Cheddar, Apple Butter, and Ham Open-Faced Sandwiches

6 slices country bread, or
6 ciabatta rolls, cut in half
horizontally

2 tablespoons olive oil

6 tablespoons apple butter
(see recipe on page 196)

4 tablespoons Dijon mustard

1½ pounds Black Forest ham,
thinly sliced (or smoked turkey)

12 ounces extra-sharp white
cheddar cheese, sliced

Fresh chives, chopped, for
garnish

Brush one side of the country bread or the cut sides of the rolls with the oil. Broil until the bread begins to brown around the edges, about 2 minutes.

In a bowl, combine the apple butter and mustard. Spread this mixture on each slice of bread or roll. Mound the ham loosely on top, and then some cheese. Broil until the cheese melts and begins to brown in spots, about 2 minutes. Sprinkle with the chopped chives and serve.

Makes 6 servings.

Heartwarming Soups

The next two recipes are guaranteed to make you feel warm and cozy. The Curried Apple Soup and the Curried Butternut and Apple Soup are variations on a theme from Champlain Orchard in Shoreham, Vermont. Both are made with apples, but they are quite different from one another.

Curried Apple Soup

2 medium onions, peeled and chopped

4 tablespoons butter

1 teaspoon freshly grated ginger

1 teaspoon dry mustard

1 teaspoon turmeric

1 teaspoon ground cumin

1 teaspoon ground coriander

¼ teaspoon cloves

¼ teaspoon cinnamon

¼ teaspoon cayenne

6 tart apples, chopped

1½ quarts chicken stock

Juice of 1 lemon

Sea salt and pepper, to taste

Sour cream, as needed

Option: Reserve 1 cup of apple pieces to add later to the soup as a garnish.

In a large skillet, sauté the onions in the butter. Add the ginger, dry mustard, turmeric, cumin, coriander, cloves, cinnamon, and cayenne. Cook briefly to toast the seasonings. Add the apples and chicken stock. Simmer until the apples are soft.

Place the soup in a blender or food processor, in batches if necessary. Puree until smooth. Add the lemon juice and season to taste. Garnish each serving with a dollop of sour cream.

Makes 6 servings.

Curried Butternut Squash and Apple Soup

6 pounds butternut squash

Oil, as needed

2 teaspoons salt

Pepper, to taste

3 cups diced onions

3 garlic cloves

4 teaspoons curry powder

3 teaspoons coriander

6 medium apples, cored and diced

4½ cups water

3 (or more) cups apple cider

Milk or cream, optional

Sour cream, yogurt, or crème fraiche, as needed

Fresh basil, for garnish

....

Note: This soup freezes very nicely.

....

Preheat oven to 350°F.

Cut the squash in half lengthwise, and remove the seeds. Brush the squash with oil, and season with salt and pepper. Roast the squash cut side down in the 350°F oven for 45 minutes, or until the squash is soft.

In a stockpot, sauté the onions in oil until golden. Add the garlic, curry powder, and coriander, stirring to toast the spices. Add the apples, water, and cider. Bring to a boil and then simmer until the apples are soft.

When the roasted squash is cool enough to handle, remove and discard the skin. Add the squash to the soup. Stir to mix well.

Using a blender, in batches if necessary, puree the soup until smooth. Add more cider or milk or cream to thin the soup to a desired consistency. Garnish each serving with a dollop of sour cream, yogurt, or crème fraiche, and a sprig of basil.

Makes 12 servings.

Best Ribs Ever

Here is one more pork dish, and this just may be the best of the bunch, from Champlain Orchard in Shoreham, Vermont. It has become a personal favorite of mine, and it's easily adaptable for cooking in your indoor oven instead of on the grill. The recipe calls for many of the products that Champlain produces. The superb basting sauce can be used on chicken as well as pork ribs.

Bourbon Apple Butter Ribs

FOR THE BASTING SAUCE:

½ cup brown sugar

¾ cup apple butter

¼ cup bourbon

¼ cup apple cider vinegar

3 tablespoons apple cider

2 tablespoons Dijon mustard

FOR THE RIBS:

1 tablespoon coarse kosher salt

1 tablespoon brown sugar

1½ teaspoons dry mustard

1½ teaspoons thyme

1 teaspoon ginger

½ teaspoon cinnamon

½ teaspoon cayenne

2 (2-pound) racks baby back pork ribs

1 large onion, diced

1 cinnamon stick, broken in half

6 thin rounds peeled fresh ginger

1½ cups apple cider

In a bowl, whisk all the basting sauce ingredients to blend. Set aside.

Mix the next 7 seasoning ingredients in a small bowl. Set aside.

Using a small sharp knife, loosen the membrane from the underside of each rib rack and remove. Or you can score the membrane with a very sharp knife. Rub 1 tablespoon of the seasoning mix into each side of each rib rack. Place the ribs in a large roasting pan. Cover and refrigerate for at least 6 hours or up to 1 day.

Preheat oven to 325°F.

Lift the ribs out of the pan. Scatter the onion, cinnamon stick, and fresh ginger in the pan. Pour in the cider. Return the ribs to the pan, meat side down. Cover the pan with foil.

Place the pan in the 325°F oven, and roast until the meat is tender and begins to pull away from the bones, about 2 hours. Uncover and cool for at least 30 minutes or up to 2 hours.

Prepare a barbecue grill. Over medium-high heat, grill the rib racks until they are heated through and lightly charred, about 5 minute per side. Brush generously on all sides with the basting sauce. Grill the ribs until the sauce becomes a sticky glaze, about 3 more minutes per side.

Transfer the rib racks to a cutting board. Cut the racks between the bones into individual ribs. Arrange the ribs on a platter and serve with the remaining sauce on the side.

Makes 4 servings.

Ginger, Ground and Fresh

From Champlain Orchards in Shoreham, Vermont, come these two dessert recipes—one for a low-fat gingerbread and one for bread pudding, both flavored with applesauce. What's interesting is that the gingerbread is made with both ground ginger and fresh ginger root, available in most supermarkets. These recipes offer good ways to use leftover applesauce.

Low-Fat Applesauce Gingerbread

1½ cups unbleached flour

1 cup whole wheat flour

⅔ cup sugar

2½ teaspoons baking soda

1 teaspoon ground ginger

1 teaspoon cinnamon

1 teaspoon ground allspice

1½ cups unsweetened applesauce

1 cup molasses

3 egg whites

1 teaspoon fresh ginger root, peeled and diced small

Preheat oven to 325°F. Coat a 9 x 13-inch baking pan with non-stick cooking spray.

In a large bowl, combine the flours, sugar, baking soda, and spices. Mix well. Whisk in the applesauce, molasses, egg whites, and fresh ginger root. Spread the batter evenly in the prepared baking pan.

Bake in the 325°F oven for 40 minutes, or until the cake tests done with a toothpick inserted into the center of the cake. Allow to cool for at least 20 minutes.

Cut into 16 squares. Serve warm or at room temperature with applesauce, vanilla yogurt, or crème fraiche.

Makes 16 servings.

Applesauce Bread Pudding

3 cups dry bread cubes (about 4 slices)

1½ cups applesauce

¼ teaspoon cinnamon

Dash of nutmeg

2 tablespoons butter, cut into small pieces

2 eggs, beaten

2 cups milk

½ cup sugar

1 teaspoon vanilla

Dash of salt

Cinnamon, to taste

Preheat oven to 350°F. Butter an 8 x 8 x 2-inch baking pan, and layer in half of the bread cubes.

In a bowl, combine the applesauce, cinnamon, and nutmeg. Spread the mixture over the bread cubes. Layer the remaining bread cubes on top. Dot with butter.

In another bowl, combine the eggs, milk, sugar, vanilla, and salt. Pour the mixture over the bread cubes. Lightly sprinkle cinnamon over the top.

Bake in the 350°F oven for about 1 hour, or until a knife inserted into the bread pudding comes out clean.

Makes 6 servings.

Cold Hollow Cider Mill

"Vermont to the core"—that's the clever motto at Cold Hollow Cider Mill in Waterbury Center, Vermont. There is much to take in here, far beyond the apples and cider made on the premises. If you're too busy to make your own cider syrup, you can pick up a bottle or two. I personally like their honey and cider vinegar. I defy anyone to walk out of their bakery without purchasing some cider doughnuts, or a Cold Hollow dog treat if you are a dog lover. This being Vermont, there's aged Vermont cheddar cheeses including a wonderful Grafton Village Sage Cheddar. All kinds of goodies are available in the store's pantry—cider barbecue sauce, cider curry mustard, pumpkin butter, and so much more. You can even watch live bees (behind glass) make honey in the mill's Honey Corner. Those are the bees that pollinate the orchards every spring when the blossoms are on the trees.

Cold Hollow Cider Mill uses the rack and cloth method to make their cider on the premises. The 1920-vintage press is in action year-round, even daily from mid-September into December. The large sample tank provides visitors with a taste of the cider while they watch the process. This is how cider was made hundreds of years ago. (See page 288 for how cider is made elsewhere in New England.)

A popular tourist destination, Cold Hollow Cider Mill is one of those rare stops that also offers a bite to eat. Open seven days a week, the Apple Core Luncheonette and Brew offers lunch options made with local products and organic greens. Adults may have hard cider or a local brew on draft to go with their meal.

The history behind Cold Hollow Cider Mill begins in 1974 when Eric and Francine Chittenden, descendants of Vermont's first governor, started making apple cider for friends. It wasn't long before they realized the business potential in making cider the old-fashioned way. In 1976, they purchased the old Gibbs Farm in Waterbury Center. A classic Vermont dairy farm, dating back to the 1800s, that house and barn combination was the start of Cold Hollow Cider Mill, which over the years has evolved into a prosperous business, and not to be missed if you are in Vermont. Here are two of their wonderful recipes. For the appetizer, all you need is some good crackers. For the dessert, all you need is leftover apple cider doughnuts.

Note: The only trouble with the bread pudding recipe is that it calls for fourteen leftover apple cider doughnuts. In our house there are never, ever any leftover apple cider doughnuts! And Cold Hollow's apple cider doughnuts were declared one of the country's four best dough-nuts by *Gourmet* magazine. So if you can find the strength to set aside fourteen apple cider doughnuts, you are in for a real treat.

Caramelized Onion and Cider Jelly Spread

3 pounds Vidalia onions, thinly sliced

3 tablespoons canola oil

1 tablespoon salt

1 cup brown sugar, divided

1 cup cider jelly

½ teaspoon red chili flakes

3 tablespoons balsamic vinegar

In a large frying pan, caramelize the onions in the oil. Once the onions begin to brown, add the salt and ½ cup brown sugar. Continue to caramelize the onions.

Add the cider jelly, red chili flakes, balsamic vinegar, and remaining ½ cup brown sugar. Cook the onion mixture an additional 5–10 minutes. Serve warm.

Makes about 2 cups.

Apple Cider Doughnut Bread Pudding

14 apple cider doughnuts, broken into pieces and dried overnight

4 large eggs, lightly beaten

2 tablespoons unsalted butter, melted

½ cup white sugar

¼ cup dark brown sugar

3 cups whole milk

1 cup apple cider

1 teaspoon vanilla extract

1 teaspoon cinnamon

¼ teaspoon nutmeg, freshly grated

1 large McIntosh apple, cored, peeled, and chopped

Preheat oven to 350°F. Grease a 9 x 13 x 2-inch loaf pan.

Place the doughnut pieces into a large mixing bowl. In a separate bowl, combine the eggs, butter, sugars, milk, cider, vanilla, cinnamon, and nutmeg. Pour the egg mixture over the doughnuts and let soak for 15 minutes. Add the chopped apple to the doughnut mixture.

Pour the entire mixture into the baking pan, and bake in the 350°F oven for 1 hour.

Makes 12 servings.

Fond of Fondue

Fondue became popular in the United States in the 1970s, and every few years it makes a comeback as a savory appetizer or sweet dessert. Long forks or skewers are needed for dipping into the hot fondue pot. The original cheese fondue was created out of necessity by residents of the Swiss Alps. They lived in isolated mountain villages and had to rely on locally made food. There was always plenty of Swiss cheese on hand as well as day-old bread, which is perfect for dipping into the hot cheesy mixture. I have two fondue pots in my cupboard. Two pots are perfect for entertaining. One pot can hold a savory cheese fondue, and the other can hold melted chocolate for a dessert of dipped fresh fruit, especially strawberries. Here we have a New England fondue, which uses apple cider instead of the usual wine, to help melt the cheese.

Cider and Cheese Fondue

¾ cup apple cider

2 cups shredded cheddar cheese

1 cup shredded Swiss cheese

1 tablespoon cornstarch

⅛ teaspoon pepper

In a large saucepan, bring the cider to a boil. Reduce heat to medium low.

In a large bowl, toss the shredded cheeses with the cornstarch and pepper. Slowly stir a quarter of the cheese mixture into the cider, using a wooden spoon. Stir constantly until the cheese is incorporated and creamy. Continue slowly adding the cheese, and stirring until all the cheese is melted.

Transfer cheese-cider mixture to a fondue pot (or a slow cooker will do if need be). Serve with cubes of crusty bread.

Makes 6 servings.

Green Mountain Orchards

The Darrow family at Green Mountain Orchards has been growing apples for more than a century—that's four generations of kinfolk. One of Vermont's largest apple orchards, it is located in the hills overlooking the charming village of Putney.

This orchard operation prospered for its first seventy-five years, but in the 1990s the apple market collapsed. Many New England orchards went out of business. The Darrows cut their acreage by nearly half and managed to survive with efficient management and

diversification. Today they have 125 acres of apple trees and nearly eighteen acres of blueberries, mostly for the wholesale market. They also grow peaches, pears, plums, pumpkins, raspberries, sweet corn, and Christmas trees. Their pick-your-own and retail business is thriving, thanks in part to the bakery that's known for its delicious pies, muffins, sticky buns, and cider doughnuts. In the fall, those cider doughnuts are warm no matter what time you stop by.

Green Mountain Orchards is also known for its fresh cider, pressed on the premises. Visitors can press their own cider, if desired, starting in September when the apples start to sweeten. Wonderful tours of the property are available as well as horse-drawn wagon and sleigh rides by appointment.

This orchard closes for the winter, reopening in July for blueberry season. But the Darrows welcome people to visit any time of the year to hike and picnic. Some folks even snowshoe through the rolling hills when snow blankets this part of New England.

Upside-down cakes are just plain fun to make, and the results are impressive. With the flip of a wrist, the luscious fresh fruit on the bottom becomes the topping. Provided by Green Mountain Orchards, this plum gingerbread version has a lot going for it. Pears or apples may be used in place of the plums. If your choice is apples, it is recommended to use Honeycrisp, Jonagold, or Golden Delicious.

Upside Down Plum Gingerbread Cake

FOR THE TOPPING:

2 pounds plums

½ stick butter

¾ cup packed light brown sugar

FOR THE CAKE:

2½ cups all-purpose flour

1½ teaspoons baking soda

1 teaspoon ground cinnamon

1 teaspoon ground ginger

½ teaspoon ground cloves

¼ teaspoon salt

1 cup mild molasses

1 cup boiling water

1 stick butter, softened

½ cup light brown sugar

1 large egg, lightly beaten

To make the topping, cut the plums in half, and remove the pits. In an oven-proof nonstick skillet over medium heat, melt the butter. Reduce the heat to low. Melt the sugar in the butter, which should take about 3 minutes. Arrange the plums skin side down in the skillet, and cook for 2–3 minutes. Remove the skillet from the heat.

To make the cake, preheat oven to 350°F.

In a large bowl, whisk together the dry ingredients. In a separate bowl, whisk together the molasses and boiling water. In a third bowl, beat the butter, sugar, and egg. Combine all the ingredients in the large bowl. Mix until smooth.

Pour the cake batter into the skillet, spreading it evenly without disturbing the plums. Bake in the 350°F oven for 40–50 minutes, or until a toothpick inserted into the cake comes out clean. (If needed, double wrap the skillet's handle in foil.)

Allow the cake to cool for 5 minutes. Run a knife around the outer edge of the cake, then, turn the skillet upside down onto a large serving plate.

Makes 6 servings.

Flan Or Fruit Squares?

Is there anything more quintessentially New England than maple syrup in the spring and apples in the fall? After a snowy winter, many New Englanders are happy to see the sap running, sap that will be transformed almost magically into maple syrup, a definite sign of spring. Apples too are waking up from their winter nap. The last of fall's crop has been in storage in a controlled atmosphere. These still have the crispness and unique flavor of a freshly picked apple. Those two key ingredients are combined in the following recipe for Vermont Apple Flan.

According to the U.S. Department of Agriculture, Vermont continues to be the number one producer of maple syrup in the nation, outdoing New York in second place and Maine in third place. Vermont averages 1.2 million gallons of maple syrup a year.

I've had this curious recipe in my files since the 1990s, and I've adapted it slightly. It comes from the Northeast McIntosh Growers Association. I say "curious" because it's made with pie dough, making it more like a pie or a baked fruit square than any flan I've ever had. For me, a flan is a custard-like dessert. But I may be wrong. I've seen other flan recipes online that are similar to this—one was for a Vermont Cheddar Flan. Let's see if you agree with my thinking on all this.

Vermont Apple Flan

1 package piecrust mix

4 McIntosh or Cortland apples

2 cups maple syrup

1 tablespoon butter

Whipped cream or ice cream (optional)

Preheat oven to 425°F.

Prepare the piecrust mix according to directions on the package. Roll out the pie dough to ⅛-inch thickness. Line and 9 x 9-inch baking pan with the pie dough. If desired, make a rolled "rope" edge around the top of the pan with the pie dough.

Peel and core the apples. Cut the apples into thick slices.

In a saucepan, heat the maple syrup to boiling. Add the apples in batches, a quarter of the apples at a time. Cook the apples until tender but not mushy. Remove each batch from the pan and place the apples in a bowl. Repeat until all the apples are cooked.

Arrange the apples on the pie dough so that the slices overlap slightly. Pour the remaining syrup over the apples. Dot with butter. Bake the flan in the 425°F oven for 35 minutes, or until the pastry is golden brown. Remove the pan from the oven and allow it to cool slightly.

Cut the flan into 3-inch squares. Serve with whipped cream or vanilla ice cream, if desired.

Makes 9 servings.

Sentinel Pine Orchards

Five hundred acres: that's a lot of land. Sentinel Pine Orchards is one of the largest orchards we came upon in our travels through New England. Located on the shores of Lake Champlain in Shoreham, Vermont, Sentinel Pine Orchards has been in the Blodgett family for nearly half a century. As part of the Vermont Land Trust, it will be preserved as agricultural land forever. Whitney and Roberta Blodgett are the current owners.

More than 200 acres are devoted to the growth of McIntosh and Macoun apples as well as other varieties. The Blodgetts are dedicated to producing the highest quality apples possible, and they work closely with Cornell University to achieve that goal. State-of-the-art technology and facilities help make that happen.

Like many other orchards, Sentinel Pine ships apples throughout the United States with customers as far away as Texas and Florida. Beginning in late August, tours are offered with lessons on the correct way to pick apples. They also provide fund-raising opportunities for local groups interested in selling apples. Here is a recipe for a dessert pizza from Roberta Blodgett.

Cinnamon Apple Pizza

¾ cup sugar, divided

Basic pizza dough (recipe follows)

1 tablespoon oil

½ cup water

5–6 apples, peeled, cored, and sliced

3–4 tablespoons cinnamon*

Mozzarella or cheddar cheese, as needed to cover the top of the pizza (optional)

....

* If that's too much cinnamon for your taste buds, use a lesser amount.

....

Preheat oven to 500°F.

Add ¼ cup sugar to the flour mixture for basic pizza dough. If you are using already shaped pizza dough, sprinkle the sugar on top.

In a lightly oiled large skillet over medium to high heat, combine the water and sliced apples, stirring occasionally until most of the water is evaporated. Add the remaining ½ cup sugar and the cinnamon to the apples. Stir and remove the skillet from the heat.

Spread the apple mixture over the pizza dough. Top with cheese, if desired.

Bake in the 500°F oven for 10–15 minutes, or until golden brown.

Makes 1 pizza, or 6 servings.

Basic Pizza Dough

2 teaspoons yeast

1¼ cups warm water, divided

4 cups flour, divided

1 teaspoon salt

2 tablespoons oil

In a bowl, combine the yeast with ¼ cup warm water. Let stand.

In a large bowl, combine 3½ cups of flour with the salt. Add the oil, the remaining 1 cup of warm water, and the yeast mixture. Stir with a spoon to mix well.

Knead the dough on a floured surface until the dough is smooth, about 10 minutes. Use the remaining flour as needed. Place the dough in a large greased bowl, cover with plastic wrap, and let stand for 1 hour.

Knead the dough again for 1 minute to deflate any air in the dough. Divide the dough into 2 balls. If making only one pizza, you can wrap the other dough ball tightly with plastic wrap and freeze for future use.

Makes enough dough for 2 pizzas.

Two Orchards on an Island

No trip to Vermont is complete without a visit to Lake Champlain, the nation's sixth largest lake, on the Vermont/New York state line. The Lake Champlain Islands, eighty in all, are a surprise to many travelers as they are dotted with small towns, wineries, and orchards. Modern bridges and old-fashioned ferries provide access to the larger islands, such as South Hero. On South Hero, you'll find two beloved orchards—Hackett's and Allenholm Farm.

Seven generations of the Allen family have been growing fruit at Allenholm Farm, ever since Reuben Allen and his son Horace moved to the island in 1870. It is the oldest commercial apple orchard in Vermont. Today the Allens grow twenty-five acres of apples plus berries and tart cherries, all of which can be found at the family farm stand along with Papa Ray Allen's legendary homemade pies, Empire applesauce, dried Empire apples, and Allenholm crab apple jelly.

Brimming with Vermont's famous maple syrup and cheeses, the farm stand is open daily from late May to December 24. The apple harvest and the pick-your-own season start in the fall. Close to twenty varieties of apples are available, including the crisp and juicy Vermont Gold for which the Allenholm Farm is known. The trip out to the orchard is via a wagon pulled by a farm tractor, much to the delight of children who also will love the adorable animals in the Petting Paddock.

While apples have been growing on their land for more than a century, Hackett's Orchard has been in the family since 1967. It's now owned by Ron and Celia Hackett. Three generations are currently involved with the 50-acre family business. More than forty varieties of apples are grown on the property and sold in a spacious red barn with white trim.

In the classic farm stand you'll find more than apples. Freshly picked vegetables in the summer, pumpkins in the fall, and Vermont products such as maple syrup and honey are available. Berries, cherries, peaches, pears, and plums are sometimes offered, but that all depends on the weather. Those fruits don't do well if Vermont has had an especially harsh winter.

In the winter, Hackett's Orchard is sometimes open "by chance" or you can make an appointment to pick up apples, take-and-bake apple crisp, and frozen cider. Yes, you can freeze cider. But you'll have to return in the summer for Hackett's famous cider slush, or the fall for fresh cider doughnuts (weekends only in November and December).

Hackett's is officially open from May 1 to December 31. The pick-your-own season begins when the apples are ripe, usually after Labor Day. Tours of the orchard by wagon are offered to small groups. A picnic area and playground are additional reasons why so many people love this orchard.

Allenholm Farm

A pound cake is actually a loaf, and it dates back to the eighteenth century. Pound cake gets its name from the original ingredients for the popular dessert—a pound of flour, a pound of butter, a pound of sugar, and a pound of eggs. That would make a pound cake that could feed a family for days. Modern-day bakers have adapted this recipe for Applesauce Pound Cake from Pam Allen at Allenholm Farm in South Hero, Vermont.

Applesauce Pound Cake

1¾ cups flour

1¼ teaspoons baking soda

1 stick butter, softened

1½ cups sugar

3 large eggs, separated and at room temperature

⅔ cup applesauce

1 teaspoon vanilla

Preheat oven to 325°F. In a bowl, sift together the flour and baking soda. Set aside.

In another bowl, cream the butter and sugar until fluffy. Add the egg yolks and beat well. Add one-third of the flour mixture and beat until well mixed. Add the applesauce and beat again. Repeat with the rest of the flour and applesauce.

In another bowl, beat the egg whites until stiff. Fold into the batter. Pour the mixture into a greased and floured loaf pan. Bake in the 325°F oven on the center rack for 1 hour, 20 minutes.

Makes 1 loaf.

Note: This pound cake freezes well.

Hackett's Orchard

These recipes from Hackett's Orchard in South Hero, Vermont, start with one of my fall favorites: Apple, Potato, and Cheddar Soup.

Apple, Potato, and Cheddar Soup

2 tablespoons extra virgin olive oil

¼ cup finely chopped onion

2 celery stalks, chopped

3 medium apples (Cortland or Crispin), peeled, cored, and chopped

3 Yukon gold potatoes, peeled and chopped

⅛ teaspoon ground thyme

¼ cup dry white wine

4 cups chicken broth

1½ cups grated sharp cheddar cheese

½ cup milk

⅛ teaspoon nutmeg

⅛ teaspoon white pepper

1 additional apple, chopped, for garnish

In a large saucepan, heat the oil. Sauté the onions and celery until translucent. Add the chopped apples, potatoes, and thyme. Stir in the wine and simmer for 2–3 minutes. Add the broth and simmer until the potatoes are tender, 30–40 minutes.

In a blender or food processor, puree the soup mixture (in batches if necessary). Return the soup to the saucepan. Over very low heat, stir in the grated cheese, milk, nutmeg, and pepper. Cook until just heated through.

Ladle the soup into warm serving bowls, and garnish with freshly chopped apples.

Makes 4 servings.

Apple-Y Appetizers

Salsa, salsa, salsa; one can never have too many salsa recipes. Here are a few, including a festive summer favorite from Hackett's Orchard in South Hero, Vermont. The pear salsa is something I've been making for years, especially around Thanksgiving time. All you need is basic tortilla chips for dipping. These salsa recipes can also be used as relishes with meat or fish dishes. Hackett's Orchard also provided two more recipes for interesting spreads. They require sturdy crackers, such as Triscuits.

Fresh Apple Salsa

1½ cups diced tomatoes

1 cup diced unpeeled apples (about 2, such as McIntosh or Paula Red)

¾ cup diced sweet yellow peppers

3 scallions, diced

3 tablespoons apple cider

1½ tablespoons good quality extra virgin olive oil or sunflower oil

Generous handful of fresh basil leaves, diced

Salt and pepper, to taste

In a bowl, combine all the ingredients. Cover and chill for 2 hours. This is at its best when served that same day with your favorite tortilla chips.

Makes about 3 cups.

Pear Salsa

1 cup fresh cranberries

4 tablespoons sugar

4 pears, peeled, cut in half with cores removed

2 teaspoons raspberry vinegar

Finely chop the cranberries, or process briefly in a food processor. In a bowl, combine the cranberries and sugar. Refrigerate at least 1 hour.

Coarsely chop the pears. Mix the chopped pears with the cranberry mixture. Add the raspberry vinegar and mix well.

Makes about 3 cups.

Apple Cheese Spread

8 ounces cream cheese, softened

1 cup grated sharp cheddar cheese

2 tablespoons apple cider

1 medium-size apple such as Golden Delicious, Ida Red, or Empire

1 teaspoon dried basil

1 teaspoon dried oregano

1 teaspoon dried thyme

¼ teaspoon freshly ground pepper

Note: This will keep for 1–2 days. It's great with bagel chips, pretzels, or celery sticks.

In a bowl, combine the cream cheese, cheddar cheese, and cider. Blend until smooth.

Peel, core, and grate the apple. Add the grated apple to the cheese mixture. Add the herbs and pepper. Mix until well combined.

Spoon the mixture into a serving bowl. Cover and chill for 1 hour.

Makes about 2 cups.

Cheddar With Caramelized Apples

1 tablespoon butter

2 tablespoons packed brown sugar

2 medium Gala apples, peeled, cored and cut into ¾-inch chunks

¼ cup raisins

4 ounces sharp cheddar, thinly sliced

Whole wheat crackers, as needed

In a medium skillet over medium heat, melt the butter until bubbly. Add the brown sugar and stir until combined. Add the sliced apples and raisins. Reduce the heat to low. Cover the pan and cook, stirring occasionally, for about 6 minutes or until apples begin to soften.

Uncover the pan and continue cooking, stirring often until apples are lightly browned and just tender. Let cool slightly.

Top each cracker with a slice of cheese and a spoonful of the warm apple mixture.

Makes about 2 cups.

Old-Time Sweets

Those with a serious sweet tooth will appreciate these two old-time desserts from Hackett's Orchard in South Hero, Vermont. Traditional hermits are large, round spice cookies made with molasses and raisins. They are also called tea cakes. Commercially made hermits, the kind you can buy at a supermarket, are usually squarish. The earliest known recipe for hermits dates back to 1877 in a cookbook from Portland, Maine. Some say the soft, brown hermits got that name because they look like the sack cloth robe often worn by the hermits of yesteryear. One thing that culinary historians agree upon is that hermits originated in the Lake Champlain region. Fudge, on the other hand, is even more of a mystery. No one knows who made the first batch of fudge, or where. It's thought to be an American invention, probably created by accident while making caramels. When the caramels did not come out as expected, the cook cried "Oh fudge!" Dictionaries from the early 1800s define "fudge" as "to bungle." This is was definitely a happy accident.

Apple Hermits

½ cup butter or margarine

1 cup brown sugar

1 egg

¼ cup milk

2 cups all-purpose flour

½ teaspoon baking soda

½ teaspoon salt

½ teaspoon cinnamon

¼ teaspoon ground cloves

2 cups peeled and shredded apples (about 3)

Preheat oven to 375°F.

In a large bowl, cream the butter and sugar. Beat in the egg and milk. Sift the dry ingredients into the creamed mixture. Stir in the shredded apples. Drop by the spoonful onto a parchment-lined baking sheet. Bake in the 375°F oven for 10–14 minutes. Allow the hermits to cool on racks.

Makes 24 cookies.

Apple Fudge Squares

2 (1-ounce) baking chocolate squares

½ cup shortening

1 cup sugar

2 eggs, beaten

⅔ cup unsweetened applesauce

1 teaspoon vanilla

1 cup flour

½ teaspoon baking powder

¼ teaspoon baking soda

¼ teaspoon salt

½ cup chopped walnuts

Preheat oven to 350°F.

In a large saucepan, melt the chocolate and shortening. Blend in the sugar, eggs, applesauce, and vanilla.

In a bowl, sift together the dry ingredients, and add to the chocolate mixture. Spread into a greased and floured 8 x 8-inch pan. Sprinkle the chopped walnuts on top.

Bake in the 350°F oven for 35–40 minutes. Allow the fudge to cool before cutting into squares.

Makes 16 fudge squares.

WALDORF SALAD

Legend has it that the classic Waldorf Salad was created at the Waldorf-Astoria Hotel in New York City in in the 1890s. Consisting simply of apples, celery, and mayonnaise, this salad eventually became a staple item in fine restaurants. By the 1920s, walnuts were added to the mix. The original recipe was vague about amounts but did call for "a good mayonnaise."

Pam Allen from Allenholm Farm in South Hero, Vermont, still makes a Waldorf Salad. She says the amount of those ingredients depends on how many people you plan to serve. Much like the way the original recipe was put down on paper, Pam says: "Mix cut-up Cortland apples (they are best because they don't turn brown), celery, walnuts, raisins, and mayo to taste. Sprinkle with paprika." For a modern touch, Pam sometimes uses craisins instead of raisins. Craisins are dried cranberries.

New Hampshire

New Hampshire is called "the Switzerland of America" because of its breathtaking scenery and skiing opportunities. This state is also known for its maple syrup and apple orchards. Did you know that it takes approximately forty gallons of sap to make approximately one gallon of maple syrup?

As for apple orchards, the state of New Hampshire designated the roads connecting five orchards in Londonderry as a scenic highway called The Apple Way. The first apple trees were planted in that area by Scotch-Irish settlers, and they became a major crop for local farmers. Londonderry's five orchards—Woodmont, Sunnycrest, Elwood, Moose Hill, and Merrill's—help to make the area worth a visit. Apple Way winds past those orchards with their old family homesteads, reminding us of times gone by.

Covered bridges, waterfalls, and skiing are just three of the many colorful sights that come to mind when one thinks about New Hampshire, a surprisingly diverse state.

Laconia is the site for Motorcycle Week every June. In recent years, more than 200,000 bikers cruised on up for the annual festivities. Only twenty miles away is the peaceful Canterbury Shaker Village. The Shakers emigrated from England to the United States in 1774 and established self-contained communities from Maine to Kentucky. The Canterbury Shaker Village is one of the oldest, most typical, and most completely preserved of the Shaker Villages. New Hampshire is also known for its International Speedway in Loudon, while people are awed by America's Stonehenge in North Salem. It is said that one can determine solar and lunar events of the year there. This state really does have something for everyone.

As for those covered bridges and waterfalls, there are more than fifty covered bridges still standing in New Hampshire. Ever wonder why these bridges were covered? Most New Hampshirites claim the bridges last longer when they're covered because they are sheltered from rain, snow, ice, and the sun. Others assert that the bridges were covered to help get skittish cattle over the rushing water of rivers and streams.

There are more than 400 waterfalls and cascades in New England, many of them in New Hampshire, from Agassiz Basin in Woodstock to Zealand Falls in Bethlehem. The best waterfall in the state is Arethusa Falls in the White Mountain National Forest, according to local experts Greg Parsons and Kate Watson (www.newenglandwaterfalls.com).

There's no select time to visit New Hampshire. It's truly beautiful any time of the year with all four seasons making a colorful appearance, especially the fall with its stunning colors.

So Many Orchards, So Little Time

There are 221 towns and thirteen cities in the state of New Hampshire. And there's at least one orchard or farm in every town, plus almost countless farm stands. Let's begin this tour of the state with the venerable Applecrest Farm Orchard, the oldest and largest.

Just about a century ago, when it was apple harvest time in New Hampshire, the "apple train" would head out of Boston with plenty of apple lovers on board. The train would stop in Hampton Falls, about a mile from Applecrest. The travelers would pick apples and then catch a train headed back to Boston. This may have been the birth of agritourism (any agriculturally based operation that attracts visitors such as cooking classes at an Italian farmhouse) in New Hampshire, and it all started at Applecrest back in the 1920s.

Agritourism continues at Applecrest although these days most people arrive by car. The 225-acre farm still offers pick-your-own apples as well as peaches, blueberries, strawberries, and raspberries. Every weekend is busy with some 15,000 visitors on a nice Sunday. They come for the hayrides, petting zoo, live music, and food festivals. The old-fashioned ice cream barn, built in 1804, is a big draw too. The farm market, with its hand-pressed apple cider and hot cider doughnuts, is open daily and year-round.

The oldest continuously operated apple orchard in the country, Applecrest has buildings that date back to the 1700s. On the newer side of things, Applecrest opened the Farm Bistro in the heart of the orchard, offering true farm-to-table dining. Already winning awards, the Bistro has a "kids eat free" policy on snow days when school is cancelled.

Four generations of the Wagner family have worked the land at Applecrest, dedicated to sustainable agriculture of the highest quality possible.

Heading north you'll find Mack's Apples, an eight-generation family-run farm with one hundred acres dedicated to apples. Voted the best pick-your-own operation in the state, Mack's is also known as Moose Orchards, established in 1732 by John Mack from Ireland. This is the oldest single family-run orchard in New Hampshire. The farm market has a long list of locally produced items, a veritable locavore heaven, from milk and eggs to cheese and maple syrup. Mack's Attic is a treat with its old photographs and artifacts.

At Hazelton Orchards in Chester, the Hazelton family has been growing apples since 1898. Today they are also known for their juicy peaches under the stewardship of Kitt and Cathy (Hazelton) Plummer. Their pick-your-own season is in full swing from September through October. That's also when they do their cider pressing. Visitors are advised to look for the guardian of the orchard, a handsome red-tailed hawk.

In stark comparison, Hackleboro Orchards is the new kid on the block, a mere twenty-five years young. This large working farm offers nine varieties of apples in the pick-your-own section, just a tractor ride away from the farm stand where you'll see fresh peaches, nectarines, plums, pears, and much more. Their fresh unpasteurized sweet cider is available along with freshly baked pies. Farm animals and a scenic picnic area make this Canterbury orchard worth a visit. This is one of those rare orchards that allows family dogs as long as they are leashed. If you forgot the leash at home, they'll gladly provide you with one.

Farther north near the Vermont state line is Poverty Lane Orchards, an interesting name for an apple operation facing hard times, but it was saved by hard cider. The first trees were planted there around 1960, basic McIntosh and Cortland varieties for whole-sale buyers. But then New England growers started losing market share to fruit from faraway places. The first bold move at this Lebanon orchard was to plant heirloom apple varieties around 1980. Next came the decision to plant Bittersweet and Bittersharp apples that no one wanted to eat, but they were ideal for making hard cider. Owners Stephen Wood and wife Louisa Spencer were way ahead of the coming hard cider wave of interest. Today, like a three-legged stool, the revived enterprise consists of the pick-your-own and retail farm stand, the wholesale shipped packs of "uncommon" apples, and Farnum Hill Ciders, gently sparkling and still (no bubbles), dry and complex.

When Steve and Nancy Bleilers moved to a small farmhouse in the town of Alexandria in the late 1970s, they were teachers with no plans to become farmers. All they hoped to do was harvest some apples off their trees for their own consumption. More than two decades went by, and now these former teachers are full-time farmers with about 1,000 trees to tend at Cardigan Mountain Orchard. Their three grown sons help out, and the entire family is involved one way or another. The more than fifteen varieties of apples include Gravenstein and Baldwin. The Cardigan Country Store offers fresh, locally grown produce and artisan-quality products. Make sure to try their "Summer in a Jar" pickled veggies.

Gould Hill Orchards in Hopkinton just may have the oldest bearing apple tree in New Hampshire. Their Gramma Baldwin tree is now more than 200 years old. That's just part of the rich history at this family-run farm. The 1810 post-and-beam barn is now home to a country store and bakery, where they like to create new items such as blueberry cookies. Of course, apple cider doughnuts are available but only on weekends because they like to serve them freshly made and hot. Since 2009, Gould Hill has been managed by the Bassett family: Tim, Amy, Hannah, Amelia, and Cameron. They have lots of plans for the future, and they hope to be growing apples, peaches, and pumpkins for many years to come.

Carter Hill Orchard

There's a lovely story behind the family-owned Carter Hill Orchard in Concord, New Hampshire. There has been an active orchard on the property since the 1700s.

Fast forward to the 1970s, when the orchard was owned by Sunnycrest Farm. As a kid, Rob Larocque grew up living across the street from Sunnycrest Farm, and he wanted to be an apple farmer more than anything. As soon as he was old enough, he started working at the farm. When Rob graduated from high school, Sunnycrest made him the manager. Rob married his high school sweetheart Annette, and the newlyweds moved into the one-room farmhouse on the property. In 1974, their son Todd was born, and five years later Nick was born. The family worked together on making major changes at the farm, and that included adding a playground area for families, walking trails, an observation tower, and a bakery for Annette.

In 1999, Sunnycrest decided to sell the orchard, which Rob and Annette wanted badly. With federal funds from the Farmland Protection Program and help from their friends and neighbors, the couple purchased the property in 2001 and renamed it Carter Hill Orchard.

Since then the Larocques have expanded the bakery and renovated the farm stand. Son Todd was named Young Farmer of the Year by the Concord Grange. Rob and his friend Rick Duane started a cider mill, New Hampshire Cider Works. And the family built a new home where Rob and Annette now live with Todd, his wife, and their children. The Larocques are hopeful that the orchard will be their family business for a long, long time to come.

What better recipe could there be in this book about New England orchards than this Orchard Cake? It calls for two pounds of fresh fruit—apples, peaches, pears, berries or whatever you have on hand.

Orchard Cake

2 eggs

¼ cup milk

1 cup sugar

Pinch of salt

1½ cups all-purpose flour

2 pounds fresh fruit

Butter for greasing pan

Preheat oven to 375°F.

In a bowl, beat the eggs and milk. Add the sugar and pinch of salt, and continue to beat. Add the flour, mixing it in thoroughly to produce a compact cake batter.

Peel and slice the fruit, removing all seeds and pits. Add the fruit to the bowl and mix well (the batter will be mostly fruit).

Grease a 9-inch pan with butter and pour in the batter. Place the pan in the upper third of the preheated oven, and bake for 50 minutes or until the top has become lightly colored.

Makes 6–8 servings.

Butternut Farm

The story behind Butternut Farm in Farmington, New Hampshire is idyllic. Giff and Mae Burnap met at the University of New Hampshire. After working for seven years at Giff's family fruit farm in New York, they decided to venture out on their own. They moved back to New Hampshire knowing it would offer everything they were looking for, and they bought Butternut Farm in 2005. When Giff saw the farm for the first time, he knew it was the perfect place.

Now raising three daughters, the Burnaps love the lifestyle farming provides. They planted sweet and sour cherry trees that are starting to produce fruit, along with berries, peaches, nectarines, plums, and apples. Thanks to their website (www .butternutfarm.net), you can have fruit all year long with tips on storing, freezing, and canning. The Burnap family is all about "being green" and "giving back." They are committed to programs and practices that honor our environment, and they support several local efforts that help their community.

Brookdale Fruit Farm

Founded in 1847 by Edwin Hardy, Brookdale Fruit Farm in Hollis, New Hampshire, has undergone major changes with every generation. The orchard trees were planted in 1910, and their first farm stand cropped up by the side of the road in the 1960s. Over the decades, the techniques of raising apple trees changed dramatically with dwarf or semi-dwarf trees planted in place of the big standard trees. Those smaller trees have resulted in better quality fruit. Today Brookdale Fruit Farm is celebrating seven generations of family farming.

The good people at Brookdale Fruit Farm say their recipes make exceptionally good apples taste even better, and they generously share those recipes with customers. First up, we have Applesauce Doughnuts, a delicious way to start the day. Then it's on to late-afternoon appetizers with before-dinner drinks. You can make these Apple Canapes with McIntosh, Cortland, Empire, Golden Delicious, and Macoun, all grown at Brookdale.

Next comes an unusual recipe for Hot Apple Soup, unlike any hot apple soup recipe I've ever seen. They call it a soup, but I'm tempted to pour it into a mug for sipping by the fireplace.

Applesauce Doughnuts

3 cups flour

1 teaspoon baking powder

½ teaspoon nutmeg

¼ teaspoon salt

1 egg

⅔ cup sugar

4 tablespoons shortening

1 cup applesauce

½ teaspoon vanilla

¾ cup buttermilk

Vegetable or canola oil, as needed

Extra sugar for coating donuts

In a large bowl, sift together the flour, baking powder, nutmeg, and salt. In another bowl, beat the egg, and add the sugar and shortening. Mix until well blended. Beat in the applesauce and vanilla. Add the dry ingredients to the wet ingredients alternating with the buttermilk.

Turn the combined mixtures onto a large floured board or work surface. Roll out gently to about ⅜-inch thick. Cut out doughnuts with a doughnut cutter. Drop the doughnuts into hot oil (375°F) and fry until golden brown, turning them over to cook evenly. Drain on paper towels. Roll the hot doughnuts in sugar.

Makes 2 dozen doughnuts.

Apple Canapes

4 ounces cream cheese

1 tablespoon sherry

½ apple, finely diced

1 celery stalk, minced

⅛ teaspoon salt

Caraway seeds, as needed

In a large bowl, combine all the ingredients except for the caraway seeds. Mix well. Roll into small balls. Roll each ball in the caraway seeds.

Makes about 15 balls.

Hot Apple Soup

1 quart apple cider

1 cup applesauce

Rinds from 1 orange and 1 lemon

2 cinnamon sticks

6 whole cloves

6 allspice cloves

1½ cups maple syrup

½ cup rum

1 cup applejack

8 spiced apple rings, for garnish

Bring the first seven ingredients to a boil in a large pot. When boiling, add the rum and applejack. Serve hot garnished with spiced apple rings.

Makes 8 servings.

Surowiec Farm

This farm in rural Sanbornton has been in the Surowiec family since 1917, when it was a dairy farm. It wasn't until 1971 when the first apple trees were planted. With spectacular views to the north and west, the farm has expanded and diversified. Today they offer pick-your-own blueberries and apples in addition to a well-stocked farm stand, all under the supervision of Stephen and Katie Surowiec. Just look for the old blue pickup truck parked out front.

Apple Hill Farm

Apple Hill Farm in Concord has undergone a massive transformation since Chuck and Diane Souther purchased the land in 1978. They planted their first apple trees that spring even before the family homestead was built. Twenty-four varieties are now grown there. The Paula Reds are the first to ripen in late August, and the Lady apples come last in late October. You can pick your own with certain varieties, and all others are available in the farm stand along with their jams, jellies, and pancake mixes. Apple Hill is a regular sight at seasonal farmer's markets in Bedford and Concord. The Southers love to share their recipes with customers. Here's just a sampling of what's cooking at Apple Hill Farm.

Apple Bacon Summer Salad

3 strips bacon

3 tablespoons olive oil

2 tablespoons red wine vinegar

1 garlic clove, minced

1 teaspoon Dijon mustard

¼ teaspoon salt

¼ teaspoon coarse pepper

5 cups salad greens (spinach or romaine work best)

¼ cup shredded cheese (your choice)

1 apple, chopped

Cook the bacon in a frying pan over medium heat until crispy, 6–8 minutes.

Drain the bacon on a paper towel.

Remove all but 2–3 tablespoons of the warm bacon fat from the frying pan, and add the olive oil to the pan. Stir to blend the fats. Crumble the cooked bacon and return it to the frying pan. Stir in the vinegar, garlic, mustard, salt and pepper.

Keep the dressing warm while you get the greens ready. In a large bowl, tear up the salad greens. Add the shredded cheese and chopped apple. Spoon the warm bacon dressing over the top and toss to coat lightly.

Makes 4–6 servings.

Crockpot Apple Cider Beef Stew

2 slices bacon

1½–2 pounds lean stew beef

½ cup chopped onions

8 carrots, sliced thin

6 medium potatoes, sliced thin

2 apples, chopped (Cortland or Northern Spy works well)

2 teaspoons salt

2 cups fresh apple cider

Note: Thicken the juices in the crockpot by adding a slurry, a mixture of flour and cold water, about 1½–2 tablespoons of flour and 2 tablespoons of water. Stir to mix well.

In a sauté pan, cook the bacon. Remove the cooked bacon and pat dry with a paper towel.

In the same pan, sauté the beef and chopped onions. Pat the beef dry and add to the crockpot with the remaining ingredients. Stir to mix, cover, and cook on low for 8 hours.

Makes 4–6 servings.

Stonybrook Farm

In the heart of New Hampshire's beautiful Lakes Region is Stonybrook Farm in Gilford. Just follow the country road with a white fence on one side and a stone wall on the other. The weathered gray farm stand holds everything you'd expect as well as their now-famous homemade apple cake, freshly pressed apple cider, local maple syrup, maple candy, and maple kettle corn. A dozen different varieties of apples (including Ginger Gold) are but a hay wagon ride away, pulled by a bright blue tractor. Overlooking Lake Winnipesaukee, the farm with its handsome birch trees is a popular venue for weddings and special events.

Pumpkin Apple Crisp

FOR THE APPLE LAYER:

3–4 medium-size tart apples

⅓ cup brown sugar (or maple sugar)

1 tablespoon cornstarch

½ teaspoon ground cinnamon

¼ teaspoon salt

⅓ cup water or sweet cider

2 tablespoons butter

FOR THE PUMPKIN LAYER:

¾ cup canned (or fresh) pureed pumpkin

¾ cup heavy cream or evaporated milk

⅓ cup granulated sugar or maple sugar

1 egg

1 teaspoon cinnamon

1 teaspoon ground ginger

¼ teaspoon ground nutmeg

¼ teaspoon cloves

¼ teaspoon salt

FOR THE CRISP TOPPING LAYER:

1 cup flour

1 cup dark brown sugar

½–¾ stick of margarine or butter, slightly softened

1 teaspoon cinnamon

FOR SERVING:

Vanilla ice cream, as needed

Peel and slice the apples. You should have enough sliced apples to fill 3 cups.

In a medium saucepan, combine the brown sugar, cornstarch, cinnamon, salt, and cider. Mix well, and then add the butter. Bring the mixture to a slow boil. Add the sliced apples and cook for 4 minutes, stirring often. Turn off the heat and allow to cool slightly.

In a large bowl, combine the ingredients for the pumpkin layer. Mix until smooth.

In a separate bowl, combine the ingredients for the crisp layer. Mix until crumbly.

Preheat oven to 350°F. Lightly coat a 9 x 13-inch baking pan with vegetable spray.

Spread the apple mixture evenly in the baking pan. Pour the pumpkin mixture on top of the apple mixture. Top with the apple crisp topping.

Bake in the 350°F oven for approximately 1 hour, or until the mixture is bubbly. Serve warm with vanilla ice cream on top.

Makes 12 servings.

Riverview Farm

Like many other orchard operations, Riverview Farm has but a short season, from August through October. So don't put off a visit to this farm in Plainfield, New Hampshire. The Barn Store is the hub of the farm, and its rear deck overlooks the Connecticut River. The store is where you can find out what's ripe for picking, and where you can catch a hayride up to the orchards. The Franklin family established Riverview Farm more than thirty years ago.

In addition to already picked produce, the Barn Store has an autumnal motif with Indian corn and dried flowers hanging from the wooden beams. All things local, honey, maple syrup, and cheese, can be found in the well-stocked store. The jams are made in the farmhouse kitchen, and the cider is freshly pressed. Feel free to pack a lunch and gather the family around one of the many picnic tables on the lawn. It's not surprising that this naturally beautiful site is available for private events such as weddings.

"Life is short. . . eat dessert first" is the motto for dessert lovers everywhere. And desserts made with the bountiful fruits from an orchard are among the best to have as your first (or last) course.

The simplest apple dessert has to be baked apples, and this is how they do it at Riverview Farm. Their recipe calls for an ovenproof skillet. If you don't have one, you can use a 9 x 13-inch baking dish, and bake as directed. They also offer recipes for an out-of-the-ordinary pie made with apples and blueberries and for the classic French dessert, the relatively easy Apple Tarte Tatin, which is an upside-down tart.

Then we move on to the pizza recipes from Riverview Farm in which apples play a major role. The first is sweet, and the second savory and more sophisticated. Everyone likes pizza, which makes a perfect appetizer or a casual dessert when cut into small pieces. One pizza goes a long way when served in that manner.

Baked Apples

7 large (about 6 ounces each) Granny Smith apples, divided

6 tablespoons unsalted butter, softened, divided

½ cup packed brown sugar

⅓ cup dried cranberries, coarsely chopped

⅓ cup coarsely chopped pecans, toasted

3 tablespoons old-fashioned rolled oats

1 teaspoon finely grated zest from 1 orange

½ teaspoon ground cinnamon

Pinch table salt

⅓ cup maple syrup

⅓ cup plus 2 tablespoons apple cider, divided

Vanilla ice cream, as needed

Adjust an oven rack to the middle position, and preheat the oven to 375°F.

Peel, core, and cut 1 apple into ¼-inch dice. In a large bowl, combine 5 tablespoons of butter with the brown sugar, cranberries, pecans, oats, orange zest, cinnamon, salt, and diced apple. Set aside.

Shave a thin slice off the bottom (blossom end) of the remaining 6 apples to allow them to sit flat. Cut the top ½ inch off the stem end of apples, and reserve. Peel the apples, and use a melon baller or small measuring spoon to remove 1½-inch diameter core, being careful not to cut through the bottom of the apple.

Melt the remaining tablespoon of butter in a 12-inch non-stick oven-safe skillet over medium heat. Once the foaming subsides, add the apples, stem-side down, and cook until the cut surface is golden brown, about 3 minutes. Flip the apples, reduce the heat to low, and spoon the filling inside, mounding the excess filling over the cavities. Top with the reserved apple caps. Add the maple syrup and ⅓ cup cider to skillet.

Transfer the skillet to 375°F oven, and bake until a skewer inserted into the apples meets little resistance, 35–40 minutes, basting every 10 minutes with the maple syrup mixture in the skillet.

Transfer the apples to a serving platter. Stir the remaining cider as needed into the sauce in the skillet to adjust the consistency. Pour the sauce over the apples and serve with vanilla ice cream, if desired.

Makes 6 servings.

Note: Six of the apples are left whole. One is diced and added to the filling.

Apple Blueberry Pie

Pastry dough for 9-inch two-crust pie

4 medium apples

2 cups blueberries

½ cup sugar

1 teaspoon cinnamon

½ teaspoon nutmeg

1 tablespoon butter, cut into small pieces

Preheat oven to 425°F.

Roll out the pastry dough for the bottom crust. Place the dough in a pie pan, and prick the bottom and sides of the dough.

Peel, core, and slice the apples. In a large bowl, mix the apple slices with the blueberries, sugar, cinnamon, and nutmeg. Pour the fruit mixture into the prepared pie pan. Dot with butter.

Roll out the dough for the top crust. Place the dough on top of the pie. Flute the entire edge of the pie, and prick holes in the top.

Bake the pie in the 425°F oven for 40–50 minutes. Cover the crimped edges of the pie with aluminum foil until the last 15 minutes of baking.

Makes 6 servings.

BERRY GOOD TIP

When making a blueberry pie, try adding a peeled and grated Granny Smith apple. Rich in pectin, the apple will help thicken the berries and juice, and it will enhance their flavor.

Apple Tarte Tatin

½ cup butter, at room temperature

2 vanilla beans

1 cup sugar

2 cinnamon sticks, broken in half

2–3 apples, peeled, cored, and sliced

Puff pastry, as needed

Confectioners' sugar, as needed

Preheat oven to 400°F.

Melt the butter in a 9-inch ovenproof frying pan.

Split the vanilla beans lengthwise, and scrape out the seeds into the cup of sugar. Mix well. Pour the sugar on top of the butter. Cook over medium heat until the butter and sugar are melted. The sugar will be a light golden color. Remove from the heat. Place the cinnamon sticks on top of the sugar so they divide the frying pan into quarters.

Place the sliced apples overlapping on top of the caramelized sugar. Cover the frying pan loosely with the puff pastry.

Bake in the 400°F oven for 20 minutes. Remove the pan from the oven, and set aside to cool slightly.

Cover the frying pan with a large plate or serving platter. Holding firmly, turn upside down so that the tarte tatin falls onto the plate. Sprinkle with confectioners' sugar and serve warm.

Makes 6 servings.

Note: You can also make "vanilla sugar" by placing a vanilla bean with a cup of sugar in a glass jar with a tight-fitting lid. Set aside for a few days to allow the vanilla to permeate the sugar.

Apple Pizza

Piecrust dough, enough to make
2 pies

6 medium to large apples

1 cup brown sugar

¾ cup flour

⅔ stick margarine or butter

½ cup shredded sharp cheddar
cheese (optional)

Make enough piecrust dough as if you were making 2 fruit
pies. (Betty Crocker's recipe is recommended.) Roll out the
dough to fit a large pizza pan, plus a little bit extra. Turn the
dough under along the edges and crimp.

Peel and slice the apples. Arrange the sliced apples in a fan
shape, overlapping slightly, all over the pan, starting at the
outside edge and working to the center.

Preheat oven to 425°F.

For the topping, combine the brown sugar, flour, and margarine until crumbly using a pastry blender. Carefully sprinkle
the topping over the sliced apples. Bake in the 425°F oven
for 25 minutes.

Makes 12 servings.

Optional: About 7 minutes before the pizza is done, remove
it from the oven, sprinkle with the shredded cheese, and
return the pizza to the oven. Continue baking just until the
cheese is melted.

Apple, Bacon, and Gorgonzola Puff Pastry Pizza

1 sheet puff pastry

4 bacon slices, fried crisp

1 shallot or ½ onion, minced

1 tablespoon honey, plus more for drizzling

Shredded mozzarella, as needed

1 apple, cored and diced

½ cup Gorgonzola

Roll out the puff pastry on a lightly floured surface to about 10 x 14 inches. Fold over the edges ½ inch. Press with a fork to keep the edges from puffing up too much. Brush the edges with water.

Preheat oven to 400°F.

After cooking the bacon, use a slotted spoon to move the bacon to paper towels on which to drain. Use that same pan to sauté the shallots until golden. Add the tablespoon of honey to the sautéed shallots. Spread the shallot-honey mixture over the puff pastry.

Sprinkle a handful of mozzarella over the entire pizza. Crumble the bacon on top. Add more mozzarella, and top with the diced apples. Drizzle honey over that and finally the Gorgonzola.

Bake in the 400°F oven for 20 minutes.

Makes 6-8 servings.

Apple Annie

Off the beaten path well describes Apple Annie, a small orchard in Brentwood. Now owned by Laurie and Wayne Loosigian, the orchard invites visitors to stroll about and picnic on the grounds. Their goal is to grow sound, healthy, tasty apples, which they achieve by using the least toxic chemicals and as little as possible. Nearly everything they sell in the farm store is made on the premises, from the unpasteurized cider to the jams and jellies. On their annual Cider Day in November, they demonstrate how to press cider and how to make hard cider, applesauce, and apple cider vinegar. About a dozen varieties of apples are grown at Apple Annie, including the yellowish Liberty and the bright red Enterprise. Look for the Fameuse variety, also known as the Snow Apple of Quebec. It's believed to be the ancestor of the ever-popular McIntosh.

New Hampshire Fruit Growers Association

The New Hampshire Fruit Growers Association describes itself as "an organization of about forty farmers who all share a passion for growing good fruit and grow New Hampshire apples with care for local customers." According to the association, there's a nearby orchard no matter where you live or play in the state, from the seacoast to the Merrimack and Connecticut River valleys to the Great North Woods. Their mission helps to maintain the rural character of New Hampshire's landscape for residents and visitors alike.

When are New Hampshire grown tree fruits ready for harvest? It begins in July with the sweet and sour cherries, followed by peaches and plums in August through September. The pears make their appearance in September. Apples, which are an important part of the state's history, ripen August through October. The apple is the official state fruit, and apple pie is the state's official dessert.

As with other New England apples, each variety has its own characteristics—what's best for fresh eating, what's best for baking, etc.? Every local orchard can tell you what they are growing and how best to use that fruit.

The New Hampshire Fruit Growers Association is also a wonderful source of recipes that have been collected from the orchards over the years. Here's a sampling, a half-dozen recipes for breakfast and dessert dishes (The apple cider syrup in New Hampshire differs from the cider syrup made right next door in Vermont.)

Let's start with apple fritters, a big thing in Connecticut, but this is how it's done up north. They can be served at breakfast or as a dessert.

Apple Fritters

1 cup sour cream

½ cup milk

1 egg, lightly beaten

2 teaspoons sugar

1 teaspoon cinnamon

1 cup flour

1½ teaspoons baking powder

½ teaspoon salt

¼ cup oil

3 baking apples, peeled and cut into ⅛-inch slices

Maple syrup or confectioners' sugar, as needed

In a bowl, combine the first 8 ingredients.

In a frying pan, heat the oil over medium high heat.

Dip the apple slices into the batter, a few at a time, and fry until golden brown, 3–4 minutes on each side. Drain on paper towels and serve with maple syrup or dust with confectioners' sugar.

Makes about 48 fritters.

....

Note: Use a melon baller or small ice cream scoop for measuring the batter and dropping it into the oil.

....

French Toast Strata with Apple Cider Syrup

FOR THE FRENCH TOAST:

1 pound French bread, cut into cubes

8 ounces cream cheese, cut into small cubes

8 eggs

2½ cups milk

6 tablespoons butter or margarine, melted

¼ cup maple syrup

FOR THE APPLE CIDER SYRUP:

1 teaspoon cinnamon

8 teaspoons cornstarch

1 cup sugar

2 tablespoons lemon juice

2 cups apple cider or apple juice (if cider is no longer in season)

4 tablespoons butter or margarine

Layer half of the bread in a greased 9 x 13-inch baking dish. Top with the cream cheese and remaining bread.

In a blender, combine the eggs, milk, butter, and maple syrup. Pour this blended mixture over the bread and cheese. Press the layers down with a spatula. Refrigerate, covered, 2–24 hours.

Preheat oven to 325°F.

Remove the baking dish from the refrigerator and bake, uncovered, in the 325°F oven for 35–40 minutes, or until the center is set and the edges are golden brown. Let stand for 10 minutes before serving.

To make the Apple Cider Syrup (which can be made one day ahead), combine the cinnamon, cornstarch, and sugar, in a small saucepan, and mix well. Stir in the lemon juice and cider. Cook over medium heat until mixture thickens and boils, stirring constantly. Cook for 2 minutes longer. Remove from heat and stir in the butter.

Drizzle syrup over the warm strata.

Makes 4 servings.

Apple Cake with Peach Topping

1 egg

1⅛ cups sugar

2 sticks butter, at room temperature

2 cups flour

½ tablespoon baking powder

Raisins and nuts, as needed (optional)

4 apples, sliced

½–⅔ cup peach preserves

Preheat oven to 350°F. Grease and flour a 9 x 13-inch baking pan.

In a bowl, cream the egg and sugar. Add the softened butter and mix well. Add the flour and baking powder, and mix well. Pour the batter into the prepared pan.

If desired, sprinkle the raisins and nuts over the batter.

Overlay the apple slices on top of the batter. Top the apples with the peach preserves.

Cooking tip: Heat the preserves for easy spreading.

Bake in the 350°F oven for 45 minutes. Allow to cool before serving.

Makes 12 servings.

Apple Pancakes

2 cups flour

3 teaspoons baking powder

1 teaspoon salt

1⅓ cups milk

2 eggs

4 tablespoons melted shortening

1 medium to large apple, peeled and grated

Butter, maple syrup, or brown sugar for topping

In a large mixing bowl, combine the flour, baking powder, and salt.

In another bowl, beat the milk, eggs, melted shortening, and grated apple. Add this mixture to the flour mixture. Mix until just blended.

Pour about ¼ cup of the batter into a hot, greased frying pan. Cook until the top of each pancake is covered with bubbles, then flip to cook the other side. When golden brown on both sides, move the pancakes onto a warm serving platter.

Serve with butter, maple syrup, or brown sugar.

Makes approximately 15 (4-inch) pancakes.

Mom's Applesauce Cake

½ cup butter

1½ cups sugar

3 eggs

2 cups flour

2 teaspoons baking soda

½ teaspoon salt

1 teaspoon cinnamon

½ teaspoon cloves

½ teaspoon nutmeg

1½ cups unsweetened applesauce

½ cup chopped nuts

1 cup raisins

Preheat oven to 350°F.

In a large bowl, cream the butter and sugar. Add the eggs, and beat until fluffy.

In another bowl, sift the dry ingredients. Add the dry ingredients and the applesauce alternately to the butter/sugar mixture. Add the nuts and raisins. Pour into a well-greased tube pan.

Bake in the 350°F oven for 1 hour.

Makes 8 servings.

Apple Cake with Cream Cheese Frosting

FOR THE CAKE:

1¾ cups sugar

¾ cup oil

3 eggs, beaten

1 teaspoon cinnamon

1 teaspoon salt

1 teaspoon baking soda

2 cups flour

1 teaspoon vanilla

3 cups peeled, grated apples

FOR THE FROSTING:

4 ounces cream cheese, softened

4 tablespoons (½ stick) margarine, softened

1 pound confectioners' sugar

1 teaspoon vanilla

Half and half or milk, as needed

Preheat oven to 350°F. Grease a 9 x 13-inch pan.

In a bowl, mix together the sugar and oil, then add the beaten eggs.

In another bowl, sift the dry ingredients and add to the sugar mixture, beating well. Add the vanilla. Fold in the grated apple.

Bake in the 350°F oven for 50–60 minutes. Allow to cool before frosting.

While the cake is baking, make the frosting. In a bowl, cream the cream cheese and margarine until well blended. Gradually add the confectioners' sugar and the vanilla. Moisten with teaspoons of half and half or milk until the frosting is the right consistency for easy spreading.

Makes 12 servings.

Alyson's Orchard

With its beautiful vistas, Alyson's Orchard is known as much for its dream weddings as for its apples. The 450-acre property in Walpole, New Hampshire, is open year round. In warm weather, you can visit the farm stand or pick your own fruit. In colder times, you can stay overnight in a country lodge and go for a horse-drawn sleigh ride in the snow.

The picturesque orchard consists of apples, peaches, pears, plums, nectarines, quince, berries, with apples by far the largest crop. Among the fifty-plus varieties, the heirloom apples have been in cultivation for more than seventy-five years. The excellent website (www.alysonsorchard.com) details what is grown and what that fruit is ideal for, such as the Winesap, which is best for making applesauce, apple pie, and cider.

Alyson's apples have been certified as Eco Apples, grown under specific practices that include advanced agricultural orchard management. Through Integrated Pest Management, fewer chemicals are applied to the fruit trees. (For more information, visit www.redtomato.org.)

Alyson's Orchard got its start in 1981 when Susan and Bob Jasse established a family retreat from the ground up. The virgin land evolved over the years into a pick-your-own orchard, so beautiful and well designed it became a popular venue for country weddings and other special events.

Sadly, Alyson's Orchard is named in memory of the youngest of Bob's seven children, who died as an infant. Bob passed away in 2008. His plans for the orchard are being carried out by his wife with a devoted staff.

More than fifty acres are dedicated to fruit-growing trees that are ready for harvesting from midsummer to late fall. The fruit from Alyson's Orchard has such a sterling reputation that it is sold in major markets in New Hampshire, Vermont, Massachusetts, and Connecticut. But that doesn't compare to shopping in person at Alyson's seasonal farm stand with its red and white exterior and dark green market umbrellas. The shelves are well stocked with every imaginable country goodie.

What makes Alyson's Orchard unique? In our travels throughout New England, it was the only one we found with an Italian bocce court on the premises. Visitors are encouraged to play a game or two while their children enjoy the nearby playground and meet the farm's friendly goats.

New England Apple Association

Who knew the humble apple could be used in so many entrees? The following dishes are from the New England Apple Association, which has eighty years of experience at promoting the fresh harvest each year through educational ventures.

The first batch of five focuses on chicken and turkey. One recipe after another sounds so delicious, you'll want to try them all. Then check out the association's meatloaf recipes in which the apple plays a starring role. Almost everyone likes meatloaf. One recipe is very simple, and the other is a bit more complex.

Next is a wonderful pork stew. On chilly nights, nothing's better than a pork stew. The New England Apple Association suggests adding apples to sweeten the pot. The stew has a long list of essential ingredients, but you toss almost all of them into a slow cooker and forget about it for eight hours. It could not be easier. The apple growers also make a basic smoked ham rather special with the addition of apples, applejack, and apple cider.

Rounding out the wonderful entrees offered by the New England Apple Association are two recipes for fish. Fish with apples, you ask? Most definitely, yes. And lastly, vegetarians may enjoy a simple stir-fry. Like all stir-fries, it's quick and easy.

Apple Chicken Stir-Fry

1 pound boneless, skinless chicken breast, cut into cubes

2 tablespoons vegetable oil, divided

½ cup sliced onions

1 cup thinly sliced carrots

1 teaspoon dried basil, crushed

1 cup fresh Chinese pea pods

1 tablespoon water

1 medium apple, cored and thinly sliced

2 cups cooked rice

½ sliced red pepper (optional)

Stir-fry the cubed chicken breast in 1 tablespoon of oil in a non-stick skillet until lightly browned and cooked through. Remove the chicken from the skillet.

Stir-fry the onions, carrots, and basil (and optional red pepper) with the remaining oil in the same skillet until the carrots are tender. Stir in the pea pods and water. Stir-fry for 2 minutes.

Remove the skillet from the heat. Stir in the apples. Add the chicken and mix well. Serve hot over cooked rice.

Makes 2 servings.

Chicken Oriental Kabobs

4 skinless, boneless chicken breasts, cut into 2-inch pieces

Pepper, to taste

2 apples, cored and quartered

8 fresh mushrooms

8 parboiled whole white onions

2 oranges, quartered

8 canned pineapple chunks

8 cherry tomatoes

1 cup cider or a (6-ounce) can frozen apple juice concentrate, thawed

1 cup dry white wine

2 tablespoons soy sauce

Dash of ground ginger

2 tablespoons vinegar

¼ cup corn oil

Sprinkle the chicken with pepper. Thread 8 skewers as follows: chicken, apple, mushroom, chicken, onion, chicken, orange quarter, chicken, pineapple chunk, cherry tomato. Place the kabobs in a shallow pan.

Combine the remaining ingredients and spoon over the kabobs. Marinate in the refrigerator for at least 1 hour. Drain and reserve the marinade.

Broil 6 inches from the heat, 15 minutes on each side, brushing often with marinade.

Makes 4 servings (2 skewers per person).

French-Style Chicken with Apples

6 boneless, skinless chicken breasts

3 apples, cored and sliced

1 onion, sliced

6 artichoke hearts, halved

1 (10-ounce) can condensed chicken or vegetable broth

3 tablespoons apple brandy, cider, or apple juice

Pinch of cinnamon and nutmeg

Salt and pepper, to taste

Fresh parsley or dill, minced, for garnish

Spray a large skillet with cooking spray. Brown the chicken breasts on both sides. Remove the chicken from the skillet and set aside.

Reserve 6 apple slices for garnish.

Using the same skillet, stir in apples, onion, artichoke hearts, broth, brandy, cinnamon, and nutmeg. Cook for 3 minutes.

Spread the chicken breasts in the skillet. Arrange the apple mixture on top of the chicken. Simmer, covered, for about 10 minutes, or until the chicken is thoroughly cooked. Season to taste.

Garnish with fresh parsley or dill and the reserved apple slices before serving.

Makes 6 servings.

Pot Roasted Chicken with Apples and Apple Cider

2 tablespoons oil

1 chicken, 4–4½ pounds, cut into 8 pieces

Flour, as needed to coat the chicken

1 onion, sliced

2 cups apple cider

Juice of 1 lemon

2 teaspoons sugar

3 apples, sliced

Pinch each of ground cloves, ginger, and sage

Warm a large skillet over medium-high heat. Add the oil to the warmed skillet. Dredge the chicken pieces in the flour. Brown the chicken pieces in the hot oil.

Add the onion and sauté until softened. Reduce the heat, and add the cider, lemon juice, and sugar. Cover and simmer for about 20 minutes. Add the apples and seasonings, and simmer an additional 15 minutes.

Serve chicken pieces in a pool of apple cider sauce.

Makes 4 servings.

Apple Turkey Sauté

½ cup flour

½ teaspoon salt

¼ teaspoon black pepper

1 pound turkey breast, cut into ¼-inch-thick slices

1 tablespoon butter

2 tablespoons olive oil

3 apples, peeled, cored, and sliced

½ cup sliced mushrooms

½ cup sliced onions

2 tablespoons capers

1 cup apple juice or cider

2 tablespoons chopped fresh parsley

In small bowl, combine the flour, salt, and pepper. Dredge the turkey slices in the flour mixture to lightly coat.

In a large skillet, heat the butter and olive oil over medium heat. Add the turkey slices and sauté, turning, until browned on both sides and cooked thoroughly.

Remove the turkey from skillet and keep warm. Add the apples, mushrooms, onions, and capers to the skillet. Sauté just until the apples are tender. Stir in the apple juice to deglaze the skillet and simmer for 5 minutes.

Arrange the turkey slices on a platter. Cover the turkey with the apple and vegetable mixture. Spoon the sauce in the skillet over the entire dish. Garnish with parsley and serve.

Makes 4 servings.

Apple Meatloaf

1 pound ground beef

1 medium Paula Red or Ginger Gold apple, peeled and finely chopped

1 medium potato, peeled and finely chopped

1 small onion, minced

1 teaspoon salt

¼ teaspoon pepper

1 egg, beaten

Preheat oven to 375°F.

In a large bowl, thoroughly mix the ground beef, apple, potato, and onion. Mix in the salt and pepper, then the beaten egg. Pack firmly into a greased 8-inch loaf pan.

Bake in the 375°F oven for about 1 hour. Serve hot with a generous amount of pan juices.

Makes 4 servings.

McIntosh Meatloaf

1 McIntosh or other New England apple, peeled and chopped

2 pounds ground beef

1 egg, beaten

⅓ cup chopped celery

1 cup fresh bread crumbs

⅓ cup minced onions

¼ cup molasses

¼ teaspoon salt

¼ cup milk (or just enough to moisten)

Pepper, to taste

½ McIntosh apple, cored and sliced

FOR THE GLAZE:

2 tablespoons ketchup

2 tablespoons molasses

1 teaspoon mustard

FOR THE SAUCE:

½ McIntosh apple, peeled and chopped

1 tablespoon horseradish

Salt and pepper, to taste

Preheat oven to 350°F.

Mix together all the main ingredients except the second (sliced) apple. Place in 9 x 5-inch loaf pan. Press the apple slices into the top of the meatloaf. Bake uncovered in the 350°F oven for 1 hour.

In a bowl, mix the ingredients for the glaze. Remove the meatloaf from the oven and glaze. Return the meatloaf to the oven and continue baking for 7–10 more minutes.

In another bowl, mix the ingredients for the sauce and serve with the meatloaf.

Makes 6–8 servings.

Pork and Apple Stew

2 pounds pork, cubed

½ cup flour

½ teaspoon salt

¼ teaspoon pepper

½ teaspoon garlic powder

2½ tablespoons olive oil

1 onion, chopped

4 carrots, peeled and sliced

1 sweet potato, peeled and cubed

3 potatoes, peeled and cut into eighths

1 pound butternut squash, peeled and cubed

1 teaspoon cinnamon

½ teaspoon thyme

¼ teaspoon nutmeg

⅛ teaspoon ground ginger

⅛ teaspoon ground cloves

1 cup apple juice or cider

2 cups water

3 cups sweet white wine

3 McIntosh or other New England apples, peeled, cored, and cut into eighths

1 cup green beans, chopped into 1-inch pieces

Combine the pork, flour, and seasonings in a sealable bag. Shake to coat well. Heat the oil in a large skillet and add the pork. Brown on all sides. Reserve the extra flour mixture.

In a slow cooker, combine the pork with the remaining ingredients except the apples and green beans. Cook on low for 8 hours. Make a paste with the reserved flour mixture dissolved in a small amount of water. Stir into the stew to thicken.

Add the apples and green beans. Cook on high for 15 minutes and serve.

Makes 6 servings.

Smoked Ham with Apple Raisin Cider Sauce

2 New England apples, such as Ida Red, Cortland, or Rome

2 teaspoons vegetable oil

1 yellow onion, sliced

½ cup raisins

½ cup applejack

2 cups ham stock or chicken broth

1 tablespoon cornstarch

½ cup apple cider, cold

2 pounds smoked ham, sliced

Peel the apples, if desired. Remove the cores, and chop the apples into small pieces.

Heat the oil in a large saucepan. Lightly sweat the onions until softened. Add the chopped apples, raisins, and apple-jack, and slowly cook until most of the liquid has reduced. Add the stock and bring to a boil.

In a bowl, combine the cornstarch and cider, and add to the stock as a thickener.

Warm the sliced ham in the oven. Serve the slices topped with the cider sauce.

Makes 6 servings.

Apple Halibut Kabobs

½ cup dry white wine or chicken broth

4 teaspoons olive oil

2 tablespoons lime juice

2 tablespoons finely chopped onions

½ teaspoon salt

½ teaspoon dried thyme, crushed

⅛ teaspoon pepper

1 apple, cored and cut in 1-inch cubes

1 medium green or sweet red pepper, cut into 1-inch squares

1 small onion, cut into 1-inch squares

1 pound halibut, cut into 1-inch cubes

In a bowl, combine wine, oil, lime juice, onions, salt, thyme, and pepper. Mix well. Marinate the remaining ingredients in this mixture for 1 or 2 hours.

Thread the apple, pepper, onion, and halibut on long metal or bamboo skewers. Repeat five times on each skewer, ending with the apple.

Broil or grill 4 or 5 inches from heat for 6–8 minutes or until fish flakes when tested with a fork. Serve warm or cold.

Makes 4 servings.

Apple Stuffed Fish Fillets

1 McIntosh or other New England apple, grated and peeled

1 carrot, grated

1 green onion, minced

2 tablespoons fresh lemon juice

¼ teaspoon ground ginger

¼ teaspoon ground mustard

¼ teaspoon salt

¼ teaspoon black pepper

¼ teaspoon dried thyme

4 sole, cod, or other white fish fillets

¼ cup water or broth

Preheat oven to 400°F.

In a medium-size bowl, combine all but last two ingredients and mix well. Spread this mixture evenly over the length of the fillets, and carefully roll them up.

Place the fillets, seam side down, in a lightly oiled roasting pan, and pour the water or broth over the fillets. Cover with foil and bake in the 400°F oven for 10–15 minutes, or until the fish flakes. If using a microwave oven, cook for 5 minutes.

Makes 4 servings.

Crunchy Apple Stir-Fry

1½ teaspoons vegetable oil

½ cup sliced onions

1 cup thinly sliced carrots

1 teaspoon dried basil, crushed

1 cup fresh Chinese pea pods

1 tablespoon water

1 apple, cored and thinly sliced

In a large skillet or wok, heat the oil. Stir-fry the onions, carrots, and basil until the carrots are tender. Stir in the pea pods and water. Stir-fry for 2 more minutes. Stir in the apples and remove from the skillet from the heat. Serve hot.

Makes 2 servings.

Maine

Maine sits at the northeastern corner of the nation, the largest of the six New England states. In fact, Maine is bigger geographically than the other five New England states combined. Yet its population of 1.3 million is just a tad more than Rhode Island, the smallest state in the Union.

Maine's most famous residents include Steven King, the famous horror storywriter who lives in Bangor, and the presidential Bush family who summers in Kennebunkport.

People new to the state are called transplants, and visitors are "from away." Mainers definitely have their own way of saying things. They don't pronounce the letter "r" so Mainer, for example, is pronounced Mainah. Ayuh means yes. Cute and adorable babies are "cunnin." And they like to use the word "wicked" as in wicked cold weather, a colloquialism that has spread into other parts of New England. The average winter temperature in Maine is 20°F, and it rarely gets above 70°F in the summer. Maine's other fun facts are pretty interesting:

- It's believed that the Vikings discovered Maine more than 1,000 years ago, long before Christopher Columbus.
- The official state insect is the honey bee, so crucial to the success of all the orchards.
- Maine is the only state name with one syllable, and it's the only state with just one other state on its border, New Hampshire. Its only other border is with Canada.
- Maine has 3,478 miles of coastline (more than California with 3,427).
- The Vacation State, as it is called, has 3,166 offshore islands and sixty-seven lighthouses, some of them said to be haunted.
- Maine is most famous for its rocky coastline, lobsters, and blueberries.

No book that explores Maine can be published without at least some words of praise for the state's famous blueberries. The blueberry is the official state fruit, and the wild Maine blueberry pie is the official state dessert. Maine produces more than 90 percent of the wild blueberry crops harvested every year in the United States.

To harvest wild blueberries, a special rake is used. Some wild blueberry farms provide those rakes to their pick-you-own customers. Just watch out for Maine's black bears. They love blueberries as much as we do, and they return year after year for the wild blueberry harvest because those berries are so wicked good.

McDougal Orchards

Charming is the first word that comes to mind when you come upon McDougal Orchards in Springvale, Maine. This is a seventh-generation family farm in the southern part of the state. Seven generations. . . there's a lot of history there.

McDougal Orchards is part of a 450-acre parcel of land purchased in 1779 by Joshua Hanson at a tax auction for 52 pounds, 10 shillings. Ever since then the property has been farmed by the same family. Through various marriages, the land has been held by the Hansons, McDougals, and now the McAdams. Most recently, in 1984, Ellen McDougal married Jack McAdam, who became a captain for the U.S. Coast Guard. They now own McDougal Orchards.

Back in the early 1930s, Alva McDougal planted 1,600 McIntosh trees in what is now the main orchard. It was believed at that time that 400 trees per child could support a family, and Alva had four children at that time. One of those children, Robert, took on the task of modernizing the orchard. Dwarf trees replaced the big standard trees, and the first pick-your-own operation was launched in 1972 when a major storm destroyed the wholesale crop.

Back then Nova Scotians would come down to Maine to pick apples every fall, and they stayed in a bunk house that evolved over the years into a warming hut for cross-country skiers. Now it's the Donut Shack, where you can find Captain Jack operating the "donut robot," a gizmo that produces apple cider donuts for a growing number of fans.

In 2005, the 284-acre farm was granted entry into the USDA Farm and Ranch Land Protection Program. This agricultural conservation easement ensures that pristine farmland will be available to future farmers.

From McDougal Orchards, here's an intriguing recipe for apple-flavored brownies. Some may argue these are really blondies because there isn't any chocolate in the recipe. But Captain Jack calls them brownies, so that's what they are.

Apple Brownies

½ cup margarine or butter

1 cup sugar

1 egg, beaten

1 cup chopped apples

½ cup chopped nuts (pecans are recommended), optional

1 cup flour

½ teaspoon baking soda

½ teaspoon of baking powder

1 teaspoon cinnamon

....

Note: This recipe may be doubled, in which case you should use a 9 x 13-inch baking pan.

....

Preheat oven to 350°F.

In a large bowl, cream the margarine or butter with the sugar. Add the egg, and mix well. Stir in the chopped apples and chopped nuts. Add the remaining dry ingredients. Mix well.

Pour the batter into an 8-inch square pan. Bake in the 350°F oven for 40–45 minutes.

Makes 8 servings.

Spiller Farm

The Spiller family has been farming since 1894 in Wells, Maine. Their 130 acres are on both sides of Route 9A, five acres set aside for berries and another four devoted to apples. The farm is owned by Anna and Bill Spiller. The farm's store is run by Jim and Jeannine Spiller.

Open daily year round, the red and white Spiller Farm store has apples, cider, and sugar pumpkins even in the dead of winter. You can also pick up some hay, shavings, and bird feed there. This is rural America at its best. On the prepared food side of things, you can also get some cider doughnuts and a lobster roll—after all, this is Maine, and the farm is not too far from its famous rocky coast. In warm weather, you can dine outside at one of the green picnic tables next to the farm's pond. Produce from Spiller Farm can also be found at the farmers' market held in Kennebunk in the summer.

Like other farms and orchards, the pick-your-own season begins in June with strawberries and moves on to apples and pumpkins into late October. A hayride tour of the farm features a small covered bridge, beehives, and wild turkeys. Tours are offered weekend afternoons in September and October. For details, check the website (www.spillerfarm.com).

A USE FOR BRUISED APPLES

If life hands you lemons, you make lemonade. And so it is with bruised apples. Anna and Bill Spiller at Spiller Farm in Wells, Maine, offer a very easy dessert made with bruised apples. Remove the core from a bruised apple, and cut the apple into equal-size pieces, with or without the skin. Put the apple slices in a saucepan with very little water. Bring the mixture to a simmer, and reduce the heat to low. Cook until the apples are softened. If desired, add sugar, spices such as cinnamon and nutmeg, or any dried fruit. Serve your bruised apples hot or cold, or as a sauce over ice cream.

Treworgy Family Orchards

What's not to like about this particular orchard? The Treworgy family is eager to show visitors what life is like on a working farm in Levant, Maine.

- Starting in the spring, goats of all sizes nuzzle up to the fence hoping to get petted, and their babies arrive in late May, much to everyone's delight.
- You can buy apples by the bag, or you can pick your own starting in the fall. There are 1,300 trees in the five-acre orchard, and they are loaded with Cortland and McIntosh apples.
- The pumpkin patch takes up another five acres, and the massive corn maze is simply amazing (pun intended).
- They freeze some of their famous apple pies so you can take one home and bake it yourself.
- Hayrides run throughout the fall season, either tractor pulled or drawn by handsome Belgian Suffolk draft horses.
- Starting on Labor Day weekend, the Orchard Café is open, and New England folk music fills the air every weekend.

This is just part of the story from Treworgy Family Orchards, owned by Gary and Patty Treworgy. Along with eighteen family members, they are always dreaming up ways to make it a fun experience for people of all ages. Their hope is that every visitor leaves feeling a little closer to the land and to family farming traditions. Here is the family recipe for an unusual applesauce made with plums.

Plum Applesauce

2 pounds McIntosh apples, quartered and cored (do not peel)

2 pounds red or black plums, quartered and pitted

¼ cup water

¼ cup sugar

In a 4- or 5-quart heavy pot, combine all the ingredients. Cover and cook over moderately low heat, stirring occasionally, until the fruit is very tender and falling apart, about 1 hour or more.

Force the cooked mixture through a large medium-mesh sieve, using a rubber spatula to press the fruit through the strainer. Discard what is left in the sieve (mostly apple peels).

Pour the plum applesauce into a container with a tight-fitting lid. This will keep in the refrigerator for 1 week, or it can be frozen.

Makes 8 servings.

Sweetser's Apple Barrel and Orchards

With a striped awning out front, Sweetser's Apple Barrel is a red and white farm stand that locals and tourists rely on for apples, apples, and more apples. The stand is open daily usually from July 1 to early December.

The sixth-generation family farm was started in 1812, and the first trees were planted in 1840. New apple and pear trees were planted as recently as 2012, when the farm celebrated its 200th anniversary. Today there are more than 1,000 apple trees on the property with a selection "second to none," according to the Sweetsers. Connie and Dick oversee day-to-day operations. Debby and Greg now own the orchard and are committed to maintaining the family heritage.

Inside the Apple Barrel, the thirty-nine varieties of apples are clearly marked so customers know whether they are looking at heirloom or limited edition apples. Old-fashioned chalkboards offer plenty of information on which varieties are available on a given day. "Today's Apples" are on display in a crisp white, wooden display case with each variety in its own cubby. Another display offers paper bags of apples, filled with a blend ideal for making pies. It's here that you will find apples that never make it to your favorite supermarket, such as Red Astrachan and Wolf River. On a warm summer day, there's nothing like their cold apple cider. In cool weather, they offer it hot and mulled.

The Apple Barrel is also stocked with freshly picked vegetables from nearby Chipman's Farm and artisan breads from Standard Baking. They even sell Maine's famous Whoopie Pies, the state's official treat.

The abundance of apples spills out of the farm stand with wooden crates brimming with fruit of all colors. Bright orange pumpkins and yellow mums complete the colorful scene.

In the summer and fall, Sweetser's is a popular venue for country weddings with vows exchanged in the orchard, receptions under a big white tent, and libations in the beautiful old barn. In the winter, the orchards go to sleep and the land becomes a delight for cross-country skiers.

North Chester Orchard

Allen and Jane LeBrun own the six-acre North Chester Orchard overlooking the Penobscot River in Chester, Maine. Their apples have such clever names, such as Zestar!, and yes, the exclamation point is part of its name. Jane says every bite of that apple tastes "like a whole bowl of fruit." The Wealthy and Sweet Sixteen trees planted in 2013 will be producing fruit in a couple of years.

The LeBruns feel blessed to be working at their orchard. Their farmhouse was built in 1886 on a foundation of fieldstones. In addition to their 1,400 apple trees (and growing), they grow pumpkins and raise bees to pollinate the crops and for honey.

Jane's recipes are as down home as can be. She makes an excellent apple crisp, applesauce that goes very well on French toast, and old-fashioned baked apples. Here are two to try, including one called Heaven and Earth with very loose directions. You can adjust that recipe to suit your preferences. The number of servings depends on your amounts—figure on one serving for every potato in the casserole.

HEAVEN AND EARTH

Layer slices of potatoes, apples, and onions in a lightly greased casserole dish. Mix in a slice or two of crumbled bacon and a dash of nutmeg. Cover and bake for 50–60 minutes in a preheated 350°F oven.

Grammie Ludden's Crab Apple Pickles

1 cup vinegar

2 cups sugar

1 cup water

5 quarts crab apples

In a large saucepan, combine the first three ingredients and bring to a boil to make a syrup.

Leave the stems on the crab apples. Cut out the blossom end, and stick a clove into each end. (The alternate method is to put a couple of cloves into each jar before filling.)

Steam the crab apples in the hot syrup just until the skins start to crack open. Pack the crab apples in hot jars. Pour the boiling syrup over the apples. Seal the jars tightly.

Makes 6–12 jars (depending on the size of your jars).

Note: 5 quarts of apples will require 3 batches of the vinegar mixture.

Thompson's Orchard

"More than 100 years"—that says a lot about Thompson's Orchard in New Gloucester, Maine. Founded in 1906, this family-owned and -operated apple orchard and farm covers 200-plus acres, and in the fall the property has been called "a New England postcard."

The farm offers home-grown fruits, local vegetables, apple trees, and a gazebo with a beautiful view where rustic weddings are held. Weekend entertainment includes horse-drawn hayrides and sleigh rides (if there's enough snow). They press their own cider and are known for their "awesome" doughnuts and apple dumplings. In the summer, look for apple cider popsicles in the freezer. In the winter, make sure to try the hot cider. In the antique-filled farm stand, don't be surprised to see octogenarians in rocking chairs near the wood-burning stove.

The U-pick orchards have dwarf apple trees for easy picking. The staff is knowledgeable and friendly. Like many other Maine orchards, they are open from Labor Day weekend in September to December 24.

Brackett's Orchard

Brackett's Orchard was established around 1783 in Limington, Maine, and is thought to be the oldest family-owned and -operated orchard in the state. Manley Brackett is the eighth generation of Bracketts to farm the scenic hilltop. Nine varieties of apples, tree-ripened peaches, and blueberries are grown on the seventy-five-acre spread.

Visitors can pick their own apples and pumpkins on weekends in September and October. Free hayrides are offered as well as rides on the Brackett Apple Express, a bright red-and-blue miniature train that offers a tour of the orchards.

Nicely decorated with bright orange pumpkins and seasonal flowers, the charming farm store is open from mid-August through May (or when they run out of apples). In the fall especially, it is well stocked with all the apple varieties, cider, honey, jams, and maple syrup.

A rather unusual feature is the authentic brick pizza oven on the premises. You can watch the experienced pizza master toss his dough into the air before topping it with pepperoni or goat cheese, and then sliding it into the Neapolitan-style wood-burning oven.

On the farm is an antique one-room schoolhouse now called the Country Collection; they sell all things country for the home and garden . Especially interesting is the espaliered apple tree fence beside the store.

Bailey's Orchard

Rod and Kay Bailey celebrated their fiftieth wedding anniversary in 2015, and for forty of those years, they have operated Bailey's Orchard in Whitefield, Maine. The property has been in the Bailey family for more than two centuries. The old barn, weathered with dark green trim, is more than 100 years old and built with wood that came from trees on the property.

Today there are more than 400 apple trees on their land with about forty-five varieties, some of them heirloom. The Baileys accomplished much over the years—adding a cider mill, apple sorting machine, and a cold storage unit to the farm. Early in the season, they use McIntosh, Cortland, and Macoun apples for their cider. Later, a larger variety goes into the mix. In all, a couple of thousand gallons are pressed in a good year. In addition to apples, the Baileys grow seven varieties of pears and three varieties of plums.

It's a family affair at Bailey's with four generations of the family actively involved every fall. In season, Bailey's Orchard is open every day, rain or shine.

Kay says the Cortland is her favorite apple—it's good for cooking and holds its shape. Here is one of Kay's favorite recipes.

Baked Apple Squares

3 eggs

1¾ cups sugar

2 cups flour

1 teaspoon cinnamon

1 teaspoon baking powder

½ teaspoon salt

¾ cup cooking oil

1 teaspoon vanilla

2 cups thinly sliced apples

1 cup chopped nuts (optional)

Preheat oven to 350°F.

In a large bowl, beat the eggs. Gradually add the sugar, and beat until light and fluffy.

Sift the dry ingredients into the egg-sugar mixture. Add the oil and vanilla. Mix well. Fold in the apple slices and nuts (if desired).

Pour the batter into a greased 9 x 13-inch baking pan. Bake in the 350°F oven for 40–45 minutes.

Makes 8 generous apple squares.

Kelly
Orchards

Art and Jill Kelly are regular figures at several farmers' markets in southern Maine during the summer and fall months. As owners of Kelly Orchards in Acton, they are eager to share their apples, peaches, berries, pumpkins, and cider with a discerning public. With a degree in plant science from the University of Massachusetts, Art has mastered growing peaches, something not easily accomplished in Maine.

Founded in 1982, Kelly Orchards produces seventeen varieties of apples from the 10,000 or so trees that grow on the thirty-acre farm. About 600 new trees are planted every year. Fruit lovers can pick their own, or they can purchase already picked fruit at the small family-run farm stand. The pick-your-own season runs from early September through October. The orchard does a very good job on their Facebook page detailing what fruit is available. And they don't mind if you sample an apple or two while picking in the orchard.

Beyond the basics, such as the crisp and sweet Gala and the pear-like Ginger Gold, Kelly Orchards offers on a limited basis antique and heritage varieties with wonderful names. That includes Caville Blanc, a French apple ideal for cider; and the Esopus Spitzenberg, Thomas Jefferson's favorite apple. They also grow the rare Cox Orange Pippin, the aromatic English dessert apple.

New England Apple Association

Bar Lois Weeks, executive director of the New England Apple Association, enthusiastically responded to my call for recipes from regional orchards, declaring this book "a wonderful project." Her nonprofit organization was founded in 1935 by a group of wholesale growers from the New England states and New York. Now devoted to New England, the association's mission is to promote the local apple industry through educational and promotional events and projects. Their website showcases the wide variety of New England apples, the nutritional value of apples, and how they are grown and prepared. So here are a half-dozen quick and easy salad recipes that make excellent use of Maine's beautiful apples.

Apple Broccoli Salad

2 New England apples

3 cups fresh raw broccoli, cut up

¼ cup chopped walnuts

1 tablespoon chopped red onion

⅓ cup raisins

½ cup vanilla low-fat yogurt

Lettuce, as needed

4 sprigs fresh parsley (optional)

Core and chop the apples into bite-size pieces. In a bowl, combine all the ingredients. Mix well. Serve on a platter over a bed of lettuce garnished with fresh parsley if desired.

Makes 4 servings.

Apple–Brown Rice Salad

FOR THE DIJON VINAIGRETTE:

3 tablespoons olive oil

¼ cup chopped parsley

3 tablespoons rice vinegar

2 teaspoons Dijon-style mustard

2 garlic cloves, minced

1 teaspoon sugar

½ teaspoon salt

Black pepper, to taste

FOR THE SALAD:

3 New England apples, cored and cut into 1-inch chunks

2 tablespoons lemon juice

3½ cups cooked brown rice

3 skinless, boneless chicken breast halves, cooked and cut into chunks

1 medium red bell pepper, seeded, trimmed, and chopped

¼ cup sliced green onions

Whisk together the vinaigrette ingredients. Set aside.

In a large bowl, gently toss the apple chunks with the lemon juice. Add the remaining ingredients and toss gently. Dress the salad with the vinaigrette. Chill until ready to serve.

Makes 4-6 servings.

Apple, Chicken, and Bleu Cheese Salad

FOR THE BLEU CHEESE DRESSING:

¼ cup fat-free mayonnaise

¼ cup crumbled bleu cheese

1½ teaspoons lemon juice

FOR THE SALAD:

3 apples, cored and cubed

3 boneless, skinless chicken breast halves, cooked and cubed

1 cup seedless red grapes, halved if large

5 cups mixed salad greens

In a bowl, whisk together the dressing ingredients.

In a large bowl, toss together the apples, chicken, and grapes with the bleu cheese dressing. Divide the salad greens evenly among 4 salad plates. Top the salad greens with a generous cupful of the apple-chicken salad.

Makes 4 servings.

Four Fruit Salad

1 New England apple, cored and chopped

1 cup seedless grapes

1 orange, in segments

1 pear, cored and chopped

....

Serving suggestions: Serve on lettuce-lined plates with a scoop of cottage cheese; serve in a glass dish with a scoop of sherbet on top; or serve in a bowl topped with plain yogurt.

....

In a bowl, toss all the ingredients together.

Makes 2 servings.

Fall Festival Fruit Salad

FOR THE SALAD:

1 New England apple, cored and thinly sliced

¼ pound seedless grapes

1 melon, seeded, pared, and cut into chunks

Pomegranate seeds, as needed

Mixed salad greens, torn into bite-size pieces

FOR THE CITRUS DRESSING:

½ cup plain yogurt

¼ cup orange juice concentrate, thawed

In a large bowl, combine the apples, grapes, melon, pomegranate seeds, and salad greens.

In a small bowl, combine the dressing ingredients. Using a wire whisk, whip until smooth. Add the citrus dressing to the fruit and salad bowl. Toss to coat well.

Makes 4 servings.

French Apple-Pear Salad

2 New England apples, cored and sliced into spears

2 pears, cored and sliced into spears

2 celery stalks, chopped

2 tablespoons lemon juice

½ teaspoon vanilla

¼ cup walnut or canola oil

Salt, to taste

2 teaspoons tarragon

½ cup toasted walnuts

Brie or bleu cheese, crumbled, as needed

In a medium bowl, combine the fruit and celery. In a small mixing bowl, whisk together the lemon juice, vanilla, oil, and salt. Pour the dressing over the salad. Top with the tarragon, walnuts, and cheese.

Makes 4 servings.

A Good Fence and a Good Dog

"Mainers," as they are called, were usually self-sufficient a century ago in rural parts of the state. Just about every farm grew apple trees for enjoyment and survival. As the world, even in rural Maine, became more modern, people began to rely on supermarkets for their food, and many orchards fell by the wayside.

In 1925, there were 35,561 farms that were raising apples in Maine, according to Gary Keough, State Statistician with the USDA National Agricultural Statistics Office. In 2007, when the most recent agricultural census was taken, only 372 apple farms were reported in Maine. Nine decades of change had brought about many challenges for Maine growers. Today these men and women must keep up to date on new methods and trends in order to survive.

One of their challenges is finding affordable and experienced labor—not an easy task, searching for skilled apple pickers wiling to work long hours in varying weather conditions. The commercial buckets carried by apple pickers can weigh forty pounds as workers climb up and down 20-foot ladders. Many orchards rely on Jamaicans who must obtain guest visas through the federally sanctioned temporary agricultural program, which involves much paperwork and critical deadlines. Some orchards have dependable Jamaicans who return year after year, for thirty years or more in some cases. Their pay for working in an American orchard for three months is more than what they can earn in an entire year back home in Jamaica.

Maine orchards have had to diversify to stay viable, and a growing number now grow more than apples. Some farmers claim climate change has enabled them to grow stone fruit (cherries, peaches, and plums) for the first time with great success.

Weather is another major challenge. Back in 2012, the fall harvest was a total loss in many parts of the state because the apple trees were budding after a very warm March and were then wiped out in an April freeze.

Another major challenge for apple farmers is dealing with disease and insects that can destroy orchards. Many farmers use Integrated Pest Management with natural predators and pesticides that have as little impact as possible on the environment. For example, selective sprays are applied only when pests are present and causing damage. Other unwanted visitors are deer, moose, bear, porcupine, and rodents. A good fence and a good dog usually keep those creatures at bay.

Pietree Orchard

This is a truly extraordinary orchard, and for so many different reasons, but first, here's the history of Pietree Orchard in Sweden, Maine. The McSherry family established the orchard around 1940. The King family purchased the orchard in 2007, and it is presently owned by Tabitha King, author of eight novels, philanthropist, and social activist.

Today the orchard produces apples, berries, peaches, plums, nectarines, pumpkins, vegetables, and flowers. The bright and modern farm stand is open daily in season and on weekends in the winter, offering "amazing" cider donuts, pies, freshly pressed cider, maple syrup, and brick-oven pizza. A green John Deere tractor pulls a brown hay wagon filled with visitors through the orchard on fall weekends. The orchard's magnificent view of the White Mountains just may slow down any planned apple picking.

The fifty-five varieties of apples, including many rare heirloom types, are under the watchful care of Farm Manager Dan Cousins and Scott Miller, who is known as "The Apple Doc." Energy-saving technology is evident with the orchard's wind turbine and solar collector.

In our travels throughout New England, this was the only orchard we found that was so welcoming to the handicapped and otherwise challenged. Naomi King, who calls herself "the Business Monkey" at Pietree, almost had to leave her job because of her dependence on a wheelchair. Working with the Maine AgrAbility program at the University of Maine, major changes were made to make her job more accessible, and that led to changes in the orchards, fields, and farm store that made them more accommodating. Even the hay bale maze was designed to be accessible for everyone.

The socially responsible and progressive Pietree Orchard also participates in various projects aimed at improving the community around the farm. The close-knit team there is dedicated to transforming the entire agricultural property into one that welcomes all, regardless of their disabilities. That team also loves good food, and here are some of their recipes.

Apple Filo Pockets

3 apples, cored and chopped

¼ cup maple syrup or honey

¾ teaspoon ground cinnamon

¼ teaspoon ground nutmeg

¼ teaspoon ground cloves.

6 tablespoons dairy or nondairy butter

1 box frozen filo dough, thawed

Ground cinnamon, as needed

Whipped cream or ice cream (optional)

Preheat oven to 350°F. Line a baking sheet with parchment paper or foil.

In a medium mixing bowl, toss the apples with the maple syrup or honey, ground cinnamon, nutmeg, and cloves.

Melt the butter.

Roll out one tube of pastry from a box of thawed filo dough. Count the number of sheets and divide by four. Lift up one-fourth of the sheets and place them on the work surface. Brush with the melted butter. Scoop one-fourth of the apple mixture toward one side of the pastry. Fold over and roll up the edges. Place on the prepared baking sheet. Brush with butter. Repeat three more times.

Sprinkle with the cinnamon. Bake in the 350°F oven for 25 minutes. Cool for 5 minutes before serving. Cut in half on diagonal. Enjoy plain or with whipped cream or ice cream.

Makes 8 servings.

Apple Stuffed Bread

2 cups nondairy or dairy milk

½ cup maple syrup or honey

2 tablespoons dry yeast

3 cups bread flour

4 cups all-purpose flour

⅓ cup ground flaxseed meal

1½ tablespoons ground cinnamon

2 teaspoons salt

⅓ cup applesauce

⅓ cup safflower oil or melted butter

3 apples

¼ cup plus 1 tablespoon dairy or nondairy butter, divided

4 tablespoons maple syrup or honey, divided

1 tablespoon ground cinnamon

1 teaspoon ground nutmeg

2 tablespoons flour, if needed

Scald the milk for 2 minutes in the microwave on high (or bring to a simmer for 2 minutes in a saucepan over medium heat). Stir in the maple syrup or honey and dry yeast.

In an extra-large mixing bowl, whisk together the bread flour, all-purpose flour, flaxseed meal, cinnamon, and salt.

Mix in the applesauce, safflower oil, or melted butter, and the yeast-milk mixture. Knead 5 minutes, until smooth and stretchy. Cover with a towel and rest in a warm place to rise, about 90 minutes, until doubled in volume.

Meanwhile, wash, core, and dice (chop into small pieces about the size of 2 peas) the apples. In a medium frying pan, melt ¼ cup butter and sauté the apples over medium-high heat for 3 minutes. Add 3 tablespoons maple syrup or honey, ground cinnamon, and nutmeg. Sauté 2 more minutes. Set aside until bread dough has finished the first rise.

Grease 2 loaf pans.

After the dough has risen once, punch down. If sticky, add the 2 tablespoons of flour and knead briefly. Divide the dough in half.

With a rolling pin, roll the dough to an 11 x 8-inch rectangle. Spoon half the apple mixture over the rectangle. Then roll the dough into a long cylinder. As you lift the dough to transfer it to a loaf pan, fold under the ends to tuck it into the pan. Repeat for second loaf, using the second half of the apple mixture.

Cover the loaves and allow the bread to rise in a warm place for about 30 minutes.

Preheat oven to 375°F.

Melt the remaining 1 tablespoon butter. Whisk in the remaining 1 tablespoon of maple syrup or honey. Brush over the top of the loaves.

Bake in the 375°F oven for 30 minutes, or until the loaf sounds hollow when tapped.

Allow the bread to cool for 10 minutes before removing from the pan. Cool for 5 more minutes on a rack. Slice and enjoy.

Makes 2 loaves.

....

Note: Freeze the second loaf or share it with a friend. This is a fun recipe on a day when you want to do other things around the house. There are three wait times in which you are free to do other things: about 75 minutes during the first rise, 30 minutes during the second rise, and 30 minutes during baking.

....

Apple and Pear Cobbler

4 apples

3–4 Asian pears

½ cup raisins or dried cranberries

½ cup maple syrup or honey

2 tablespoons arrowroot or cornstarch

¾ teaspoon ground ginger

¾ teaspoon ground nutmeg, divided

⅛ teaspoon ground cardamom or allspice

Pinch plus ¼ teaspoon salt, divided

1¾ cups whole wheat flour (or gluten-free flour blend mixed with 1½ teaspoons xanthan gum, or ¾ cup sorghum flour, ½ cup brown rice flour, and ½ cup amaranth flour

¼ cup masa harina

½ cup brown sugar

2 teaspoons baking powder

8 tablespoons dairy or nondairy butter

¼–⅓ cup hot water

Preheat oven to 400°F.

Wash, core, and thinly slice the apples and pears.

In a large bowl, combine the sliced apples, pears, raisins or dried cranberries, maple syrup or honey, arrowroot or cornstarch, ground ginger, ½ teaspoon nutmeg, cardamom or allspice, and the pinch of salt. Transfer the mixture to a 9 x 13-inch baking dish.

In another bowl, whisk together whole wheat flour (or gluten-free flour blend), the masa harina, brown sugar, baking powder, ¼ teaspoon nutmeg, and ¼ teaspoon salt.

With a pastry cutter or two knives cutting in opposite directions, cut in the butter until there are no pieces larger than a small pea.

Mix in the hot water to make a biscuit dough. If too crumbly, add more water 1 tablespoon at a time. Drop clumps of the dough in big spoonfuls over the top of the apples and pears.

Bake in the 400°F oven for 40–45 minutes, or until baked through and bubbly.

Makes 12 servings.

Lodi Apple Panini

1 round loaf focaccia (Pietree focaccia is recommended)

Olive oil or walnut oil, as needed

4 ounces cheddar cheese or 3 ounces hummus

2 Lodi apples, peeled, cored, and thinly sliced

¼ medium-size onion, sliced into rings

2 tablespoons walnuts or pecans, optional

Slice the focaccia in half widthwise so you have 2 large rounds, a bottom and a top. Brush each cut side with the olive or walnut oil.

Spread the cheddar cheese or hummus across the bottom half. Spread the apple slices and onion rings across the cheese or hummus. If using, sprinkle with the walnuts or pecans before putting the top half of the focaccia over the bottom.

On a hot grill, put the whole stuffed focaccia bottom side down, and grill until the bread is toasted and the cheese is melted. Carefully holding sides together with tongs, turn over the panini on the grill, and grill 1 or 2 more minutes for grill marks and heating the sandwich through.

Makes 2 servings.

Note: If you have a panini press, you will not have to turn the sandwich over.

Sandy River Apples

Maine's "Apple Man" died in 2015, just two months shy of his 100th birthday. Francis Fenton passed away in the same room in which he was born on the family farm in Mercer, Maine. Sandy River Apple Orchard has been in the Fenton family since 1852. Six generations have tended the land, surrounded by 200 acres of pine forests.

The farm had sat vacant for thirty years until Francis retired from the navy in 1972, and he returned home to save the orchards. With his wife Dollie Lea, he brought Sandy River Apples, as it is now called, back into full production.

Nestled near the banks of the Sandy River, the farm is now run by Francis's daughter, Carol Fenton Gilbert, and her husband Jim. They grow forty-plus varieties of apples, from Arkansas Black with a purple to nearly black hue, to the Twenty Ounce apple that can easily weigh more than a pound and is great for baking.

Making this orchard unique is its Quilted Apple Retreat, a weekend getaway program for quilters in the refurbished 200-year-old barn. Food and lodging are provided in the 1790s farmhouse across the street from the barn. In the fall, each attendee is given a peck of freshly picked heritage apples from the orchard—a memorable keepsake from a special time in Maine.

Apple Acres Farm

Apple Acres Farm in South Hiram, Maine, has been in the Johnson family since 1949. Bill Johnson took over the business from his father thirty years later. Today, Bill and his wife Marilyn, with four children and more grandchildren, run the farm. They offer pick-your-own apples from August through October on their ten-acre spread, and their annual Bluegrass Festival is a foot-stomping treat not to be missed.

The Johnson family makes a healthy line of apple baking mixes, syrups, and granolas using their sweet apples, cider, and all-natural ingredients. All their products are produced and packaged at the farm by members of the family.

Here are some of their recipes that include apple cider syrup (also known as boiled cider) as the main flavor ingredient. That syrup comes in a quaint old-fashioned bottle, one that you will want to keep. If you can't find apple cider syrup in your local markets, you can purchase it at their farm store or order it online at www.appleacresfarm.com.

Please note that the apple cider syrup from Apple Acres is different from the traditional cider syrup you find elsewhere. Described as "liquid gold," the Johnson formula results in a lighter, more versatile syrup.

For breakfast, the Johnson family suggests making Apple & Cinnamon French Toast when you have the morning munchies. Dip slices of your favorite bread into a mixture of 4 eggs, ½ cup milk, ¼ teaspoon cinnamon, a pinch of nutmeg, and 3 tablespoons of finely chopped apples. Make your French toast as usual on the griddle or in a large frying pan. Drizzle your French toast with Apple Acres Apple Cider Syrup just before serving.

The Johnsons also offer three dinnertime recipes—a lively salad dressing with a touch of wasabi and two pork dishes that are pretty special when served with rosemary roasted vegetables and herbed mashed potatoes.

Lastly, they say there's not much to do in Maine during the dead of winter so it's no wonder that Bill and Marilyn have come up with a half-dozen cocktails, a little "northern comfort" to sip by the fire on those frigid nights. Their apple cider syrup is the key ingredient in these mixed drink recipes. They don't fool around in Maine—they make many of these before and after dinner drinks by the pitcher.

Pork Tenderloin with Caramelized Onions and Apples

1 pork tenderloin

3 apples, thinly sliced

4 onions, sliced and caramelized

1 cup apple cider syrup, divided

Preheat oven to 350°F.

Cut open the pork tenderloin lengthwise so that it unrolls. Place the thinly sliced apples and caramelized onions inside the tenderloin. Drizzle the tenderloin with ¼ cup of apple cider syrup. Roll up the tenderloin and secure with kitchen twine.

Reduce the oven temperature to 325°F, and roast the tenderloin for 45–60 minutes. Remove the tenderloin from the oven, and baste the tenderloin with the remaining apple cider syrup.

Return the tenderloin to the oven, and roast at 325°F with the pan juices until they begin to caramelize, about 15 minutes. Allow the tenderloin to rest a few minutes before slicing.

Makes 4 servings.

Salad Dressing with a Kick!

½ cup apple cider syrup

½ cup apple cider vinegar
(or balsamic)

¼ cup olive oil

¼ cup tamari or soy sauce

¼ cup lime juice

Wasabi powder to taste
(1 teaspoon is recommended)

Mix all the ingredients together in a bottle. Cover and shake.

Makes 1¾ cups.

Note: If you like a thicker salad dressing, add ½ teaspoon cornstarch to the mixture.

How Cider Is Made

Just how is cider made? This is how they do it at Carlson Orchards in Harvard, Massachusetts.

To make their premium blend cider, the folks at Carlson first gather a special blend of apple varieties and give them a thorough washing. The apples are then crushed into a juicy mash. Rice hulls are added to the mash to help with the pressing of the apples. The rice hulls keep the apple juices flowing under the pressure of the press.

The mash is then put into one of forty-five porous bags that hang vertically in the press. Each bag is surrounded on each side by a plate, and these plates are squeezed together with a maximum of 2,000 pounds per square inch of pressure to get the juice out.

All of their pressed cider is pasteurized prior to bottling. Their entire operation is governed by a strict HACCP (Hazard Analysis and Critical Control Point) plan that ensures quality and safety at every point in the production cycle.

Pasteurization is just one of many critical points maintained to ensure a high level of quality for the consumer. Flash pasteurization brings the juice from a chilly 45°F up to 165°F and then back down to an even chillier 38°F, all in about ninety seconds.

Once the cider is pasteurized, bottles are prepared with the Carlson Orchards label and sent along the bottling line to be filled. The newly pasteurized apple cider flows freely into gallon, half-gallon, quart, and pint containers. On a busy fall day, Carlson Orchards will bottle upwards of 8,000 gallons.

The patriarch of the Carlson family started farming in 1936 on a remote hilltop in Harvard. That spot turned out to be a perfect place for growing apples, and those apples are ideal for making cider.

The folks at Poverty Lane Orchards in Lebanon, New Hampshire, are very particular about the apples used in making their cider. They use bittersweet apples that have high tannins and sugars (Dabinett, Yarlington Mill, Chisel Jersey, Ellis Bitter, Ashton Bitter, Somerset Redstreak, and Medaille d'Or) and bittersharp apples with their high tannins and acid (Kingston Black, Stoke Red, and Foxwhelp). A small percentage of their heirloom varieties are vital for their fermented cider blends. The Golden Russett, which dates back to the pre-Revolution era in America, is relied upon for good fermentation, while newer apples such as Ida Red and Elstar help in the quest for acid. All these apples contribute specific aromas and flavors.

At Bear Swamp Orchard & Cidery in Ashfield, Massachusetts, the Gougeon family offers certified organic apple, hard cider, sweet cider, raw vinegar, and more. With three generations of Gougeons on the property, their land has been an orchard, on and off, for more than a century. There are two cider mills on site, one old and one a state-of-the-art facility constructed by Steve Gougeon in 2008. The cider mill and apple storage area are solar powered. Their process begins with a bushel of apples, which is hand-picked of branches and leaves, and then hand-washed in a large sink. The clean apples are hand-fed into a wall-mounted grinder that turns the apples into a chunky applesauce. That "applesauce" is dumped into their apple press, which is a water press that uses regular household water pressure to fill a rubber water bladder in the center of the stainless cylinder that presses the crushed apples against the walls of the cylinder. The cider runs out into a fountain where it is collected in buckets by hand. At Bear Swamp, some of that sweet cider is turned into hard cider.

Cider Hill Farm in Amesbury, Massachusetts, makes an award-winning unpasteurized cider made from a blend of seven to twelve varieties of apples, selected for their excellent balance of sweet, tart, astringent, and aromatic tones. Their fruit goes through a washing and polishing line before being chopped and fed into a state-of-the-art horizontal Goodnature Press. This press has no wood racks and is easy to sanitize. It is typical for raw ciders to have a shelf life of seven to ten days, but Cider Hill Farm routinely can be kept for three to four weeks as long as the cider is refrigerated. They press one day a week and can make up to 1,300 gallons during the busiest point in the season from mid-September to mid-October. The cider is never heated, pasteurized, UV treated, chemically preserved or altered. It's just 100 percent cold pressed.

Wood's Cider Mill in Springfield, Vermont, does it the old-fashioned way. Their twin-screw cider press was purchased in 1882 and originally run by waterpower. The press is now housed in a new structure, built in 2003, and is worked by hand and with electricity. They make about 200 gallons of cider per pressing. The Wood family proudly says that, while much has changed in the past century, a returning ancestor would quickly see how much has remained the same.

Cider aficionados ask when is the best time for cider. Most orchards and cider mills begin pressing their apples in early September, and that cider is a bit on the tart side. October and November ciders offer the fruitiest, deepest, and most complex flavors.

The recipe on page 291 is the only way I make hot mulled cider whenever friends come over to watch the New England Patriots play football on TV and for family get-togethers during the holidays. It tastes good, warms the soul, and makes our house smell delicious.

Cider Pork Chops with Sweet Potatoes and Apples

4 pork chops

3 tablespoons shortening

2 large sweet potatoes, partially cooked and cut into pieces

2 large apples (Cortland, if possible), sliced

½ cup cider syrup

¼ teaspoon cinnamon

¼ teaspoon nutmeg

In a large skillet, brown the pork chops in the melted shortening. Move the chops to one side of the skillet, and add the sweet potatoes. Place the sliced apples on top of the sweet potatoes. Cover the apples and sweet potatoes with the cider syrup, and sprinkle with the cinnamon and nutmeg.

Turn the heat down to low, cover with a lid, and cook slowly until the apples are steamed and the sweet potatoes are glazed.

Baste everything with the syrup in the bottom of the pan several times while cooking.

Makes 4 servings.

Old-Fashioned Hot Mulled Cider

Old-Fashioned Hot Mulled Cider

½ gallon fresh apple cider

½ cup brown sugar

1 teaspoon ground allspice

1 teaspoon ground cinnamon

1 apple studded with cloves

In a large saucepan, combine the cider, brown sugar, and spices. Float the clove-studded apple in the cider mixture. Bring to a boil, reduce the heat, and simmer for 10 minutes. Serve in mugs. This can also be prepared in a slow cooker or crockpot.

Makes 8–10 servings.

Cider Smash

1 cup apple cider syrup

1 cup fresh lemon juice

1 cup good bourbon

1 lemon, sliced (optional)

Combine all the ingredients. Heat the combined ingredients to serve warm, or simply serve poured over ice. Garnish with a slice of lemon if desired.

Makes 6 servings.

Cider Smash

Adam's Fall

Apple cider syrup

Tequila

Seltzer

Fresh limes, for garnish

In a pitcher, combine equal parts of each of the liquid ingredients. Pour over ice, strain, and serve with a wedge of lime.

Makes 1 pitcher.

Eve's Revenge

Apple cider syrup

Dark rum

Cointreau

In a pitcher, combine equal parts of the three ingredients. Serve over ice.

Makes 1 pitcher.

Apple Daiquiri

1 tablespoon apple cider syrup

1 ounce lime juice (more or less to taste)

1 teaspoon sugar

2 ounces good rum

Combine all the ingredients. Pour into a glass filled with crushed ice.

Makes 1 serving.

Brandied Apple Fizz

1 ounce apple cider syrup

1 ounce apricot brandy

3 ounces seltzer

Combine all the ingredients, pour over crushed ice, strain, and serve.

Makes 1 serving.

Hiram's Hot Apple Ale

⅓ cup apple cider syrup

2½ pints strong ale

¼ teaspoon nutmeg

1 teaspoon ginger

Sugar (white or brown), to taste

Mix all together in a pot, heat slowly, and serve in mugs.

Makes 6 servings.

The Symbolic Apple

The New England Apple Association has been around for eighty years educating all those interested in the iconic American apple. They feel that no other food appeals to us as much as the apple. When you think about it, apples are central to so many legends and idioms. An apple a day keeps the doctor away. "The apple of my eye" is a compliment. Sir Isaac Newton discovered gravity after being hit in the head with an apple falling from a tree. New York is called The Big Apple. The Beatles recorded on the Apple label. Apple is the name Steve Jobs selected for his computer company in 1976, and one of their signature products is called a Mac, as in McIntosh. With all that to ponder, from the New England Apple Association come these two recipes for delicious non-alcoholic drinks.

Apple Cooler

1 quart apple cider
2 cups apricot nectar
Juice of 6 limes
2 liters club soda
6 sprigs fresh mint (optional)

In a pitcher, combine the cider, nectar, and juice. Pour into 6 tall glasses filled with ice. Fill glasses with club soda. Garnish with mint sprig if desired

Makes 6 servings.

Apple Honey Shake

1 quart chilled apple cider or juice
2 cups chilled orange juice
¼ cup honey
2 teaspoons grated orange rind

Combine all ingredients and shake to blend. Pour over ice in 6 tall glasses. Garnish with mint sprig, apple slice, or long peel of orange.

Makes 6 servings.

Libby & Son U-Picks

Wild blueberries are smaller than their cultivated cousins, and they have a more intense flavor, sweet and tangy. The bushes produce berries every other year with their harvest time being July and August. At Libby & Son U-Picks in Limerick, there are twelve cultivated blueberry varieties to pick, from Early Blue to Aurora. They have 10,000 bushes on eighteen acres with plans to plant more. That family-owned and -operated farm has been growing blueberries and more since the 1950s. Aaron Libby provided this excellent recipe for his Aunt Lisa's blueberry muffins.

Blueberry Coffee Cake Muffins

FOR THE MUFFINS:

1 cup sugar

1 stick butter

2 eggs

1 pint sour cream

1 teaspoon vanilla

2 cups flour

1 teaspoon baking soda

1 teaspoon baking powder

2 cups blueberries (fresh is best and the larger the better)

FOR THE TOPPING:

½ cup crushed walnuts

¼ cup sugar

1 teaspoon cinnamon

Preheat oven to 350°F.

In a large bowl, combine the sugar and butter. With an electric hand mixer, cream together until smooth. Add the eggs, sour cream, and vanilla, mixing well.

In a separate bowl, combine the flour, baking soda, and baking powder. Mix well.

Add the flour mixture to the sugar-butter mixture a little at a time, and mix until smooth. Fold the blueberries into the batter, and divide the mixture evenly in a cupcake tin.

In a separate bowl, combine the crushed walnuts, sugar, and cinnamon, and mix well. Sprinkle the topping mixture on the tops of the muffins.

Bake in the 350°F oven for 25–28 minutes. You will be able to tell if the muffins are done when a toothpick comes out clean after being inserted into the center of a muffin.

Makes 12 muffins.

The Best Apple Cider Doughnuts In Maine

Not in the mood to pick your own apples? How about pick-your-own apple cider doughnuts, some of the best Maine has to offer, in alphabetical order:

Apple Acres Farm
363 Durgintown Road, Hiram
207-625-4777
www.appleacresfarm.com

Brackett Orchard
224 Sokokis Avenue, Limington
207-730-9169
www.brackettorchard.com

Holy Donuts
194 Park Avenue, Portland
207-874-7774
and,
7 Exchange Street, Portland
207-775-7776
www.theholydonut.com

Lakeside Orchards
318 Readfield Road, Manchester
207-622-2479
www.lakesideorchards.com

Libby & Son
86 Sawyer Mountain Road, Limerick
207-793-4749
www.libbysonupicks.com

McDougal Orchards
201 Hanson Ridge Road, Springvale
207-324-5054
www.mcdouglaorchrds.com

Orchard Hill Farm
36 Orchard Road, Cumberland Center
207-829-3581
www.orchardhillfarmmaine.com

Ricker Hill Orchard
295 Buckfield Road, Turner
207-225-5552
www.rickerhill.com

Rocky Ridge Orchard and Bakery
38 Rocky Ridge Lane, Bowdoin
207-666-5786
www.rockyridgeorchard.com

Rowe's Orchards
333 Moosehead Trail, Newport
207-368-4777
www.roweorchards.com

Thompson's Orchard
276 Gloucester Hill Road, New Gloucester
207-926-4738
www.thompsonsorchard.com

Wallingford's Apple Orchard
1240 Perkins Ridge Road, Auburn
207-754-5169
www.wallingfordsorchard.com

Appendix A: Directory of Orchards

CONNECTICUT

Beardsley's Cider Mill and Orchard
278 Leavenworth Road (Route 110)
Shelton, CT 06484
203-926-1098
www.beardsleyscidermill.com

Belltown Hill Orchards
483 Matson Hill Road
South Glastonbury, CT 06073
860-633-2789
www.belltownhillorchards.com

B.F. Clyde's Cider Mill
129 N. Stonington Road
Old Mystic, CT 06355
860-536-3354
www.bfclydescidermill.com

Bishop's Orchards
1355 Boston Post Road
Guilford, CT 06437
203-453-2338
www.bishopsorchards.com

Blue Jay Orchards
125 Plumtrees Road
Bethel, CT 06801
203-748-0119
www.bluejayorchardsct.com

Buell's Orchard
108 Crystal Pond Road
Eastford, CT 06242
860-974-1150
www.buellsorchard.com

Drazen Orchards
251 Wallingford Road
Cheshire, CT 06410
203-272-7985
www.drazenorchards.com

Ellsworth Hill Orchard and Berry Farm
461 Cornwall Bridge Road
Sharon, CT 06069
860-364-0025
www.ellsworthfarm.com

Holmberg Orchards
12 Orchard Lane
Gales Ferry, CT 06335
860-464-7305
www.holmbergorchards.com

Karabin Farms
894 Andrews Street
Southington, CT 06489
860-620-0194
www.karabinfarms.com

Lyman Orchards
32 Reeds Gap Road
Middlefield, CT 06455
860-349-1793
www.lymanorchards.com

Roger Orchards
336 Longbottom Road
Southington, CT 06489
860-229-4240
www.rogersorchards.com

Silverman's Farm
451 Sport Hill Road
Easton, CT 06612
203-261-3306
www.silvermansfarm.com

MAINE

Apple Acres Farm
363 Durgintown Road
Hiram, ME 04041
207-625-4777
www.appleacresfarm.com

Bailey's Orchard
255 N. Hunts Meadow Road
Whitefield, ME 04353
207-549-7680
www.facebook.com/pages/
Baileys-Orchard

Brackett's Orchard
224 Sokokis Avenue
Limington, ME 04049
207-730-9169
www.brackettorchard.com

Doles Orchard
187 Doles Ridge Road
Limington, ME 04049
207-793-4409
www.dolesorchard.com

Kelly Orchards
82 Sanborn Road
Acton, ME 04001
207-636-1601
www.kellyorchards.com

Lakeside Orchards
318 Readfield Road (Route 17)
Manchester, ME 04351
207-622-2479
www.lakesideorchards.com

Libby & Son U-Picks
86 Sawyer Mountain Road
Limerick, ME 04048
207-793-4749
www.libbysonupicks.com

Mc Dougal Orchards
201 Hanson Ridge Road
Springvale, ME 04083
207-324-5054
www.mcdougalorchards.com

North Chester Orchard
460 North Chester Road
Chester, ME 04457
207-794-3547
www.northchesterorchard.com

Orchard Hill Farm
36 Orchard Road
Cumberland Center, ME 04021
207-829-3581
www.orchardhillfarmmaine.com

Pietree Orchard
803 Waterford Road
Sweden, ME 04040
207-647-9419
www.pietreeorchards.com

Ricker Hill Orchard
295 Buckfield Road (Route 117)
Turner, ME 04282
207-225-5552
www.rickerhill.com

Rocky Ridge Orchard
38 Rocky Ridge Lane
Bowdoin, ME 04287
207-666-5786
www.rockyridgeorchard.com

Rowe Orchards
333 Moosehead Trail
Newport, ME 04953
207-368-4777
www.roweorchards.com

Sandy River Apples
240 W. Sandry River Road
Mercer, ME 04957
207-587-2563
www.sandryriverapples.com

Spiller Farm
85 Spiller Farm Lane
Wells, ME 04090
207-985-3383
www.spillerfarm.com

Sweetser's Apple Barrel and Orchards
19 Blanchard Road
Cumberland Center, ME 04021
207-829-6599
www.facebook.com/pages/
Sweetsers-Apple-Barrel-and-
Orchards

Thompson's Orchard
276 Gloucester Hill Road
New Gloucester, ME 04260
207-926-4738
www.thomponsorchard.com

Treworgy Family Orchards
3876 Union Street
Levant, ME 04456
207-884-8354
www.treworgyorchards.com

Wallingford's Apple Orchard
1240 Perkins Ridge Road
Auburn, ME 04210
207-754-5169
www.wallingfordsorchard.com

MASSACHUSETTS

Autumn Hills Orchard
495 Chicopee Row
Groton, MA 01450
978-448-8388
www.autumnhillsorchard.com

The Big Apple
207 Arnold Street
Wrentham, MA 02093
508-384-3055
www.thebigapplefarm.com

Carlson Orchards
115 Oak Hill Road
Harvard, MA 01451
800-286-3916
www.carlsonorchards.com

Cider Hill Farm
45 Fern Avenue
Amesbury, MA 01913
978-388-5525
www.ciderhill.com

Clarkdale Fruit Farms
303 Upper Road
Deerfield, MA 01342
413-772-6797
www.clarkdalefruitfarms.com

Fairmount Fruit Farm
887 Lincoln Street
Franklin, MA 02038
508-533-8737
www.fairmountfruit.com

George Hill Orchards
582 George Hill Road
South Lancaster, MA 01561
978-365-4331
www.georgehillorchards.com

Honey Pot Hill Orchards
144 Sudbury Road
Stow, MA 01775
978-562-5666
www.honeypothill.com

Keown Orchards
10 McClellan Road
Sutton, MA 01590
508-865-6706
www.keownorchards.com

Parlee Farm
95 Farwell Road
Tyngsboro, MA 01879
978-649-3854
www.parleefarms.com

Russell Orchards
143 Argilla Road
Ipswich, MA 01938
978-356-5366
www.russellorchards.com

Smolak Farms
315 S. Bradford Street
North Andover, MA 01845
978-682-6332
www.smolakfarms.com

Tougas Family Farm
234 Ball Street
Northboro, MA 01532
508-393-6406
www.tougasfarm.com

Westward Orchards
178 Massachusetts Avenue
Harvard, MA 01451
978-456-8363
www.westwardorchards.com

Wilson Farm
10 Pleasant Street
Lexington, MA 02421
781-862-3900
www.wilsonfarm.com

NEW HAMPSHIRE

Alyson's Orchard
57 Alyson's Lane
Walpole, NH 03608
603-756-9800
www.alysonsorchard.com

Apple Annie
66 Rowell Road
Brentwood, NH 03833
603-778-3127
www.appleannienh.com

Applecrest Farm Orchard
133 Exeter Road (Route 88)
Hampton Falls, NH 03844
603-926-3721
www.applecrest.com

Apple Hill Farm
580 Mountain Road (Route 132)
Concord, NH 03301
603-224-8862
www.applehillfarmnh.com

Brookdale Fruit Farm
41 Broad Street
Hollis, NH 03049
603-465-2240
www.brookdalefruitfarm.com

Butternut Farm
195 Meaderboro Road
Farmington, NH 03835
603-335-4705
www.butternutfarm.net

Cardigan Mountain Orchard
1540 Mt. Cardigan Road
Alexandria, NH 03222
603-744-2248
www.cardiganmtnorchard.com

Carter Hill Orchard
73 Carter Hill Road
Concord, NH 03303
603-225-2625
www.carterhillapples.com

Elwood Orchards
54 Elwood Road
Londonderry, NH 03053
603-434-6017
www.elwoodorchards.com

Gould Hill Orchards
656 Gould Hill Road
Contoocook, NH 03229
603-747-3811
www.gouldhillfarm.com

Hackleboro Orchards
61 Orchard Road
Canterbury, NH 03224
603-783-4248
www.hackleboroorchards.com

Hazelton Orchards
20 Harantis Lake Road
Chester, NH 03036
603-493-4804
www.hazeltonorchards.com

Mack's Apples
230 Mammoth Road
Londonderry, NH 03053
603-434-7619
www.macksapples.com

Merrill's Farm
569 Mammoth Road
Londonderry, NH 03053
603-622-6636

Moose Hill Orchard
Home of Mack's Apples
230 Mammoth Road
Londonderry, NH 03053
603-434-7619

Poverty Lane Orchards
98 Poverty Lane
Lebanon, NH 03766
603-448-1511
www.povertylaneorchards.com

Riverview Farm
141 River Road
Plainfield, NH 03781
603-298-8519
www.riverviewnh.com

Stonybrook Farm
128 Glidden Road
Gilford, NH 03249
603-293-4300
www.stonybrookfarmnh.com

Sunnycrest Farm
59 High Range Road
Londonderry, NH 03053
603-432-9652
www.suncrestfarmnh.com

Surowiec Farm
53 Perley Hill Road
Sanbornton, NH 03269
603-286-4069
www.surowiecfarm.com

RHODE ISLAND

Appleland Orchard
135 Smith Avenue
Smithfield, RI 02828
401-949-3690
www.applelandorchardri.com

Barden Family Orchard
56 Elmdale Road
North Scituate, RI 02857
401-934-1413
www.bardenfamilyorchard.com

Dame Farm and Orchard
91B Brown Avenue
Johnston, RI 02919
401-949-3657
www.damefarmandorchards.com

Elwood Orchard
58 Snake Hill Road
North Scituate, RI 02857
401-949-0390
www.elwoodorchard.com

Goodwin Brothers Farm Stand
458 Greenville Road
North Smithfield, RI 02896
401-765-0368
www.goodwinsfarm.com

Harmony Farms
359 Saw Mill Road
North Scituate, RI 02857
401-934-0741
www.harmonyfarmsri.com

Hill Orchards
86 Winsor Avenue
Johnston, RI 02919
401-949-2940
www.hillorchards.com

Jaswell's Farm
50 Swan Road
Smithfield, RI 02917
401-231-9043
www.jaswellsfarm.com

Knight Farm
1 Snake Hill Road
North Scituate, RI 02857
401-349-4408
www.knightfarm.com

Narrow Lane Orchard
213 Narrow Lane
North Kingstown. RI 02852
401-294-3584
www.facebook.com/
NarrowLaneOrchard

Phantom Farms
2920 Diamond Hill Road
Cumberland, RI 02864
401-333-2240
www.phantomfarms.com

Pippin Orchards
751 Pippin Orchard Road
Cranston, RI 02921
401-943-7096
www.facebook.com/PippinOrchard

Rocky Brook Orchard
997 Wapping Road
Middletown, RI 02842
401-851-7989
www.rockybrookorchard.com

Steere Orchard
150 Austin Avenue
Smithfield, RI 02828
401-949-1456
www.steereorchard.com

Sunset Orchards
244 Gleaner Chapel Road
North Scituate, RI 02857
401-934-1900
www.sunsetorchards.freeservers
.com

Sweet Berry Farm
915 Mitchell's Lane
Middletown, RI 02842
401-847-3912
www.sweetberryfarmri.com

White Oak Farm
74 White Oak Lane
North Scituate, RI 02857
401-934-3018
www.farmfresh.org

Young Family Farm
260 West Main Road
Little Compton, RI 02837
401-635-0110
www.youngfamilyfarm.com

VERMONT

Allenholm Farm
111 South Street
South Hero, VT 05486
802-372-5566
www.allenholm.com

Burtt's Apple Orchard
283 Cabot Plains Road
Cabot, VT 05647
802-917-2614

Champlain Orchards
3597 Vermont Rt. 74 West
Shoreham, VT 05770
802-897-2777
www.champlainorchards.com

Chapin Orchard
150 Chapin Road
Essex, VT 05452
802-879-6210
www.chapinorchard.com

Cold Hollow Cider Mill
3600 Waterbury-Stowe Road
Waterbury Center, VT 05677
800-327-7539
www.coldhollow.com

Dwight Miller Orchards
511 Miller Road
East Dummerston, VT 05346
802-254-9635
www.dwightmillerorchards.com

Eagle Peak Farm
3748 Eagle Peak Road
West Brookfield, VT 05060
802-505-0080

Green Mountain Orchards
130 West Hill Road
Putney, VT 05346
802-387-5851
www.greenmountainorchards.com

Hackett's Orchard
86 South Street
South Hero, VT 05486
802-372-4848
www.hackettsorchard.com

Moore's Orchard
Corner of Johnson Road and
Pomfret Road
North Pomfret, VT 05053
802-457-2994

Scott Farm Orchards
707 Kipling Road
Dummerston, VT 05301
802-254-6868
www.scottfarmvermont.com

Sentinel Pine Orchards
832 Witherell Road
Shoreham, VT 05770
802-897-7931
www.sentinelpineorchard.com

Shelburne Orchards
216 Orchard Road
Shelburne, VT 05482
802-985-2753
www.shelburneorchards.com

Valley Dream Farm
5901 Pleasant Valley Road
Cambridge, VT 05444
802-644-6598
www.valleydreamfarm.com

Wellwood Orchards
529 Wellwood Orchard Road
Springfield, VT 05156
802-263-5200
www.wellwoodorchards.com

Windswept Farm
2417 May Pond Road
Barton, VT 05822
802-525-8849
www.windsweptfarmvermont.net

Woodman Hill Orchard
175 Plank Road
Vergennes, VT 05491
802-989-2310

Wood's Cider Mill
1482 Weathersfield Center Road
Springfield, VT 05156
802-263-5547
www.woodscidermill.com

Appendix B: Pick Your Own Cherries in New England

Here are ten places where you can pick-your-own cherries in New England. Their season is short, so plan accordingly. It's always wise to call ahead to check on availability.

Belltown Hill Orchards
483 Matson Hill Road
South Glastonbury, CT 06073
860-633-2789
www.belltownhillorchards.com

Brookdale Fruit Farm
41 Broad Street
Hollis, NH 03049
603-465-2240
www.brookdalefruitfarm.com

Butternut Farm
195 Meaderboro Road
Farmington, NH 03835
603-335-4705
www.butternutfarm.net

Doles Orchard
197 Doles Ridge Road
Limington, ME 04049
www.dolesorchard.com

Ellsworth Hill Orchard and Berry Farm
461 Cornwall Bridge Road
Sharon, CT 06069
860-364-0025
www.ellsworthfarm.com

Parlee Farm
95 Farwell Road
Tyngsboro, MA 01879
978-649-3854
www.parleefarms.com

Russell Orchards
143 Argilla Road
Ipswich, MA 01938
978-356-5366
www.russellorchards.com

Smolak Farms
315 S. Bradford Street
North Andover, MA 01845
978-682-6332
www.smolakfarms.com

Sunnycrest Farm
59 High Range Road
Londonderry, NH 03053
603-432-7753
www.sunnycrestfarmnhcom

Tougas Family Farm
234 Ball Street
Northboro, MA 01532
508-393-6406
www.tougasfarm.com

Index

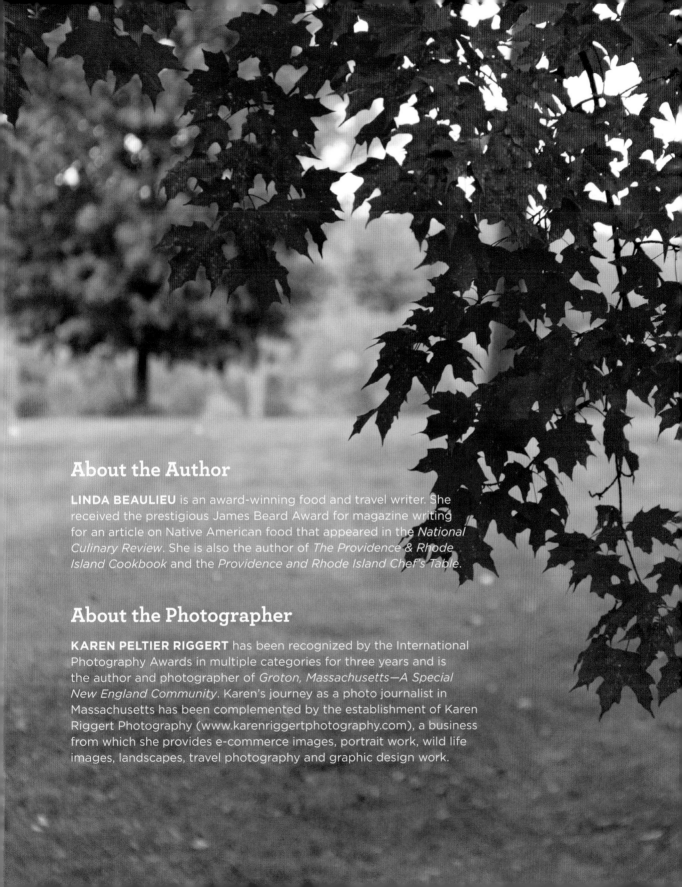

About the Author

LINDA BEAULIEU is an award-winning food and travel writer. She received the prestigious James Beard Award for magazine writing for an article on Native American food that appeared in the *National Culinary Review*. She is also the author of *The Providence & Rhode Island Cookbook* and the *Providence and Rhode Island Chef's Table*.

About the Photographer

KAREN PELTIER RIGGERT has been recognized by the International Photography Awards in multiple categories for three years and is the author and photographer of *Groton, Massachusetts—A Special New England Community*. Karen's journey as a photo journalist in Massachusetts has been complemented by the establishment of Karen Riggert Photography (www.karenriggertphotography.com), a business from which she provides e-commerce images, portrait work, wild life images, landscapes, travel photography and graphic design work.

"And when you crush an apple with your teeth, say to it in your heart:

Your seeds shall live in my body,

And the buds of your tomorrow shall blossom in my heart,

And your fragrance shall be my breath,

And together we shall rejoice through all the seasons."

—KAHLIL GIBRAN